TELL ME A STORY

r

TELL ME A
STORY

*Fifty Years
and 60 Minutes
in Television*

DON HEWITT

PUBLICAFFAIRS · NEW YORK

PublicAffairs books are available at special discounts for bulk purchases in the
U.S. by corporations, institutions, and other organizations. For more information,
please contact the Special Markets Department at The Perseus Books Group, 11
Cambridge Center, Cambridge MA 02142, or call (617) 252-5298..

Book design and composition by Mark McGarry.
Set in Electra.

Library of Congress Cataloging-in-Publication Data
Hewitt, Don.
Tell me a story : fifty years and 60 minutes in television / Don Hewitt.
p. cm.
ISBN 1-58648-141-x (pbk)
1. Hewitt, Don. 2. Television producers and directors—United States—
Biography. 3. 60 minutes (Television program) I. Title.
PN1992.4H49 A3 2001
791.45'0232'092—dc21
[B] 200101622

10 9 8 7 6 5 4 3 2 1

To Mike Wallace, the late Harry Reasoner, Morley Safer, Ed Bradley, Steve Kroft, Lesley Stahl, Andy Rooney, Bob Simon, Christiane Amanpour, Dan Rather, and (for a time) Diane Sawyer and Meredith Vieira, without whom there would have been no 60 Minutes.

And to Phil Scheffler, the late Palmer Williams, Merri Lieberthal, Esther Kartiganer, Josh Howard, Arthur Bloom, Vicki Gordon, Joe Illigasch, Robert Corujo, Joel Dulberg, Allan Wegman, the late Kenneth Dalglish, Beverly Morgan, and all the wonderful people who work with them and for them, without whom there would have been no Don Hewitt.

And to four CBS executives I relied on to keep me on an even keel when the wind blew too hard and the waves got too big—Bill Leonard, Sig Mickelson, Howard Stringer, and Frank Stanton.

Finally, to Bill Paley, the legend who created CBS, made it the Tiffany Network, and became my dear friend.

Bless them, one and all.

Contents

Acknowledgments ix

Prologue 1

1 Forty-five Minutes from Broadway 13

2 Oh, What a Lovely War 21

3 The Emerald City 43

4 New Frontiers 69

5 The Battle of the TV Executives 85

6 60 Minutes of Prime Time 107

7 What Makes a Great Story 119

8 Hitting Our Stride 135

9 Corporate Politics and Holy Wars 161

10 Razzle Dazzle 179

11 Big Tobacco 191

CONTENTS

12 Striking the Right Balance   211

13 News Business, Show Business, and Nobody's Business   223

14 The Televised Future   241

    Epilogue   255

    The 60 Minutes *Honor Roll*   259

    Index   261

Acknowledgments

Don't I have enough to do getting 60 Minutes on the air every Sunday? I thought so until Peter Osnos, the publisher of PublicAffairs, suggested to me that after a half-century in television in which I had seen it all and done it all, there had to be a book lurking inside me. After arguing that there wasn't, I came to the conclusion that there was. Peter would have had an easier time convincing me if I had known he was going to make available to me two of the best editors it has ever been my pleasure to work with: his own executive editor at PublicAffairs, Paul Golob, and the editor of the editorial page of the *Milwaukee Journal Sentinel*, Michael Ruby.

I'd also like to acknowledge that I have included in this book stories that I've told many times before to friends and family, some of which appeared in a book about 60 Minutes I wrote almost twenty years ago. Frankly, they are so much a part of me that they fall naturally into any telling of my career in journalism, and I hope no one will mind my repeating a few of them.

TELL ME A STORY

Prologue

There probably are luckier people in the world, but I don't know them. My life has been blessed by good fortune, good friends, a wonderful family, great professional colleagues, and more luck than anyone has a right to expect. I've even managed to reach that plateau called "elder statesman" without, I think, too much to be ashamed of.

I am keenly aware that you don't get where I got without some of what made Ed Murrow Ed Murrow, Walter Cronkite Walter Cronkite, and Mike Wallace Mike Wallace rubbing off on you. I am also keenly aware that *60 Minutes* works because fate bestowed on me the most talented men and women in the broadcast news business and just enough good sense to know what to do with them. Ideas in television are a dime a dozen. People who can execute those ideas are a precious commodity, and the people of *60 Minutes* are pure gold.

The formula is simple, and it's reduced to four words every kid in the world knows: Tell me a story. It's that easy.

Before *60 Minutes*, with the exception of Edward R. Murrow's *See It Now*, the accepted wisdom was that television writers put words to pictures. That's ass-backwards. What *60 Minutes* is going to do, I said, is put the pictures to the words. If we don't do it that way, all we're doing is writing captions.

Do we try to tell our stories with flair? You bet we do — just as the newsmagazines and newspapers do. Our ticking stopwatch and what has come to be known as "teases" at the beginning of *60 Minutes* are the way we do it. Newspapers also use "teases"; only they call them "headlines." Now, I've never denied that there's some theatricality in the casting of our correspondents. For better or worse, that's been part of television news from the beginning: All other things being equal, it certainly helps if the man or woman in front of the camera looks the part.

Take Ed Murrow. He not only sounded authoritative on radio, he looked authoritative on television. And it didn't hurt that this very appealing man, almost a matinee idol, looked like Walter Pidgeon playing Ed Murrow. If you auditioned fifty actors to play him, and Murrow showed up as one of them, and you'd never seen him before, he'd get the part. You couldn't say the same about Lowell Thomas. Great voice, but Lowell Thomas didn't look the way Lowell Thomas sounded.

That Mike Wallace, Morley Safer, Ed Bradley, Steve Kroft, Lesley Stahl, and Andy Rooney look and sound right for *60 Minutes* takes nothing away from their reporting skills. The way they look and sound enables them to establish a rapport with the audience that makes it easier for them to communicate. But it's not enough to look and sound like a good journalist. You have to *be* a good journalist. And they are. If they weren't, that ticking stopwatch would have stopped years ago.

The stories that *60 Minutes* producers and correspondents find *for real* turn out to be as fascinating as anything television drama or the movies can cook up. That's why hardly a Monday morning passes without a call from some Hollywood producer who wants to make a movie about someone he saw the night before on *60 Minutes*, which tells me the stories we do are getting the two reactions I want from an audience: "I didn't know that," and "Wasn't that guy on *60 Minutes* fascinating?"

What follows is a frank and honest look at the world I have been a part of for more than half a century. I have been a television journalist almost from the beginning, and I have watched the news evolve from a service to a business.

Bill Leonard, who was the vice president in charge of *60 Minutes* before he became president of CBS News, gave us our marching orders in 1968: "Make us proud." Which may well be the last time anyone ever said "make us proud" to anyone else in television. Because Leonard said "make us proud" and not "make us money," we were able to do both, which I think makes us unique in the annals of television—so unique that in 1978, when someone said to me, "You know, you guys are in the top ten." I said, "The top ten what?" I didn't know what in hell he was talking about. Back then, none of us who worked in news knew anything about ratings. It was not how we or the people we worked for measured what we were worth to the company.

Today, everyone's consumed with ratings, and people in my business—the TV news business—bitch constantly about the emphasis on Nielsen numbers and how it's not only about journalism anymore. Let's stop kidding ourselves; of course it isn't. The anchors make millions of dollars a year, producers make hundreds of thousands a year and, yes, I make more money than I ever imagined I would. Where does everyone think the money comes from? Of course, it's not only about journalism anymore. If it were only about journalism, they wouldn't pay these incredible salaries. But let's be fair about this, too. It was never entirely about journalism even in the good old days. William S. Paley of CBS, David Sarnoff of NBC, and Leonard Goldenson of ABC were businessmen, and the companies they headed were then and are today profit-making enterprises. The difference between then and now is that they were obliged to give something back in exchange for their use of the public airwaves. That was what the Federal Communications Commission demanded. So if news was a loss leader, that was the price of doing business.

60 Minutes ended that. We got ratings and CBS made a fortune, maybe $2 billion over the thirty-plus years of the program. By getting awards and making money, we proved that it was possible for a television show to be a financial success and do good at the same time. And we're not the only ones who think that. The Maryland legislature labels bills that are passed on Monday morning after an issue was raised on Sunday night as "*60 Minutes* bills."

During the more than thirty years since I hit up on the idea of producing a televised weekly newsmagazine and calling it *60 Minutes,* my politics, such as they are, have been challenged from right, left, and center. When Spiro Agnew was vice president, I was "a nattering nabob of negativism." A couple of decades later, a *60 Minutes* viewer who thought I had something to do with Michael Dukakis's defeat by George Bush in 1988, called me a "puppet of the power structure." Along the way, I've been tagged as a bleeding-heart liberal and as an ultra-right-wing conservative and everything in between.

Don't you find, as I do, that the words "liberal" and "conservative" have ceased to have much meaning? Why, for instance, is it "liberal" to endorse a strict adherence to the First Amendment and "conservative" to feel the same about the Second Amendment? Still, since people apparently have to be one thing or another, I guess I'm both—a liberal and a conservative.

I voted once for Adlai Stevenson, once for Dwight Eisenhower, for Jack Kennedy over Richard Nixon, for Hubert Humphrey over Nixon, for Nixon over George McGovern, had a tough time choosing between Gerald Ford and Jimmy Carter, but had no trouble voting for Ronald Reagan twice. I don't know why I voted for Bush in '88, and Clinton in '92, but I did. And if given a chance, I would have voted for FDR ad nauseam.

About Al Gore and George W. Bush in the election of 2000: I couldn't get up a full head of steam about either one of them, and even in the polling place I was still undecided—Gore? Bush? Or neither? But, when push came to shove, I did what most Americans did. I pulled the lever for Gore. Do I think Bush won fair and square? I don't, but I'm not devastated by it. He turned out to be pretty good, which I'm afraid is the best we could have hoped for, no matter who won.

Was there nothing good to be said about the 2000 election? How about that Pat Buchanan got no more than one-half of 1 percent of the vote?

If I've been all over the lot politically, I've also been all over the lot philosophically. I don't think murder and abortion are one and the same thing but then I don't think murder and the death penalty are either. During the Vietnam War, I didn't mind kids burning their draft cards, but I got angry when they burned the flag. In the winter of 2002, a book about CBS called *Bias*, written by a former colleague of mine, was published, excoriating the network for being too "liberal" and an affront to "conservatives." When it hit the best-seller list and climbed to the top, I surmised that it got there because there is nothing an American likes more than lowering the boom on another American and pounding him into the ground with "You liberal, you! What do you know about being an American?" or "You conservative, you!" Why don't you go home and read the Constitution?"

How we do carry on about those two words! It's a sad fact of life in the United States that our knack for expressing ourselves has come down to throwing two epithets at one another. And, when they don't sting enough, modifying them with, for example, "limousine"—as in "limousine liberal," which has replaced "parlor pink" but isn't half as bad as "bleeding heart." Not to be undone, and to get their digs in, the so-called liberals bite back with "Neanderthal" and "fat cat."

Frankly, I don't know what is liberal about so-called "liberals" and conservative about so-called "conservatives." What I do know is that you can't sum up anyone in one word. We're all much too complicated for that, and I suggest that we would be a better country and a better people if we raised the level of the public discourse and stopped slinging "liberal" and "conservative" at each other at every turn. I liked it better when we called each other a "son of a bitch," and I liked it better when we made the case for or against abortion in lecture halls and newspaper editorials and not on bumper stickers that proclaim a "right to life" or a "woman's choice"—as if good guys believe in "choice" and bad guys believe in "life" (or vice versa). To me, the words "liberal" and "conservative" are, to borrow from *Macbeth*, "sound and fury signifying nothing." You can't sum up anyone in one word and we're too damned lazy to do anything other than that. What do I propose we do about it? Well, a pretty good start would be for us journalists to take the lead in lowering the temperature and raising the level of the nation's discourse by refraining from letting those buzz words stand on their own, because the plain, unvarnished truth is that they don't.

How can someone who calls himself or herself a "liberal" decide—absolutely and unequivocally—what someone else is permitted to say that is "politically correct" or can't say that is "politically incorrect"? Polite, yes. Liberal, no. Or how can someone be against "conservation" and call himself or herself a "conservative"? If I believe—as I do, wholeheartedly—that it is un-American to deny anyone a job based on the color of his or her skin, I am a "liberal"; however, if the "anyone" in question is a white fireman who was denied a job because of affirmative action (which I imagine he would call "negative action"), I am a "conservative." So let me slide over to the so-called "liberal" side and refer to what the late civil rights leader Bayard Rustin said so well and so wisely: "It behooves white America to make the same concerted effort to include us that it once made to exclude us." But now grapple with this: whose side are you on—Bayard Rustin's or the white fireman's? Applying the word "conservative" to the plight of the white fireman or applying the word "liberal" to the plea of the black civil rights leader makes no sense. "Humanitarian" is the word for both.

When it comes to guns, the side of me that so-called "liberals" find "conservative" is the side of me that has no problem with a gun owner sporting an NRA sticker on the front window of his car. The side of me that so-called "conservatives" find "liberal" is my incredulity that the guy with the NRA sticker on his *front* window has a "Support Your Local Police" sticker on his *rear* window. Didn't anyone ever tell him that it's the cops, more than anyone else, who are threatened by guns? I think the worst example of name-calling that gets us nowhere is the meaningless epithets that pro-gun and anti-gun Americans use to disarm each other without disarming the thugs who threaten both of them. I've always thought that if we could cool down the rhetoric, reasonable Americans would find a way to get rid of the illegal handguns flooding our cities and still pre-

7

serve a safe and sane way for a hunter to own a gun. The fact of the matter is that while NRA types and anti-NRA types fire broadsides at each other, the kind of people that both sides agree shouldn't have guns fire bullets at each other—and sometimes at us! If George Mitchell could get Irish Catholics and Irish Protestants to work out a solution that both sides could live with and make Ireland a safer place to live, then why can't somebody do the same with pro-gun Americans and anti-gun Americans—and make America a safer place to live, for "liberals" and "conservatives"?

And maybe I wasn't in school the day they taught it, but I didn't understand what was conservative about selling arms to an ayatollah and liberal about wanting to find out how in hell it happened. And I never understood how anyone as smart as Bill Clinton didn't know that a twenty-one-year-old White House intern would find it irresistible to brag about having it off with the president. To me, his problem was more cerebral than sexual.

It astonishes me that black Americans, less than a century out of legal slavery, were never captivated by Communism, as so many white Americans were when it was in fashion during the 1930s and early '40s. Frankly, it gives me hope that so many black Americans have faith that they will "overcome someday." And they well might. A generation ago, Americans had to go to the movies to see *Guess Who's Coming to Dinner?* In the years since, *Guess Who's Coming to Dinner?* became *Guess Who We Just Named a National Holiday After?* or *Guess Who Won the Masters at Augusta?* (In Georgia of all places.) or *Guess Who Became the Captain of the United States Davis Cup Team?* And now, *Guess Who's Our Secretary of State and Who's Our National Security Adviser?* Guess who's coming to dinner, indeed!

I think of the American flag as a symbol of what's best in our country. I also think it's middle-class Americans, Lions and Rotarians and

Kiwanians and the like, who give us the ballast we need to stay upright. Every time the ship of state starts to tip left or right, it's the great American middle class that rights it and keeps it from capsizing. So I love to see the flag displayed, but not by motorists who seem oblivious to the fact that they more than likely just filled up their car with gasoline that came from the same country the 9/11 hijackers came from.

About gay Americans: I don't think same-sex marriages are a way of life whose time has come, but on the other hand, I might be mistaken. After all, straight marriages don't have that much going for them either, not if you look at the divorce rate.

So that's where I am, in the middle most of the time, which is where you're likely to end up if you play both sides of the street, which I frankly admit I do.

For instance, on one of the anniversaries of the first Nixon-Kennedy debate, which I produced and directed, I was asked to speak at the Reagan Library. Afterwards, sitting with Nancy Reagan and her Republican friends at lunch, I was asked how important I thought that first debate was to Jack Kennedy's election victory and—no fool I, especially in that crowd—responded: "Not as important as his father buying him Cook County." That got the reaction I was looking for. Now, I had to find a way to get to the other side of the street. And I did, when someone asked me if I had disliked Richard Nixon, to which I replied, "Not as much as Barry Goldwater did." It popped into my head and out my mouth and, presto, I was back in the middle, where I prefer to be.

The plain truth is that I don't hold in disdain people I disagree with. I just disagree with them.

How did *60 Minutes* get where it got? And what makes it different? If there are two kinds of news regularly on television—news as it happens, or almost as it happens, on cable news channels and the news of the last twenty-four hours on the evening newscasts—*60 Minutes* seldom concerns itself with either. We are more interested in the news of the times in which we live. Among the things we do best, I think, is shine lights into dark corners, and if people in dark corners are doing things they shouldn't be doing, all we've done is turn the lights on. In the movie *Network*, a newscaster tells his viewers to throw open the window and yell, "I'm mad as hell, and I'm not going to take it anymore." Nobody does that; they ask *60 Minutes* to do it for them.

About our audience and who watches us, it does not displease me that newspaper people, other broadcasters, prominent politicians, big business types, and dot-com millionaires watch *60 Minutes*. But we don't broadcast for them. We broadcast for Lions and Rotarians and schoolteachers and hard hats and office clerks and firemen.

If there was a working model for *60 Minutes*, it was *Life* magazine—the old *Life* that came out weekly and was regarded as a family friend in the homes of millions of Americans. It made the kind of connection with the audience I wanted, and I wasn't above stealing the idea lock, stock, and barrel. If *Life* could be on every coffee table in America, why couldn't we be on every television set in America?

Sometimes when immodesty gets the better of me, I flatter myself into thinking that there might be in me a small bit of "the intuitive grasp of America" that Irving Howe, in his book *World of Our Fathers*, said was in Hollywood moguls like Sam Goldwyn, Louis B. Mayer, Jesse Lasky, and Adolph Zukor. They were immigrants from Eastern Europe who arrived here with very little schooling but had a certain undefinable something that enabled them to put on celluloid the lives of American icons—from the wizard of Menlo Park, Thomas Alva Edison; to the wizard of South Bend, Knute Rockne; from the Sultan of Swat, Babe Ruth; to the King of Swing, Benny Goodman; from the man who put us all on the telephone, Alexander Graham Bell; to the man who took us all to the circus, P. T. Barnum. It was their love affair with America.

My own began in New Rochelle, a midsize suburb of New York City, where I grew up in the 1920s and 1930s. For what it's worth, there's still a lot of New Rochelle in me, and by extension, in *60 Minutes*—especially the respect it and I have for the best America has to offer. I'm sure I could get an argument about that from someone who thinks he was shafted by us, but if you're one of the millions who tunes in every Sunday night, you know we try always to tell it straight. And that's what I propose to do in this book.

CHAPTER ONE

Forty-five Minutes from Broadway

New Rochelle, New York, could have passed for a small town and did when George M. Cohan wrote about it and sang about it in the 1906 musical, *Forty-five Minutes from Broadway*, the title song of which proclaimed:

> *Forty-five minutes from Broadway*
> *Think of the changes it brings*
> *For the short time it takes*
> *What a difference it makes*
> *In the ways of the people and things.*
>
> *Oh, what a fine bunch of Rubens*
> *Oh, what a gay atmosphere*
> *They have whiskers like hay*
> *Imagine Broadway*
> *Only forty-five minutes from here.*

With due respect to George M. Cohan, New Rochelle wasn't all that small a town. But he did have a point. It had 60,000 people, and it seemed that all 60,000 knew one another. And everybody I knew did "small town" things like joining the Boy Scouts, marching in the Fourth of July parade, playing baseball in an empty lot where anything that went over the fence into the yard next door was a ground-rule double, walking along the railroad tracks and waving to the people in the dining car of the Yankee Clipper and the Merchants Limited as they barreled their way through town on their way to and from Boston, and collecting the baseball cards that came with a pack of bubble gum ("I'll trade you two Mel Otts and a Dizzy Dean for one Lou Gehrig"). I wasn't exactly Tom Sawyer or Huck Finn, but I built a raft and sailed it on a pond in the north end of town and fished with worms and cut school to go hear Tommy Dorsey at the Paramount.

Nobody was a soccer mom. Baseball, football, basketball were American. Soccer was someone else's cup of tea.

Jogging was something you did to your memory. Need a little fresh air, feel like a workout? Get the kid next door and take turns going out for forward passes.

Nobody I knew smoked cigarettes. At twenty-five cents a pack for Camels or Lucky Strikes, who could afford to smoke anything other than dry leaves in a corncob pipe?

When we weren't smoking dry leaves in the woods, we "necked" in parked cards—and "petted" if we got lucky. Necking was, as I recall, hugging and kissing. Petting, if I got it right, was groping and grasping. Nobody got laid—not that we weren't moved to, but I don't think any of us really knew how to do it. ("Doing it," incidentally, was what it was called.) Fantasizing about it, everybody did. My fantasies were never about what were called "sex pots" but about girls (yes, Virginia, it was all right to call them "girls") who had wholesome good looks like the ones whose pictures hung in every delicatessen that sold beer. They were the Cindy Crawfords and the Elle MacPhersons of their day and were vying for the title of Miss Rheingold.

The first time I met a real-life Miss Rheingold (except in my dreams) was forty years later. This Miss Rheingold, Hillie Mahoney, was the wife of David Mahoney, the chairman of Norton Simon, Inc. He was the best man and she was the matron of honor at my wedding to Marilyn Berger. While Marilyn's picture, unlike Hillie's, never hung in Estelle Glatman's mother's delicatessen (next to Dan Mafucci's barbershop), it was beamed almost nightly from Washington when she was NBC's White House correspondent.

I remember like it was yesterday (you mean it wasn't?) the signs that one day sprang up in store windows asking and answering at one and the same time: "Wasn't the depression awful?" It was my first lesson in the power of positive thinking. The Great Depression wasn't over, but if they could make you think it was, maybe they could also make you believe that prosperity was, as they put it, just around the corner.

Along with most of the other people in town, my family was just barely middle class. If a strong wind had come up, it would have blown us back into the lower class. In those days, when you signed a new lease, they gave you a two-month concession: In effect, you paid for only ten months on a one-year lease. As a result, we moved a lot, and it always felt like we were one jump ahead of the sheriff.

My parents, Frieda and Ely Hewitt, were not really mismatched, but she was German-Jewish and he was Russian-Jewish, which in those days was considered a mixed marriage. She was born in New York City, but he came here from Russia as an infant. When I was born on December 14, 1922, we were living in Manhattan, but we soon moved to Boston, where my father had taken a job as the classified advertising manager for the *Boston Herald American*. When I was four years old, we moved to Milwaukee, where my dad worked for the old *Wisconsin News*. Then, a year or so later, we moved back to New York City and he went into business with his brother, my uncle Henry, who ran a company that distributed circulars door-to-door. In those days, before radio and television had taken hold of America, that's how people got their commercials—door-to-door. Sometime after that, we moved to the suburbs, to New Rochelle. Along the way, in 1927, my brother, Richard, was born, and we were just far apart enough in age to run with different crowds.

Though we were Jewish, we weren't very religious. I was never bar mitzvahed but I was confirmed at Temple Israel in New Rochelle, but not before the temple sisterhood called a special meeting to decide—because I ran for the Catholic Youth Organization track team—whether they would allow me to be confirmed. In the end, they did.

Growing up in New Rochelle, the only overt anti-Semitism I remember came from German Jews who found my Russian-born father not to their liking. Although, to his Gentile friends and business associates, he was eminently acceptable as their guest at the New York Athletic Club, he wasn't accepted at Century, Old Oaks, and Quaker Ridge, where German Jews played golf only with German Jews. Looking back, I think that's why I considered being Jewish not all that big a deal. It just was. I stayed home from school on Rosh Hashanah and Yom Kippur and went to my grandfather's for Passover, but I also got Christmas presents and went to dances at the North Avenue Presbyterian Church. Yom Kippur, Easter, Rosh Hashanah, Christmas were all my holidays.

About God, if there is one—and I'm inclined to think there very well might be, in some form or another—I can't bring myself to believe that, whatever it is, it either needs or wants my worship. Needing to be worshiped is a human failing, and I think God is probably above that. So, I don't hold very much with religion, organized or unorganized, and I am reasonably certain that I would feel the same if I had been born Catholic, Protestant, or Muslim.

Race wasn't much of an issue in my world either, at least not one that registered with me as a subject of deep concern. My high school was integrated, and I certainly was aware of black people. But I can't recall thinking much about race, except for those times I would read about one of those terrible lynchings in the South. White people seemed to have more money than black people, but I guess I just assumed, naively, that whites were fat, rich, and happy, and blacks were fat, poor, and happy. Talk about callow youth!

My father had two particular heroes, Joe Louis and Eleanor Roosevelt. When Joe Louis knocked out Max Schmeling, my father let out a whoop and did a little dance in front of the radio, and when Westbrook Pegler beat up on Mrs. Roosevelt, he fumed. In our crowd that seemed to be the measure of how liberal you were—how much you liked Mrs. Roosevelt and how hard you rooted for Joe Louis. That's about as far as it went. The people who went farther were called "commies" and nobody wanted to be called one of *those*, so we never got very much involved in social issues. I think it was because we were chicken and not because we didn't know better.

I also sold magazines—*Liberty*, *Collier's*, and the *Woman's Home Companion*—and made enough money to go to the movies every Saturday on the trolley with enough left over for a frozen Milky Way. With very little effort you could spend most of a Saturday at the movies. The trolley ride was a nickel, and a double feature at the Cameo on Third Street in Mount Vernon was fifteen cents. What's more, they threw in a newsreel that brazenly announced itself as "The Eyes and Ears of the World" and a Tarzan or a Tom Mix short that was the first thing I remember coming on the installment plan, leaving you no choice but to come back next Saturday to see whether Tarzan and Jane had escaped from the "unga-unga-unga" cannibals who were about to eat them, or whether Tom Mix had gotten away from the "white-man-speak-with-forked-tongue" Indians who were about to scalp him. Politically correct they weren't.

To me and the kids I grew up with, the local movie house in New Rochelle was part pleasure palace and part classroom. That's where I learned about an earthquake that all but destroyed San Francisco—from Clark Gable, Spencer Tracy, and Jeanette MacDonald. That's where I got a course in what the Nazis were doing in North

Africa—from Humphrey Bogart, Ingrid Bergman, Claude Rains, and Peter Lorre. That's where I learned about the war in Europe—from Walter Pidgeon and Greer Garson. It was where we all learned how to hold a cigarette, how to hold a girl, even how to hold a conversation. It seemed to me that I led two lives: the life I imagined was waiting for me when I watched Clark Gable, Tyrone Power, David Niven, and Charles Boyer; and the more mundane one that I had to return to when the movie was over. Through it all, I never knew which character I really wanted to be—Hildy Johnson, the reporter in *The Front Page*, or Julian Marsh, the Broadway producer in *42nd Street*. I would have settled for either one, with a slight nod toward Hildy Johnson. Because along with the movies, I had another passion: to be a reporter. Maybe it was because my father worked for newspapers all his life (albeit on the business side), but while other kids were playing cops and robbers or cowboys and Indians, I was playing reporter.

And one day it paid off. I was in seventh grade at Albert Leonard Junior High in New Rochelle when our homeroom teacher, Mrs. Robeson, announced to the class that the new edition of *Junior Scholastic* had arrived and that one of their classmates—me—had won the contest for "best editorial." The piece was called "Press Drives Lindbergh to Self-Exile," which was a high falutin' title and a high falutin' subject for a sixth-grader. But Charles Lindbergh was a hero to me then. I still remember, if only vaguely, standing on a scaffold of a partly finished building in 1927 to watch the parade for Charles Lindbergh, the first man to fly the Atlantic solo. None of us knew then that this American hero was going to end up playing footsie with a guy named Adolf Hitler—more than that, who had even heard of Adolf Hitler? But everybody had heard of Lindbergh. I still recall that the very first time I heard a newsboy holler "EXTRA!" it was followed by: "READ ALL ABOUT IT, LINDBERGH BABY

KIDNAPPED!" I was only nine years old, but I could imagine myself as a reporter writing stories that some kid would shout "EXTRA!" about.

At New Rochelle High School, I wrote a sports column for the school newspaper which I called "Athlete's Footnotes." My faculty adviser, however, considered my work pretty underwhelming—except for the title of my column. Listen, kid, he said, you may be thinking about the wrong business. You'll never make it in newspaper work, so maybe you should think about something else. But "something else" had no appeal. What did at the moment was a movie called *Foreign Correspondent*, directed by Alfred Hitchcock and starring Joel McCrea, who played a reporter covering the Nazis. It was shortly after the war started in Europe, and I wanted nothing more than to be there in uniform—but the uniform I had in mind was a trench coat and a pipe. I didn't know then that my infatuation with the movies and my infatuation with journalism would lead me to where I ended up.

CHAPTER TWO

Oh, What a Lovely War

On December 7, 1942, a year to the day after Pearl Harbor and seven days before my twentieth birthday, I arrived as a cadet at the Merchant Marine Academy at Kings Point, New York. I was about to embark on a very different sort of education from the one I had had the year before.

After graduating from New Rochelle High School in 1940, I went to New York University on a track scholarship, having been captain of the track team in high school. NYU had the best track coach in America in those days, a guy named Emil Von Elling, and I had visions of being good enough to make the Olympic team. It wasn't to be. By the middle of my sophomore year, my grades were so lousy that they dropped the scholarship and I dropped out of NYU.

The previous summer, I'd been a counselor for a couple of kids up in the Berkshire Mountains of western Massachusetts. The kids' parents had as a houseguest one weekend, Arthur Perrin, who was at the time assistant sports editor of the *New York Herald Tribune*. I told Perrin of my infatuation with journalism, and he invited me to come see him. After NYU, I did.

And so it was that by the dumb luck of a chance meeting I got the job I wanted more than any in the world: copyboy at the *New York Herald Tribune*, for $15 a week, with 15 cents deducted for Social Security. The *Trib* had a relatively short history, dating back to a 1924 merger of the *New York Herald* and the *New York Tribune*. The *Herald* went back to 1835 and the *New York Tribune* to 1841. I know it sounds corny, but when I walked into that building on Forty-first Street and heard the presses, I thought I had died and gone to

ELL ME A STORY

heaven, or at the very least had gone to sleep and awakened on a
movie set. The people who worked there all looked as if they had
come from central casting. God, how I loved that place. Sometimes
I think it was the best job I ever had.

I worked a late shift at the *Trib* because I was also working days for
a weekly newspaper in Pelham, New York (not far from New
Rochelle), called the *Pelham Sun*. The *Sun* had a very small staff—in
fact, I was practically it, except for a society editor who covered garden
parties and weddings—and I did everything: reporting, editing, sometimes even going into the composing room and setting type. The
owner, Tom Kennett, was very set in his ways and was so turned off by
pretension that when I wrote a story about a prominent man in town
named Smythe, Kennett ordered me to spell his name S-M-I-T-H,
because "Smythe" was, he said, a little too pretentious for his newspaper, even though Pelham was sometimes referred to as "a populated
golf course between New Rochelle and Mount Vernon."

After a full day's work at the *Sun*, I arrived at the *Trib* at four and
left at midnight. Because our lunch hour came right after the first
edition was locked up, it also came at the time the chorus girls at the
National Theater next door were changing for the second act. What
we copyboys soon discovered was if you went into an alleyway outside the press room, you could look into the girls' dressing-room window, which was below street level. One night, a sandwich in one
hand and a soda pop bottle in the other, I was peering in the window
(no wonder I thought I had died and gone to heaven), when I got too
close and fell into the ten-foot-deep window well. As I lay there in
the darkness I could hear the girls shouting that there was a prowler
in the alley, and all I could see was a headline on my hometown
newspaper: FORMER CAPTAIN OF HIGH SCHOOL TRACK
TEAM ARRESTED AS PEEPING TOM. When I managed to dis-
cover a ladder and scramble out of there, ahead of the cops, dirty and

disheveled, I found a phone in the press room and told the city desk that I had suddenly gotten sick and had to go home. When my father took one look at me, torn and tattered, he said, "What happened to you?" That called for a little ingenuity. So I lied. "I was hit by a taxi," I said. "But the driver got away before I could get his number."

The nights when we copyboys didn't spend our lunch hours peeping at the chorus girls, we went to a *Herald Tribune* hangout called The Artists & Writers on Fortieth Street—everybody called it Bleeck's. It was the bar where Spencer Tracy and Katharine Hepburn did their drinking in the movie *Woman of the Year*. (I could never seem to get away from the movies.) If I was lucky, someone would buy me a beer. After all, I was making only $15 a week and some of those reporters were already up to $75.

Before the war, copyboys at the *Herald Tribune*, as at the *New York Times*, were culled from Yale, Harvard, or Princeton graduates. And here I was, this nineteen-year-old kid who couldn't even stay in college, but in short order became *head* copyboy. Pure talent? Maybe it had more to do with the fact that the best and the brightest were being drafted. In any event, I quickly learned that one of the jobs of copyboy was to go downstairs to Bleeck's and help the publisher, Ogden Reid, negotiate an unsteady (to say the least) trip back to his office. But what I remember most was the city room and shuttling between the copy desk and the desks of legends like Tex O'Reilly, Homer Bigart, Red Smith, and Marguerite Higgins. It was the best staff of reporters in town, and the whole scene was right out of *The Front Page*, honest to God.

It was there that I had my first political set-to, when the admittedly left-wing Newspaper Guild, which everybody was obligated to join, circulated a petition in the newsroom to open a second front in Europe to help the beleaguered Russians. That infuriated me, and prompted me to go to my first Guild meeting and, superpatriot that

I fancied myself, sound off. "If you guys want to open a second front," I said, "why don't you enlist in the army and go over there and *open* a second front? Better yet, why don't you join the Russian army?" Nothing on the far left or the far right ever appealed to me, and that outburst did not endear me to my colleagues. But I already knew that my days were numbered at the *Herald Tribune*, not because I was being fired but because guys my age were going into the service.

Rather than go into the army, I decided to enroll at the Merchant Marine Academy. It wasn't Annapolis, but it was the next best thing. The academy didn't waste a lot of time before sending us to sea. In March 1943, just three months after I got there, on St. Patrick's Eve, I was a cadet on one of forty-odd ships making up a North Atlantic convoy that was all but wiped out by a wolf pack of German subs. After all those frigid morning lifeboat drills on Long Island Sound at the academy, the only thing I remember praying for was, "Please God, let 'em hit us amidships. I don't want to freeze to death in a lifeboat."

We managed to survive, either because they ran out of torpedoes or our rusty old tub wasn't worth wasting one on. It's funny, but I wasn't frightened until an ammunition ship got hit and exploded in a horrific fireball. Anyway, comes the dawn and our escort ships are gone and we're rolling in the North Atlantic like a buoy in rough chop. That's when I noticed two dots on the horizon—a couple of RAF planes coming to escort us in. As the two dots got bigger, all I could think was: Where's the music? Without a Hollywood score to go with it, it wasn't happening. That's what comes from going to too many movies.

But in many respects, my war *seemed* like a movie. From Scotland, we were convoyed down to London where we had maybe ten days before we would be headed back to the States for another cargo and another port of destination to deliver it to. While I was there, I made the rounds of the newspaper offices, figuring there might be some way to cover this thing as a war correspondent. At *Stars & Stripes*, I found a former *Herald Tribune* reporter named Bob Moora, who was now editor of *Stars & Stripes*, and his assistant, Bud Hutton. There was also a reporter named Andy Rooney, who for all the world looked like one of those typical American kids on a recruiting poster. He wasn't around very much — he spent a lot of time covering the Eighth Air Force, along with some of the more recognized war correspondents like Homer Bigart of the *Herald Tribune*. Looking back, it never dawned on me that his life and mine would converge again a quarter of a century later.

How I talked Moora and Hutton into believing that they needed someone to cover the Merchant Marine is beyond me, but I did, and they agreed to grease the way for me. So they talked to the officer in charge, Ensley Llewellyn, and got him to write a "To Whom It May Concern" letter requesting my services to fill what he said was (but what we both knew wasn't) the "desperately needed" post of merchant marine editor.

I hand-carried Llewellyn's letter back on the return trip to New York, a voyage almost as eventful as the trip over. We were driven way up north into a field of icebergs by German subs and took a torpedo midships. We saw it knifing its way through the water and figured we were going down for sure. But the damn thing hit the side of the ship, didn't explode, and sank to the bottom. It was a dud. Now I was convinced more than ever that I was leading a charmed life.

Homework for the academy cadets was the order of the day on the trip back, but I didn't do any of it. I was that sure the job in London was mine. When we arrived, we were met by officers of the Maritime Service who asked me for my homework. "Well, sir, I didn't do it," I said, and I handed one of the officers the letter from *Stars &*

Stripes. He read it, perplexed and angry. "What the hell is this? This doesn't mean anything to us," he barked.

"Well," I said, "I think it's supposed to go to someone in Washington."

"Okay, we'll pass it on," he said, "but you're in a lot of trouble for not doing any of your homework."

The next thing I knew I got a call from the head of public relations for the Maritime Service in Washington asking me to come down to discuss the job. To my surprise, he hired me and told me to arrange for credentials as a war correspondent. By July 1943, I was back in London, accredited to the Supreme Headquarters, Allied Expeditionary Force (SHAEF), and at work covering the merchant marine under the auspices of the War Shipping Administration. In effect, I did double duty: I issued press releases for the WSA and I served as merchant marine editor for *Stars & Stripes*, handling breaking news and feature stories. The posting also carried with it something called the "simulated rank" of second lieutenant. That, among other things, enabled us to eat in the officers' mess (and sometimes by mistake being saluted by GIs). At twenty, this college dropout was the youngest correspondent accredited to General Dwight David Eisenhower's SHAEF headquarters.

In addition to writing for *Stars & Stripes*, there were opportunities to plant my stories with hometown newspapers all over America. I would go out on a rescue ship, for example, that had picked up men out of the water who had been torpedoed on the run to Murmansk, a Soviet port on the Arctic Ocean that you couldn't get to without running a gauntlet of German U-boats. What I usually did was interview the crew about what it was like the night they got hit, then write ten different leads for ten different hometown newspapers and send them out.

In many ways, I operated more or less like a freelance. The day usually began at the office, checking to see whether there were any torpedoed ships in the area. Most of the time, I was on my own. Invoking the *Stars & Stripes* name, I'd call somebody at the British navy and tell them I wanted to do a story on how they were protecting convoys in the North Sea. Or I'd ring up the RAF and ask to fly antisub patrol between Ireland and Iceland. Or I'd hear about an American ferryboat that ended up in London as a hospital ship and figure that it would make a good story.

Getting an interview with "Monty"—General Bernard Law Montgomery, who was the best known of the British generals after his victory at El Alamein in North Africa—was my big coup. I have no idea why he agreed to see me, but he did, and he gave me an hour or so of his time, talking about the way the American merchant marine was doing the job of keeping the supply lines open. I called the piece, "The Man Who Hit 'Em for Six," which is a cricket term, akin to hitting a home run, and was something Montgomery loved to say he was going to do to Germany.

The photographer assigned to me was an unprepossessing little guy who bitched constantly about the slow progress of the war and how D-Day was never going to happen and that London was getting boring. Finally, he left and headed back to the States. I figured he had chickened out and wanted to duck D-Day, so I started referring to him as "Chicken Joe."

But it turned out that Chicken Joe was anything but chicken. He went home to the States all right, but then he headed for the Pacific and wound up shooting the most famous photograph of World War II—the marines raising the flag on Iwo Jima on February 23, 1945. His real name, as everyone would soon know, was Joe Rosenthal.

After the war ended I was in the press club in San Francisco having a drink with Bill Hipple of *Newsweek* when who walks in but Rosenthal, and, in an effort to introduce them to each other, I said,

"Joe, you know Bill Hipple?" And Joe said, "Do I know Bill Hipple? I was sitting on a log on a beach at Iwo Jima minding my own business when Hipple walked over, tapped me on the shoulder, pointed to a hill behind us and said, 'Joe, why don't you get off your ass, climb up that hill and take a picture of those marines raising the flag?' And you ask me, 'Do I know Bill Hipple?' "

In London, I knocked around at first, living in a couple of nondescript flats, before managing to find lodgings in the White House, a fancy block of flats near Regent's Park that played host to a collection of reporters, actors, bandleaders, and showgirls. It was an amazing time. If there was a London West End show during World War I called *Oh, What a Lovely War*, World War II, I'm ashamed to say, was also *Oh, What a Lovely War*—at least for me. I would go out with the British navy on Hunt-class destroyers looking for German E-boats in the North Sea or fly with the RAF on antisub patrols looking for German U-boats, come back, change clothes, and go tea dancing at Claridge's. Unreal!

It's a part of me I can't seem to shake. So, over and above all the other emotions I felt in the wake of the terrorist attacks on September 11, 2001, was a strange connection to the two years I spent in London in 1943 and 1944, during which I became convinced that the Londoner who lived through the blitz, shaking his fist at the Luftwaffe overhead and ducking the V–1 and V–2 pilotless bombers that all but decimated his city, was a breed of man the world would never see again. How wrong I was! Since September 11 I have seen him over and over and over again in my city, New York—cops and firemen and rescue workers and just plain citizens of New York rising to the occasion as Londoners did more than fifty years ago.

One day, not too long after September 11, Ed Bradley and one of his producers, Michael Radutzky, came to me and told me about what they called "the city within a city," which was the incredible story of the volunteers who tended to the needs of the rescue workers at Ground Zero—like, in Ed's words, "the vice president of an investment bank who puts in a full day's work and then spends nearly all night organizing the relief effort; the computer programmer, who left his job and his family in Florida and drove a truck to New York to deliver supplies to Ground Zero; a group of Texans who set up a twenty-four-hour sidewalk barbecue stand to feed emergency personnel; the massage therapist who gave up her regular business to set up shop at Ground Zero, where she felt she was more needed than anywhere else; and a food caterer who left his paying job to volunteer in the rescue effort."

The story was too delicious to pass up, and when it was finally put on tape, it turned out to be one of the most poignant stories we or any other broadcast aired in the wake of the terrorist attacks. I'll always remember the words of one volunteer, Margie Edwards, who explained why she went to Ground Zero every day after work, handing out supplies to the workers digging through the rubble of what was once the World Trade Center. "It's very personal for me," she said. "My friend Todd is—is in there. When I come down here, I talk to him, and I want him to know that I'll be here with him, that he's not alone." Another volunteer, a man from Texas who was serving barbecue to the rescue workers, summed up the scene better than anyone else: "I've never seen a people come together like has happened around here. It's been incredible. I mean, there's no more Southern hospitality in Texas than in New York tonight. I'm telling you, it's awesome. Even though this is a horrific tragedy, this is New York's finest hour."

It wasn't long after we ran that piece that another televised sight all but broke my heart: the sons and daughters and the grandsons and granddaughters of those wartime Londoners I so loved parading through the streets of London protesting America's bombing of the

Taliban. Watching them, I became angrier and angrier. Didn't they know that if it weren't for the bombing missions of the American B–17s and their own RAF more than a half century ago during their war for survival, there might very well have been no streets of London for them to parade through—or, at the very least, parading through those same streets today might be not protesters but stormtroopers. Hadn't they ever heard Winston Churchill's short, sweet, and to-the-point paean of praise to their own RAF—"Never have so many owed so much to so few"?

I remember well those heroes of the Battle of Britain, who came to London to relax between missions. With their handlebar mustaches and chests full of ribbons, they were a rakish lot as they walked through Grosvenor Square or window-shopped on Regent Street. But when it came to girls, they were no match for the American Eighth Air Force pilots, who came to town loaded down with American cigarettes and nylon stockings. It really wasn't a fair fight. That's principally why Anglo-American relations in London in 1943 were in such a serious state of disrepair. So the brass—ours and theirs—decided to put on a show. What they decided to do was to have an American general decorate six British sailors and a British admiral decorate six American soldiers. There, in a mansion on London's Park Lane, under crossed British and American flags, the admiral and his staff and the general and his staff gathered to hand out the medals in front of the combined British and American press. I have told this story many times before, and I'm repeating it here because it says so much about diplomacy.

As the American general shook hands with the British admiral to start the festivities, the photographers banged away. They all got their shots except for a cameraman from the U.S. Army Pictorial Service. He kept clicking away but nothing happened. Finally, the American general, realizing that the GI was holding up this important display of British-American friendship, said, "What's the matter, son? Something wrong with your camera?"

"No, sir," the GI replied. "It's these damned Limey bulbs!"

That broke the tension. The British contingent burst out laughing, realizing what a silly exercise they were involved in. We all went back to the pubs, the Limeys and the Yanks, and continued to fight—over girls.

While I was in London, I hung around an officers' club called the Charles Street Club, where the better known of the newsmen hung out. One day, a guy showed up from Moscow, where he had been the United Press's bureau chief. Before you knew it, you could hear people saying, "You know who that is? That's Walter Cronkite." (Today, fifty years later, people still say, "You know who that is? That's Walter Cronkite.") I only knew him by reputation, and who could have imagined that someday he and I would work together in something called television, but damned if we didn't.

The reporters I knew worked hard, sometimes in harm's way, and played harder. For young men interested in young women, it was a fool's paradise—beguiling, silly, and often outrageous. I managed to fall seriously in love three or four times in less than fifteen months, writing my folks that this girl, then the next, was the one, even as I pledged allegiance to Mildred, the girl back home.

One of them was a showgirl named Pauline Waddington, who stripped under the name Joan White. Why, I don't know. Pauline seemed like a better name for a stripper than Joan. Anyway, a photographer friend, another Yank who had done some work in New York for the biggest name on Broadway, the impresario Billy Rose, joined me one Saturday night at the Windmill Theatre just off Piccadilly Circus, the home of London's best girlie show, where the girls were allowed to pose nude if—and that "if" was the law in London at the time—they didn't move a muscle.

To impress the stunning and statuesque Miss White and another chorine whose name we learned was Trixie something-or-other, we sent a note backstage telling them that we were two Yanks in the audience and that one of us had worked for Billy Rose.

Apparently that did it. First thing you know a note came back via an usher for us to meet them at the stage door after the show.

And so began yet another affair. Some months into it, while lying in bed one night, the beautiful Miss White turned to me and said, "May I ask you a question?"

"Sure," I said.

"Who," she asked, "is Billy Rose?"

Back home, it turned out, my parents were pack rats, saving almost all of my letters home. Reading them now, more than a half-century later, I do admit to feeling both pride and amusement—pride that I was a small part of what Tom Brokaw has called "the greatest generation" and amused that I shared with my parents every one of my many love affairs. There are references to many women (including Mildred, the girl back home) because, remember, I was twenty and single in London, a city where young unattached Yanks were much in demand. Plays, musicals, and movies were a rich part of life in London, even though it was tough to go to a movie or a play without it being interrupted by a buzz bomb, those V-1 pilotless drones that the Germans sent over London. When you heard the motor conk out, you knew—it was going to come down somewhere in the neighborhood, hopefully not on top of the theater. They came so often that if you were indoors when you heard the motor conk out, you usually ignored it.

Money, too, played a role in my letters. My mother was in and out of the hospital, and had had a breast removed. My father had some business difficulties during the war, and money was an issue in the family. I was making $100 a week, good money in those days, and with so many of my expenses taken care of by the military or service organizations, I couldn't come close to spending it all. So about half my pay went to the home front in New Rochelle.

At one point, I learned from a family friend that my folks had been recounting my adventures in London to just about everyone, including mothers of my friends on the front lines. It troubled me enough to beg them to stop: "I hope you aren't telling people too much about what I'm doing," I wrote them. "After all, Mrs. Markell, Mrs. Whitelaw, Mrs. Meyers, etc., are concerned with only one thing these days and it makes me look like a heel to be having such a wonderful time when Mike, Whitey and Dodie may not come back.... Please from now on let's keep these letters just between ourselves. Put yourself in the position of the Whitelaws or the Meyers and you can see how really little you would care about the 'great times' anyone else was having."

July 18

Dear Mom and Dad,

Still no mail from you, but I guess that's because of the delay not because you haven't written. I am still terribly anxious to hear about Mom.

......Am still a little unsettled but things should be all ironed out by the end of the week and I'll be ready to knock out a couple of stories a week. My name will be in the masthead as Merchant Marine editor.

Here is the big shock. I'm going to bring you home a daughter-in-law. No, we're not married yet, but will be by the time I leave here. Her name is Tamara Mapplebeck. She works at the

American embassy. Her mother is a Russian countess and her father a captain in the British Army.......Tamara is probably the most beautiful girl in all England and I'm sure you'd love her.... Haven't written and told Mildred yet—that's going to be difficult....

August 5

Dear Mom and Dad,

Tamara and I have called it off. I guess it's still Mildred. The other night Tamara and I went to see William Saroyan's "Human Comedy"—she didn't like it, and I told her if she didn't like Saroyan she wouldn't like America—and then I realized that she just wasn't the girl for me....

Incidentally, I went up to see a Public Relations officer...the other day, a Lt. Meredith. Could have sworn I knew him from somewhere. I glanced down on his desk and saw a sign: "Lt. Burgess Meredith." Then I knew where I'd seen him!

August 23

Dear Mom and Dad,

I'm so darned happy to hear that mom is back to normal. That had me pretty worried.

I think going to the movies makes me the most homesick. Sitting at the picture you forget where you are and it could be Loew's or Proctor's or even the Alden. Then when you come out on the street and you see a sign "Regent St." instead of Main Street you wake up with a thud, and realize how damned far away you are....

August 25

Dear Folks,

Before I go any further let's get one thing straight—that money
I am sending home is for you to do anything you want with,
and not for any "nest egg." ...I have about $200 a month
which is more than enough and certainly doesn't leave
me short.

December 6, 1943

Dear Mom, Dad and Dick,

As you have no doubt been reading in the papers there is much
talk of Jerry shelling London. We, here, of course, put little
stock in it, and if he should please don't get panicky as I am
quite capable of taking care of myself.

　　Had lunch Friday with Lady Astor down aboard one of our
ships. She struck me as a crazy old bitch, and is reputed to be
quite pro-Nazi, but exceedingly congenial.... She gave me her
address here in London, and told me to get in touch with her
sometime and spend a weekend down at Cliveden, her country estate.... Six months ago I would have cut off my arm for
the chance, but I guess I'm getting to be a regular nonchalant
newspaper man—and refuse to be awed by celebrities. Ho
hum—lackaday....

Dec. 23

Dear Mom, Dad and Dick,

Last week I was away for three days and nights on a British
destroyer on anti-E-boat patrol in the North Sea, the story of
which I cabled back and which will run in *Stars & Stripes* as

soon as I can get some pictures from the Admiralty to illustrate the story.

Had a swell time and got a good story. Merchant Marine angle was that we escorted a convoy down the coast. Described the dangers of these heavily mined waters which merchant seamen have to run through. We had a bit of a do with German E-boats (which are like our P.T.'s), but we drove them off before they could do any harm. Also we sunk a mine.

...All the action is at night so you mostly sleep in the daytime and stay on deck at night. The British are allowed liquor aboard their ships, and so a good time was had by all!!! (Note to censor: the above stuff has all been passed by the press censor—in case you want to check.) ...

[Undated; postmarked January 13, 1944]

Dear Folks,

...There's a lot of talk about the Americans being here helping Anglo-American relations. That's a lot of hokum. The Americans over here never want to see Britain again and the British don't ever want to see us again.

I am more than ever convinced that America is the greatest place in the world, but Americans are by no means the greatest people in the world, and by their always bragging and shouting about how great they are, they are going to make many enemies.

The British know they are years behind us, but they resent the fact that they can't go into a pub for a quiet glass of beer without some Yank throwing it up to them about "how great we are."

The flag waving that is so typical of America is a big joke to them and is sometimes very embarrassing.

'nuff of this stuff. Gotta get a haircut....

February 4, 1944

Dear Mom, Dad and Dick,

...Last night I got one of the biggest thrills of my life. Took Eda and her mother to see the Lunts in "There Shall Be No Night." Sitting directly in front of us (right in the next row) was Winston Churchill. Of course, I've seen him quite a bit—up at Parliament etc., but the real thrill was seeing him moved by the same dialogue that moved me. It is something I will not forget for a long time....

Eda is a real sweetheart, and though you may laugh at this, for the first time in life I'm *really* in love....

Monday, Feb. 28

Dear Mom, Dad and Dick,

About these raids. You will be happy to know, Mom, that the place where I'm living is considered to be one of the safest places in London, and at night when things get heavy everybody goes down to the second floor which is a natural shelter as it is an eight story building (here, that's a skyscraper). I, of course, wouldn't bother to get out of bed except that it's so much fun. Everybody in bathrobes and house coats.... I usually go up on the roof afterward to see the fires. But I hope you will be relieved to know that the building is so safe....

Pop, about keeping my nose clean. I will. Though it's damned difficult. Have some terrific stories to tell you when I get home—I think I'm growing up. 'nuff said....

April 14

Dear Mom, Dad and Dick,

...Can't help but be a little worried about my draft status with this new tightening up. If my classification is changed, explain

to them, will you, that I come under the category of Merchant
Marine personnel away at sea, as I'm traveling in war zones with
them.... Point out to them that I am attached to the army and
that I've been waiting here for ten months to do a specific job
for the government and it would be a bitch if I got recalled just
before the big show came off. From Ike's statements to the air
force boys the other day, which you must have read, it shouldn't
be long now.... Boy after all the things I've been through—RAF,
Royal Navy, air raids, convoys and lots I haven't been able to
write you about—I don't know how I could sit on my behind in
some army camp in the States....

It must seem from this letter that I am awfully worried. It's
just that I've spent ten months getting this Merchant Marine
proper publicity in the event of an invasion, and this would be a
hell of a time to get drafted....

Saturday April 29

Dear Folks,

If all of a sudden you stop hearing from me please don't worry.
That's all I can say. Will cable you soon as I get back. When that
will be I can't say, but when the mail starts getting slow and you
start reading in the papers about things popping here, you'll
know that I'm at a place where I can't write....

In the spring of 1944, everyone knew D-Day was coming; I wanted a
piece of it and stressed to the navy how important it was for the home
front to know of the merchant marine's contribution to the invasion.
One day in late May 1944, I was summoned to a navy public relations
office, told to sit down and listen up. We've been tailing you for a
week and we know you're all right, the navy PR man said. Go home,
pack your bag and get a train to Oban, Scotland. Which I did. In

Oban, I was met by another navy man, who took me to the harbor where dozens of the sorriest tubs anyone had ever seen were at anchor.

The ships, the one I boarded and all the others, were riding very high, so it was clear there was no cargo. And no fighting men either. Even the captain didn't know what was going on: He had sealed orders. Finally, at the designated time, he opened his orders and called me to the wheelhouse. The ships, he said, were loaded with dynamite and we were going to sink them off the French coast to make a breakwater after the initial invasion so that the follow-on forces — hundreds of thousands of troops and thousands of tons of materiel — could land in calm waters or, at worse, a light chop. With us aboard? No, the captain said, we'd be taken off before the demolition teams blew up the ships.

So there we were, lying off the beach on D-Day plus one, waiting for our orders to go in. On D-Day plus three, they said, okay, everyone get ready — and in a flash, the LCTs, the landing craft, were alongside taking us off. At that point, we must have been 100 yards from the beach, maybe less, and the LCTs started heading away from land. Wait, wait, I shouted, let's head for the beach. We did, just briefly enough for me to jump out, touch my feet on that hallowed ground and reboard. We were out of there before they blew the ships.

Sunday, June 11

Dear Mom, Dad and Dick,

Well, here I am back in my flat safe and sound....

I got back Friday. Came back on an LCT. Held off writing in the hopes that the censor would release my story and I could tell you a bit of what went on.

This much I can say—I was at the beachhead nearest Cherbourg, and as rough as it was, it wasn't as bad as I thought it would be. I got there the morning of D-plus-1....

I have an exclusive on a story which is still classified top secret and which is a humdinger. So much so that CBS called New York and had them cancel a program to give me fifteen minutes on the air with my story, but the Navy killed my script. When the story finally does break it should hit page one nationally with my byline....

I only wish some people at home who are worried about an extra gallon of gas could have seen the casualties we brought back. You know I've always been rational about this war. I couldn't hate anyone, not even the Japs.

At least that was the way I felt until a Coast Guard launch pulled alongside our LCT with 24 casualties lying out on the deck. I wanted to grab a rifle and kill every Heinie in the world. Now I know how soldiers get keyed up in battle....

As we moved up to the beach, the battleships were throwing salvo after salvo over our heads into the German positions. The Luftwaffe didn't bother us too much in the daytime cause we had pretty much control of the skies. An ME109 did come in about an hour after we anchored and he looked like a bastard at a family reunion. He buggered off after dropping his bombs like a bat out of hell. The bay was being shelled when we got there, but the cruiser and battleships soon knocked out the heavy guns....

A letter arrived less than a week after I returned to London—returned from the greatest invasion in military history. Greetings, it said; you've been drafted. Jumping from uncompleted service in the merchant marine to a civilian job with temporary rank in the navy had left me eligible for the draft. Now, even though I'd just come back from the beach at Normandy, the army wanted me. I did not want the army, however, so in September 1944, I returned to the United States and managed to get sworn in as an ensign in the naval reserve. It meant that I'd go back to sea, but as a pharmacist's mate.

Although the war didn't end officially until we dropped an atomic bomb on Hiroshima, it ended for me some months earlier in a cemetery on Saipan in the Marianas, a chain of islands in the South Pacific that American marines had taken in some of the bloodiest battles of World War II.

Walking among the grave markers, I couldn't help but think back to a Sunday afternoon in December 1941 when my pal Bobby Whitelaw and I, carrying BB guns with which we were popping tin cans in the woods, stopped at a gas station to warm up and were told by the owner, "You'd better learn how to use one of them things. The Japs just bombed Pearl Harbor."

What brought that Sunday afternoon crashing back on me was finding the grave I was looking for, the grave marked "PFC Robert Whitelaw, USMC." Bobby, I learned, had been killed by a sniper— a Japanese kid who might very well have been told on that same Sunday afternoon, "You better learn how to use one of them things. We just bombed Pearl Harbor."

Many years later, I would visit another American military cemetery—this one in Normandy—where, at low tide, you can still see the remains of the old tubs we sank, maybe a hundred yards off-shore. And I thought of how, like millions of other young men, I was molded by World War II in ways that endure to this day. It shaped my values, my sense of right and wrong, and it also quickened my pulse to be a reporter.

CHAPTER THREE

The Emerald City

I was in the *Stars & Stripes* offices in New York City when the wires moved the story that an atomic bomb had been detonated over Hiroshima. A week later, the war was over and it was time to find civilian work again.

I fancied myself becoming a foreign correspondent, and I had spent a great deal of time and energy during my months in London trying to make the kind of contacts that would help me realize this dream once the war was over.

What could have been more rewarding, satisfying, and glamorous than returning to Europe and writing for the Paris edition of the *Herald Tribune*? Unfortunately, there was one problem. The Paris edition's editor, Eric Hawkins, didn't share my pipe dream.

Okay, I thought, forget about going to work at 33, rue de Berri. Go West, young man, back to West Forty-first Street to the *Herald Tribune* mother ship, where you apprenticed as a copyboy—not just *a* copyboy, but *the head* copyboy. Surely they would find something for this up-and-coming journalist that would be commensurate with who and what he had been during the war. And they did! They said I could have my old job back and I wouldn't have to work for $15 a week. The job, I was told, now paid the princely sum of $25 a week.

That's when I bid the *HT* goodbye and trundled over to the AP. I got hired on the spot to become night editor of the Associated Press bureau in Memphis, Tennessee—where from an office right off the city room (my idea of heaven) of the Memphis *Commercial Appeal* I ran the night side of the AP's tristate wire. Tennessee, Mississippi, and Arkansas — oh, yeah, now I was in the big time. This job had taken me all the way to $50 a week, enough to get married on.

My new bride, Mary Weaver, a native Tennessean, decided there were better fish to fry in New York than in Memphis and if I could get the job of editor of the *Pelham Sun*, the weekly I had worked for during the day in 1942 while serving as a *Herald Tribune* copyboy at night, we could blow the South and raise a family up north.

Mary had a point, and it came home to me not long afterward, when Harry Snyder, the AP bureau chief in Nashville, came to Memphis one day and told me what a great job I was doing, how impressed he was with what I was turning out, and that, although he didn't want me to get my hopes up too high, there was a possibility that someday I could be promoted to the bureau in Nashville — not to count on it, but it wasn't out of the realm of possibility. And then he said that there have also been instances when someone has moved from Nashville to Atlanta — not often, but it had happened. And all I could think was, "My God, I could be an old man by the time I worked my way through every tank town in the South to get back to New York." Which was where the best jobs were and where I wanted to be — if I couldn't be in London or Paris.

So I got the job in Pelham and we headed north.

Pelham was a lot closer to New York City than Memphis, but not much happened there either, and six months or so after I arrived I left to become the night telephoto editor for Acme Newspictures, then the picture arm of the United Press, which was a better stepping-stone to the kind of job I wanted. Acme occupied a floor in a nondescript office building on Manhattan's Eighth Avenue, a block or two below the garment district, and what I did was select pictures shot by Acme photographers, write captions for them, and then transmit them by wire to newspaper offices all over the country. Sounds like the big time, but it didn't look like it. The place was musty, and so was the job, and if this was journalism, I thought, maybe I'd better start looking for something more exciting.

One day it came, out of the blue. A friend, Bob Rogow, who had worked with me at the *Trib*, was now working for CBS Radio and had heard about an opening at CBS for someone with picture experience.

"What does radio want with someone with picture experience?" I asked him.

"Not radio," he said. "Television."

"*Whata*-vision?" I asked.

"Television!" he said.

"You mean, where you sit at home and watch little pictures in a box?" I asked.

"That's it," he replied. "They got it. I saw it."

"The hell you did."

"The hell I didn't."

"Where did you see it?" I asked.

"Upstairs over Grand Central."

So I went down to Grand Central Terminal and damned if they didn't have it, up on the top floor—little pictures in a box. They also had cameras and lights and makeup artists and stage managers and microphone booms just like in the movies, and I was hooked. I had been passing through Grand Central every day on my way to work at Acme and never knew that upstairs over the trains and the waiting room and the information booth was an attic stuffed with the most fabulous toys anyone ever had to play with.

I was mesmerized. As a child of the movies, I was torn between wanting to be Julian Marsh, the Broadway producer in *42nd Street*, who was up to his ass in showgirls, and Hildy Johnson, the hellbent-for-leather reporter in *The Front Page*, who was up to his ass in news stories. Oh my God, I thought, in television, I could be *both* of them.

While waiting to see the top guy at CBS, a charmer named Bob

Bendick, who was one of television's pioneers, I looked around at the lights, the booms, the cameras, the makeup artists, the prop masters, and the wardrobe mistresses and I felt like Dorothy in the Emerald City. I got the job for $80 a week—$20 a week less than I was getting at Acme.

How, with a wife and baby and a second one on the way, can you take a cut in pay?

Oh, what the hell, I thought, nothing ventured, nothing gained. Sometimes, to this day, more than half a century later, I get cold chills thinking how close I came to opting *not* to take the $20-a-week pay cut and letting television go on its merry way without me.

At any rate, I went back to Acme and told Boyd Lewis, the executive editor who had hired me, that I was leaving.

"For what?" he said.

"Television," I told him.

"Television?" he said. "That's a fad. It won't last."

He was half right. It was a fad, but it lasted.

After CBS hired me, I bought my first television set, but there weren't many of them around. In '48, television was being watched mainly in the windows of appliance stores, where enterprising salesmen tried to talk customers who came in for vacuum cleaners and air conditioners into splurging on the latest in home appliances: television sets. If you knew someone who owned one—a black-and-white Westinghouse, Philco, or Dumont—and they liked you, you got invited over to their house to watch the only two things that were worth watching: Milton Berle's *Texaco Star Theater* and the occasional Joe Louis heavyweight fight.

My first job at CBS was to work on a live, fifteen-minute newscast, sponsored by Oldsmobile. Douglas Edwards would begin reading the news at 6:45 P.M. and, as often as not, he would not end precisely at 7—we always got hell for running over. Today if you run over, a computer will cut you off. In 1948, no one knew what a computer was. Three hours later, at 9:45 P.M., we'd do it all over again for the West Coast. For the handful of us putting out television's first daily newscast, it was enough that a picture—no matter how snowy—got from Studio 41 above Grand Central Terminal to an apartment house in the Bronx. Sending the picture all the way to the West Coast on the coaxial cable seemed like a miracle.

The title they gave me was associate director. The other ADs included some names that may be more familiar—names like Sidney Lumet and John Frankenheimer and Yul Brynner. All three of them soon decamped for Hollywood, where Lumet and Frankenheimer became prominent film directors. Brynner became the King of Siam and made the shaved head a fashion statement long before Michael Jordan did.

Six months later, they made me a director, along with a guy named Frank Shaffner, who I always thought looked more like a matinee idol than a director. He also left for Hollywood, where he directed Steve McQueen in *Papillon* and George C. Scott in *Patton*. With talent like that out of the picture, it was perhaps a case of the flatness of the ground around me. But at any rate, I was now the sole and only director of the *CBS Evening News*, and then the producer as well.

It's curious that television news took its titles from Hollywood rather than from newspapers. It was always "director" instead of "managing editor" and "producer" instead of "executive editor." Today, I am the executive producer of *60 Minutes* even though I function as executive editor of the program. Our table of organization calls for six correspondents, counting Andy Rooney, twenty-two producers and twenty-two associate producers. But we are all reporters. A half-dozen of us talk better than the rest so we put them on the air. But maybe the Hollywood influence was inevitable, given the nature of the medium. I've got to admit that one of the things that initially appealed to me about television was the cross between news and entertainment.

Still, in my serious moments, I had real doubts about whether television had a future. None of us knew whether television would become a match for radio. If Henry Ford had taken Americans out of the house and put them on the road, radio put them back in the house. And I wondered if television could really give radio a run for its money, let alone overwhelm it.

Douglas Edwards was the ultimate broadcaster, but unfortunately, not the ultimate journalist. And the powers that be never saw him as the voice of CBS Television as they saw Edward R. Murrow as the voice of CBS Radio. Our competition was John Cameron Swayze at NBC, who NBC also didn't see as a permanent fixture if and when television took off the way they wanted it to. Doug was easy to work with and unlike others in the business, did not have an ego that got in the way of our operating as a team. We were pretty good friends and shared a ritual. It was before videotape and, as I said, we had to do the broadcast twice—once at 6:45 for the eastern and central time zones, and then again three hours later for the West Coast. What did two guys on the loose in New York every weekday night do with themselves? They went to the Hudson Burlesque in Union City, New Jersey, where they became as much of a fixture as the strippers. No matter what the enticements, we had to be back in the studio for that West Coast feed. Today, when people talk about the marvel of videotape, I think it was better without it. How else would you get to a burlesque every night?

The year 1948 also marked the first time television covered a political convention. By today's standards, or even the standards of the '60s these were stone-age affairs, with cumbersome cameras, overhead booms and miles and miles of wires. Both the Democrats and the Republicans met in Philadelphia, so we only had to set up our equipment once. Because there were only two coaxial cables at the time, and one of them was designated to carry the television pool, the networks would rotate: We'd get it for twenty minutes, then NBC would get it for twenty minutes, then it would be ABC's turn. And if we ran over our twenty minutes, we would be cut off, sometimes in midsentence.

What I didn't know when I came to CBS News was that the guy in charge, a fellow named William S. Paley, was a broadcasting genius, part P. T. Barnum and part Henry Luce. This handsome matinee-idol pioneer had grown up in Chicago as the son of a successful tobacco merchant—of La Palina cigars—and after graduating from the Wharton School at the University of Pennsylvania, he bought the struggling CBS Radio Network in 1929 and immediately began to expand it.

Paley worked hand-in-glove with another genius named Frank Stanton, who was president of CBS, and as I said at a recent dinner honoring him, "If broadcasting had a patron saint, it would be Frank Stanton." He was in day-to-day charge of CBS, which wasn't easy when you had a chairman like Paley, who always thought he was in charge. And sad to say, as close as the two of them were in business, socially they seldom if ever saw each other outside the office. But inside the office, they saw eye to eye on the role they thought broadcasting played in American life. More than anybody, Frank Stanton kept broadcasting on a high plane, and he patterned a lot of what he expected of us on the way the BBC had carved out a niche for itself in its part of the world.

Bill Paley erected two towers of power, one for entertainment and one for news. And he decreed that there would be no bridge between them. In one, Paley the showman gave America Jack Benny, Jackie Gleason, Ed Sullivan, Lucille Ball, Mary Tyler Moore, Alan Alda, Carroll O'Connor, Red Skelton, and dozens of others. In the other, Paley the newsman gave America William L. Shirer, Howard K. Smith, Elmer Davis, Eric Sevareid, David Schoenbrun, Charles Collingwood, Walter Cronkite, Dan Rather, and, of course, my team. In short, Paley was the guy who put Frank Sinatra and Edward R. Murrow on the radio and 60 *Minutes* on television.

It was a different time and a different business, and Paley and Stanton knew that if they kept the two towers separate and apart, the prestige of a Ed Murrow would rub off on a Lucille Ball and vice versa, and both stars would shine even brighter.

In charge of making sure CBS exercised its public-service responsibilities for using the public airwaves was a man named Paul White, who retired before I got there, before television began to compete with radio for the attention of the public. With the support of Paley and Stanton, White had the job of building a radio news team second to none. He did that and more. The people he and Paley brought together, with heavy prodding from Murrow, weren't the best journalists in broadcasting—they were the best journalists in journalism. Even the *New York Times* couldn't touch them. They were the best radio had to offer, and they all but gave the back of their hand to me and the little band of brothers who were putting out *Douglas Edwards with the News* on television. They thought television was for kids—*Howdy Doody* and *Romper Room*. They were journalist-scholars, and to them, radio was where you did serious reporting. They made their reputation covering World War II, and they didn't want to come to terms with the fact that the war was over. But with some difficulty, they adjusted.

In the 1950s, radio was still the place to be if you were in news, until a man named Sig Mickelson arrived from WCCO, the CBS-owned-and-operated affiliate in Minneapolis. Mickelson determined that television could achieve the same prestige in broadcast journalism that radio had. At the time, there was no president of the news division, but he was a vice president of the company assigned to run the news division, which he did superbly and made the necessary changes that eventually ushered in the television age. He hired first-class journalists, filling the ranks of producers and directors with people who could better be characterized as reporters and editors.

The reporters at CBS evoked a certain age and a certain era when "ladies" and "gentlemen" were still in vogue. One day, around the turn of the century, something-or-other happened at the Vanderbilt mansion and when the press descended on the house, the butler, so the story goes, said to Mrs. Vanderbilt, "Madam, there are several reporters at the door and a gentleman from the *Herald*." Well, that's how I felt about Ed Murrow's team of Eric Sevareid, Charles Collingwood, Howard K. Smith, David Schoenbrun, Winston Burdett, Larry LeSeuer, Richard C. Hottelet, and Bill Downs. They were a breed apart. To me they were "the gentlemen from CBS." Any time anyone asks me how 60 *Minutes* stayed on top all those years, I have one answer: "We come from good stock."

You seldom, if ever, saw one of them in a television studio. What TV was doing at the time was not, they thought, serious enough for them. They thought that we were too caught up in the theatrics of television to pay attention to the serious side of broadcast journalism. And they may have been right. Among the things I concerned myself with was how to let Doug Edwards communicate the news of the day to the public while looking down at a script and not looking them in the eye. To solve that problem, I put the script on a poster-sized card held by a stage hand, so Doug could more or less look at it and the camera lens at the same time. That went on until a guy named Irving Kahn walked into the studio one day and demonstrated something he called a "teleprompter." It solved the problem, and just in time, because I was trying at that moment to convince Doug to learn Braille. If that sounds ridiculous, think about it. If you could run your hands over a script printed in Braille, you would never have to look down and could keep looking at the audience. I thought it was a great idea. Everybody else thought it was off-the-wall. To this day, I think I'm right and they're wrong. And if the teleprompter had never been invented, I'm convinced that the Rathers, the Brokaws, and the Jenningses would all be reading their scripts in Braille.

It wasn't until June 1951 that attitudes among the radio journalists began to shift. That was when Fred Friendly and Murrow decided to end their popular radio program *Hear It Now*, which offered a compilation of interviews, opinion, and sometimes just old-fashioned reporting, and decided to try their hand at a television version of the program, called, you guessed it, *See It Now*.

I worked on *See It Now* on Sunday afternoons for several years in the 1950s while at the same time working weeknights as the producer-director of *Douglas Edwards with the News*. As much as I would like to take some credit for *See It Now's* success, the truth is that all I did was act as its studio director—acting more or less like a traffic cop on the live broadcast, making sure that the production ran smoothly and that when Murrow cued up a film or a live remote, that there was no embarrassing wait between the time he called for it and the time it appeared. Because the show originated from a control room, I was often caught on camera sitting alongside Murrow, which made people think I had a bigger hand in it than I actually had.

Along with Murrow, credit for that show belonged to Fred Friendly, a big bear of a man, a truly spectacular piece of talent who made *See It Now* television's most prestigious broadcast, attracting awards and accolades and more applause than television had heard before. Before I knew it, Friendly had replaced me at the head of the class.

That didn't bother me too much. Television was expanding, and I figured there was enough glory around for the two of us. Besides, when *See It Now* moved out of its Sunday afternoon slot because it couldn't compete with *Amos 'n Andy* on several NBC stations, I lucked into a wonderful new assignment, directing special events for the very prestigious Sunday afternoon broadcast, *Omnibus*. This program was presided over by one of broadcasting's legends, Alistair Cooke. Among the stories I handled for them was a visit to Sagamore Farms, home of the great race horse Native Dancer, who the *Daily Racing Form* called "the best horse who ever ran in the Kentucky Derby without winning," and who was perhaps the best race horse ever. I foolishly asked the jockey, Eric Guerin, if he wouldn't wear a wireless microphone and let us hear what he said to the horse when he talked to him during a race. To which he replied, "Talk to the horse? I don't talk to the horse. When I want him to do something, I hit him with the whip." (Again, because I'd been to so many movies, I couldn't imagine Mickey Rooney doing anything like that.)

By the time the 1952 presidential campaign came around, television news had become more sophisticated, but we were still feeling our way and making it up as we went along. A lot of what we think of as television's basic tools and terminology came out of our coverage of that campaign. I remember a meeting, before the Republican convention that summer, when our production team was sitting around a table at the Stockyards Inn in Chicago with convention producer, Paul Levitan, discussing our coverage of the upcoming event. Our main man at the convention was going to be Walter Cronkite, who had just come over to the network after a short stint as a local broadcaster in Washington. I remembered Cronkite as a great print journalist from my days in London during the war, and knew that Frank Stanton saw Cronkite as Douglas Edwards's successor as the front man of the *CBS Evening News*. What no one foresaw was that, from that summer on, everybody who did what Walter Cronkite did would be called an "anchorman." Sig Mickelson, our boss, later claimed paternity for the term and may well have been right that he coined the phrase "anchorman," even though I thought I had. At any rate, it had nothing to do with boats, but had everything to do with a relay team. Our plan was to use four broadcasters: John Daly (who later became president of ABC News), Quincy Howe (one of the great names of the radio era), and my guy, Doug Edwards, along with the new kid on the block, Walter Cronkite. The idea was that they would hand off the coverage to each other, more or less the way a relay team hands off a baton. And just as the fastest man on a relay team runs the "anchor leg," Cronkite would run the anchor leg for us and became from that day on, not just "an anchorman," but "*the* anchorman." And now, "anchorman" is what everybody calls anyone, man or woman, who sits at what has come to be known as an "anchor desk" and presides over a newscast. I'm willing to bet that until they read this book, most of them have no idea where the term came from. To add to the silliness, anchors who also go out and report stories are called "floating anchors."

Just as the idea of a calling a broadcaster an anchorman came out of the blue, so did another idea I had, which I am happy to say makes more sense to me than the first one. It was in a Chicago diner during the same 1952 convention. I was having breakfast and pondering the problem of how to identify people on screen so that viewers at home would know who was being shown without the studio having to lower the audio from the rostrum, so Cronkite could come in and tell them, "That's Nelson Rockefeller sitting there, and that's

Bob Taft walking down the aisle." What I thought would be ideal would be to superimpose the names on the screen, but by the time anyone could set up the type to do it, the shot would be gone, and we would have moved on to something else. I was mulling over this problem when the waitress came over to ask what I wanted to eat. I looked past her up at a board on the wall listing the menu — little white letters stuck on a black background. It suddenly hit me: white letters superimposed on a black background is the way you superimpose names on the screen because the camera will not pick up the black, and you can superimpose that shot over anything you want to and show the letters and the picture simultaneously. Bingo!

"I'll have the board," I said.

"What board?" she said.

"The one up there on the wall, the one that says, 'Hamburgers 35 cents, soup 25 cents.'" (Remember, it was 1952.)

She went to get the manager. He came over and I asked him the same question. The transaction cost me $45 — $35 for the board, $10 for the stick-on letters.

I went back to the studio and told our guys, "Hey, look at this. The same letters that they use in diners to spell out S-O-U-P we can use to spell out T-A-F-T or R-O-C-K-E-F-E-L-L-E-R. Just leave off the prices and we can identify everybody at the convention without Cronkite having to say a word." And that's how the super — today it's called a chyron — was invented.

In those days, improvisation was our middle name. When the Soviets sent up Sputnik in the late '50s, I wanted to show how it passed over different parts of the world. But how? Remember, it was long before computer graphics. I got myself a black metal hanger, opened it up, and sent someone down to a sporting goods store to pick up a white cloth golf ball. I stuck the ball on the end of the black hangar, which, like the menu board, was invisible to the camera. I then hooked the hanger with the white ball on the end to a motor that turned a wheel, and then I electronically superimposed the white golf ball over a spinning globe. There we were, our own Sputnik.

We also were fierce in our competition with the other networks for breaking news and interviews. Right after the Republicans chose Richard Nixon to be Dwight Eisenhower's running mate, Nixon was holding an impromptu news conference in a hallway leading from the convention floor. NBC, ABC, and CBS, among others, were carrying the news conference live on radio and television. As usual, it was a mob scene. Our man in the crowd was Bill Downs, who was wearing a headset on which he could hear Walter Cronkite and Ed Murrow in the anchor booth and me when I wanted to cut in and tell him something. He was also holding the microphone over which we were picking up what Nixon was saying. All of a sudden I was struck with a crazy thought. "Take off your headset, Bill," I said, "and put it on Nixon before he has a chance to know what's happening, and tell him Cronkite and Murrow want to talk to him."

Downs couldn't answer because his mike was "hot" and Nixon was speaking into it, as he was speaking into a dozen or so other mikes that were stuck in his face. Bill thought I had lost my mind, but he did what I told him. He took off his headset and stuck it on Nixon's head, handed him his mike and told him, "Walter Cronkite and Ed Murrow want to talk to you."

Because it happened so fast and because it happened live in front of millions, Nixon had no chance to think about it. The other reporters didn't know what to do because there was nothing they *could* do. Here was Richard Nixon, wearing a CBS headset and holding a CBS microphone, talking to Murrow and Cronkite live on NBC and ABC as well as on CBS. We, of course, could carry both ends of the conversation. What the others got were only long pauses and then Nixon's answers, which began, "Well, Ed," or "Well, Walter." It was delicious.

Putting a headset on news personalities at news events so they could talk to Cronkite became a CBS trademark, and later, a joke. Hughes Rudd, one of our reporters during the '60s and '70s once said he'd had a dream that I told him to take off his headset and put it on Cronkite so Walter could have a conversation with himself.

In the spring of 1953, I was chosen for a plum assignment: to produce and direct CBS's coverage of the coronation of Queen Elizabeth II at London's Westminster Abbey. I felt like I was going home, to the city I had fallen in love with during World War II, to work with two of the biggest names in broadcast journalism: Edward R. Murrow and Richard Dimbleby, who was almost as well known in Britain as Winston Churchill.

It was not only years before the first transatlantic satellite, it was before anyone (except perhaps a couple of dreamers in a lab) had even thought of the possibility of satellites, let alone satellite television. It was even before videotape, so we were stuck with editing something called a kinescope, a film that was made by focusing a motion picture camera on a television set. In a stunt dreamed up by Sig Mickelson, we chartered a BOAC Stratocruiser, pulled out most of the seats and replaced them with editing equipment called movieolas so we could put the show together in the air over the Atlantic and have it ready for broadcast when the plane landed in New York.

Why all the trouble and expense to show the American people what was essentially a parade of gilded carriages and plumed Welsh Guardsmen in a procession of Knights of the Realm and Dukes and Duchesses of Whatever? So what! And who cared?

Remember, this was only eight years after the end of World War II, and so many of us remembered having watched Hitler's soldiers parade down the Champs-Elysées in Paris, that for a long time there was the frightening possibility that we would also see Hitler's soldiers parading through Whitehall or marching across London Bridge—and the world, as we knew it, would have been lost to us and to everyone else who fell before the might of the Wehrmacht.

But of course, it didn't happen that way. The Americans and British had stopped Hitler in his tracks—and the monarchy and the world as we knew it were still alive and well. And this panoply of pomp and circumstance was testimony to the fact that God was still in his heaven and everything, once more, was right with the world. In many ways, Queen Elizabeth's coronation was the closing ceremony of World War II, and Americans were glued to their television sets to watch it unfold.

On a similar day a few years later, much the same panoply of gilded carriages and royal folderol led Drew Middleton of *The New York Times* to write, "For a brief moment today, the terrible strident pace of the twentieth century slowed to the trot of cavalry horses." Dream copy, for a dream wedding that turned into a nightmare: England's Princess Margaret's ill-fated wedding to the Earl of Snowden, Anthony Armstrong-Jones, who made a lousy husband but was a brilliant photographer.

Tony and I would get to know each other when he worked for me in the 1960s on a documentary about old age. I remember the first time I was invited to dine with him and Princess Margaret at Kensington Palace. I was staying at the Savoy, where I picked up a taxi and told the driver, "Kensington Palace, please."

Figuring he had some American wacko in his cab, the driver turned around slowly and said, "You mean the Kensington Palace Hotel, right?"

"Wrong," I said. "I mean the Kensington Palace Palace!"

When I told the story to Princess Margaret at dinner, she told me, "Don't worry about it. Happens to all my guests."

Back home, the triumph of World War II had given way to the tensions of the cold war, and it was here that television journalism—especially at CBS—came of age. Ed Murrow's devastating examination of Joseph R. McCarthy in 1954, in the wake of all the damage the Wisconsin senator had done with his Communist witch-hunts, demonstrated how powerful the medium could be as a force for change—in this case, change for the better. Murrow's *See It Now* used film of McCarthy in action, of course, but relied heavily on McCarthy's own words to tie the noose that would help to hang him. In the end, Murrow looked the viewers in the eye and said, "This is no time for men who oppose his methods to keep silent. We can deny our heritage and our history, but we cannot escape responsibility for the result."

McCarthy immediately demanded equal time for rebuttal, and got it a few weeks later. But his ramblings and outrageous charges against Murrow only tightened the rope around his neck, especially after Ed, who got a copy of the recording the day before and had stayed up all night working on his response, answered McCarthy. "When the record is finally written, as it will one day," Ed said, "it will answer the question, who has helped the Communist cause and who has served his country better, Senator McCarthy or I? I would like to be remembered by the answer to that question." Murrow had retained his dignity and exposed McCarthy irredeemably as a demagogue and a bully.

Murrow was nothing less than the conscience of America at a critical time. Eight months later, McCarthy was finished when the Senate voted 67–22 to censure him. The senator from Wisconsin, the censure resolution said, "tended to bring the Senate into dishonor and disrespect, to obstruct the Constitutional processes of the Senate and to impair its dignity, and such conduct is hereby condemned."

It was a terrible time. Loyalty oaths were the order of the day, and we had one at CBS. I heard there were colleagues of mine who admitted that they had been members of the Party, but I didn't know who they were. Maybe I was naive, but I didn't know anybody who I ever knew to be a card-carrying member of the Party.

CBS News was hardly touched by the Red Scare. The only person I remember being called before the House Un-American Activities Committee was CBS's Rome bureau chief, Winston Burdett. He was told to cooperate if he wanted to keep working, and he wound up naming names of Communists or suspected Communists he knew. This, in turn, infuriated his and my colleague David Schoenbrun, our Paris bureau chief, to whom I said, "David, don't be so fucking high and mighty. If you've never faced what Burdett is facing, if somebody told you, 'You better cooperate with the House Un-American Activities Committee unless you want to spend the rest of your life on an unemployment line,' you don't know—and I don't know—exactly what we would do. Get off your high horse."

He never did, which was a disappointment, because David and I had been close. Among other things, we had covered Grace Kelly's wedding to Prince Rainier of Monaco together. In the 1950s and 60s, I was lucky enough to be in demand to produce broadcasts like that, in addition to the presidential trips to Europe and Asia that I got to go on with Eisenhower, Kennedy, and Johnson, when I wasn't producing and directing the CBS Evening News in New York.

How lucky can you get—lucky that all the first-class talent that I might have had to compete with for those plum assignments had scampered off to Hollywood and left me to attend to all the assorted presidents, queens, and popes who popped up on the television screen in the 1950s.

In the course of doing just that, in 1956, I managed to pull a very large rabbit out of a very small hat.

The *Andrea Doria*, an Italian transatlantic luxury liner, was making its way to New York the evening of July 25 when it was hit on its starboard side by the *Stockholm*, a Swedish-American liner bound for Scandinavia. The *Stockholm's* reinforced steel bow ripped a thirty-foot gash in the *Andrea Doria*, and it was only a matter of time before the great Italian liner would sink. In the tragedy, fifty-two people lost their lives.

That night I heard about the accident on my car radio, and I immediately went to a phone booth and called Doug Edwards. I told him I would pick him up at his home in Weston, Connecticut. I then called the CBS news desk and told them to have a film crew meet us at the Naval Air Station at Quonset Point, Rhode Island. Doug and I were on our way, and figured that if we managed not to get pulled over for speeding, we could make it in about two hours. But as we pulled up at the Naval Air Station, all the other cameramen and reporters, who had already flown out over the ship, were heading back to their newspapers and radio and television stations. They said there was nothing much left to report, other than that the ship was still afloat and would probably stay that way for another day or two. I figured, what the hell, we should take a look anyway. I hated not to be first, but at least we could get an eyewitness account of the big liner wallowing in the sea.

I talked a navy pilot into flying me, Doug, and our film crew out over the North Atlantic to see what we could see; he took pity on us and said he'd fly us out to the site even though the regular press flight had been there almost an hour before. Twenty minutes or so later we were airborne.

As we approached the wreck, we opened the door of the chopper and Doug stood in the opening so we could film him in the foreground with the ship below us.

"How long do you think she'll stay afloat?" I asked the pilot, figuring he would say "a few days, maybe a week."

Instead, he said, "Don't stop that camera. She looks like she's going down."

And sure enough, with our camera grinding away and Doug looking down and describing it, the *Andrea Doria* rolled over like a big dead elephant, and as the water emptied out of its swimming pools, she sank. I couldn't quite believe I had seen what I had seen. One minute she was there and the next she was gone. When we landed we called the news desk. "Tough luck," the editor said. "Everybody else has already been on the air with pictures of the ship. The only thing we can do now is go back in a few days and catch it as she sinks."

"She already has," I said, "and Doug and I have it all on film." That night, CBS News had its biggest exclusive of the year.

My maritime adventures continued a few years later, when a plane taking off from LaGuardia Airport crashed in New York's East River. It happened during a tugboat strike, and nothing was moving on the river except for a tug from New Haven whose crew was outside the jurisdiction of the unions involved in the strike. By the time I got to where the tug was bringing in bodies, the other networks, as well as all the independents and the wire services and newspapers, were setting up to interview the tugboat captain about what he had seen out there at the crash site.

What happened next has become legendary at CBS. We all packed into the wheelhouse and the captain began telling his story. About the time he got to the goriest part, with all the newsmen hanging on his every word, I interrupted his account of the "burning bodies" and "groaning survivors" with what struck the rest of the crowd as a completely irrelevant question.

"Who owns this tug?" I asked.

"For Christ sake, Hewitt," the news guys said. "Who cares?"

"New Haven Tug," the captain said.

"Okay, Hewitt," the boys said. "No more dumb questions. Captain, please start again."

As he started again, about the "burning bodies" and the "groaning survivors," I sneaked out of the wheelhouse and went to a phone booth on the dock.

"Call New Haven Tug," I told the editor on duty back in the CBS newsroom, "and tell them we want to charter their boat."

When I got back to the wheelhouse the captain was still going strong and they all gave me the "shush" sign and whispered not to interrupt again with meaningless questions.

Meaningless to you guys, I thought, not to me.

Before the captain had finished, the phone rang in the wheelhouse and he stopped to answer it.

"Which one of you guys is Hewitt?" the captain asked.

"I am."

"Okay, the boat is under charter to you. What do you want to do?"

"First thing I want to do is get these guys off my boat."

You could get killed doing things like that, but the tug crew was put to work clearing the decks of everyone except the CBS camera crew. They even found one or two stowaways before we sailed off at first light for the scene of the wreck, with an angry mob on the dock shaking their fists at us.

The captain, incidentally, thought it was great fun. About an hour later an NBC crew came out in a rowboat with an outboard motor and a small transmitter with which they hoped to get pictures back to the *Today* show.

I looked over the side at their little boat and then I got a nasty idea. "If we maneuver between them and the Empire State Building," I told the captain, "they won't be able to get a signal back to NBC."

As I said, the captain was having fun and he thought that was a dandy idea. But during the maneuver he rammed them accidentally. No harm was done but they were pissed off.

When I got back, my boss, John Day, Mickelson's second-in-command, said, "What the hell is the matter with you?"

"What do you mean—what's the matter with me?"

"We got a call from NBC that you tried to sink their boat in the East River."

"Crybabies," I said.

And NBC got even more pissed off during Nikita Khrushchev's visit to the United States in 1959, when I pulled perhaps my wildest stunt. Harry Reasoner, Charles Kuralt, and I had gone to Iowa to cover Khrushchev's visit to a farm owned by a man named Garst, and we had with us a young desk assistant named Robert Wussler, who later became the president of CBS. But it's a miracle that both our careers, his and mine, didn't end right there in a cornfield in Iowa. After staying up most of the night going over how we were going to deploy our cameras to cover the Russian premier's visit, we went out to the Garst farm at about six the next morning to see if we had overlooked anything. It was barely dawn when we came across an NBC remote truck parked on a dirt road near the farm. A remote truck is a giant van that houses a complete control room and everything else needed to put on a broadcast. Mostly they're used for sports events. I don't know why, but that remote truck with its big NBC lettering on the side looked particularly inviting sitting there all alone in the early morning sun. What made it more inviting were the keys in the ignition.

Without saying a word, I looked at Wussler. I didn't have to say anything; he knew what I was thinking.

"You wouldn't dare," he said.

"Try me," I said.

"You don't have the guts."

"I have the guts," I told him, "but what in hell would we do with it?"

"Hide it in a cornfield," Wussler said. "They won't find it until they harvest the corn in August."

With that, I got into the driver's seat, started the engine and started to drive off, when it dawned on me what lunacy this was. We were hijacking NBC's remote truck. Before we left the scene of the almost crime, Wussler took out his handkerchief and wiped off our fingerprints on the keys. It was maybe the nuttiest thing either of us ever did, but the competition between CBS and NBC was so fierce in 1959 that for a moment, at least, it seemed like the thing to do.

When I had gotten to Iowa the day before, I did what I always do when I get to an unfamiliar town. I went looking for someone who could show me around, could open doors and point me in the right direction. So, I made an appointment with the chief of police and asked him if he had an off-duty cop available who might want to be the CBS driver for the next couple of days. He said he hadn't, but why not try the ex-chief, who had just retired and knew the town better than anyone? He got him on the phone and we made a deal contingent on the new chief letting the old chief wear the uniform he had just put away in the closet.

Now we were set. There wasn't anywhere we couldn't go. Who was going to stop Harry Reasoner, Charles Kuralt, and me if we were riding with the chief? But what to do when he wasn't with us?

"I know," the chief said, "we'll make you an honorary sheriff." The next day, wearing my new Stetson and new badge, I went out to the Garst farm again. The NBC remote truck was in place, and the crew was busy setting up their cameras. I sauntered over. The crew had been sent out from Omaha and hadn't the slightest idea who I was.

"Morning, sheriff," one of them said.

"Morning, boys," I said. "What's goin' on?"

"Come on, we'll show you," one of the NBC cameramen said, and proceeded to fill me in on every detail of their coverage. He had just finished spilling the beans about what they were going to do to CBS when one of the NBC directors from New York arrived and recognized me. The jig was up. When I got back to the hotel I had a message to call John Day in New York.

"We've had another complaint about you," he said. "NBC is charging you with impersonating a police officer."

"Not so," I said. "I'm not impersonating anything. I'm an honorary sheriff and I've got the hat and badge to prove it."

CHAPTER FOUR

New Frontiers

When convention time rolled around in the summer of 1960, CBS was bursting with confidence. After all, we had owned convention coverage in the '50s: Even then, Walter Cronkite projected the image of an avuncular authority figure whom viewers reflexively trusted. Television was beginning to gain purchase as a popular and powerful force in American life, and the political theater of national conventions brought into living rooms across the country was novel and exciting. But at the 1960 conventions, NBC hit us with something new—two somethings, in fact—a team of anchormen. One, Chet Huntley, had this rich baritone voice and looked like he belonged on Mount Rushmore. The other, David Brinkley, wasn't as handsome, but he had a twinkle in his eye and a wonderfully wry sense of humor. They had been around in '56, but that was still Cronkite's year. Nineteen sixty was their year; Huntley and Brinkley played perfectly as a team and buried us in the ratings.

In the movie *Butch Cassidy and the Sundance Kid*, when Paul Newman and Robert Redford are being chased relentlessly by bounty hunters, one of them turns to the other and says, "Who *are* those guys?" That's what I felt about Huntley and Brinkley: Who *are* those guys?

I panicked and went to Sig Mickelson early in the '60 convention and told him we had to team Cronkite with *someone*, and I suggested it be Murrow. And we did. But there was a problem: Cronkite and Murrow didn't work well as a team. Each of them was too strong to play second fiddle. And in a situation like that, from time to time someone has to play second fiddle. It turned out to be a terrible idea, a complete disaster. If it seemed awkward to us, think of how it seemed to the audience. Two first violinists, each brilliant as a soloist, but who couldn't carry a tune when they played together.

The presidential race that year was between John F. Kennedy, the Democratic senator from Massachusetts, and Richard M. Nixon, the Republican vice president. I had met Nixon a couple of times in the course of his political career, but I didn't know Jack Kennedy and had never met him until I got involved with that first television debate between him and Nixon in September of that year. What I particularly remember about that night was that Kennedy took it a lot more seriously than Nixon did. Kennedy, for instance, spent the afternoon of the first "debate" resting in his Chicago hotel room and preparing himself for what turned out to be the seminal event of the 1960 campaign.

A week before the debate, Kennedy had interrupted his campaign to make a stop at Chicago's Midway Field, where we met in a hangar so I could brief him in the nuts and bolts of what he was about to get himself into, the minutiae of the process. He asked all the right questions: Do we stand or do we sit? Can we have notes or do we just wing it? How much time do we have for each answer? Kennedy knew just how important it was going to be to his campaign, and he didn't want to leave anything to chance.

Nixon, on the other hand, treated it as just another campaign appearance. On the day of the debate, instead of resting up and saving his energy that was already sapped by a staphylococcus infection, Nixon met with the Plumbers' Union—not realizing that the meeting was peanuts compared with what he had committed himself to do that evening.

I never saw Nixon until his limo pulled into the garage of the WBBM studios in Chicago the night of the debate, and was in the midst of briefing him on some of the same things Kennedy had asked about a week earlier when I saw out of the corner of my eye that Kennedy had unobtrusively slipped into the studio and was listening in—like a fighter listening to a referee laying out the rules before a heavyweight bout.

The only thing I could think to say was, "I assume you two guys know each other." They allowed as how they did, then retired to two private offices that had been set aside for them to confer with their seconds and get ready to do battle.

Before they went off to their respective "corners," I asked them if they wanted makeup. Kennedy, who had just come from California where he had been campaigning in an open convertible, looked tan and fit and said, "No thanks." Nixon, who needed some to cover up a sallow complexion and a growth of beard, also said, "No thanks." I think he thought it wouldn't be good for his image if the public knew he was made-up and Kennedy wasn't.

At any rate, his handlers did a dumb thing. Instead of availing themselves of the services of one of television's best makeup artists, Frances Arvold, who had flown to Chicago from New York to work her magic on one or the other or both, Nixon's guys smeared him with a slapdash layer of something called "shavestick" that looked so terrible that, after looking at him on camera, I called the CBS president, Frank Stanton, into the control room to take a look.

That's when he turned to Nixon's television adviser, Ted Rogers, and asked: "Are you satisfied with the way Mr. Nixon looks?" Rogers said he was, and Stanton decided, then and there, to leave well enough alone.

But as every student of politics knows, that "debate" —like a Miss America contest—turned on who made the better appearance, not with what he said but with how he looked. Kennedy won hands down (but not on radio, where looks didn't count). Nixon never recovered from that disastrous first round and the lousy makeup job that did him in.

There are several postscripts to that night in Chicago. Right after Jack Kennedy was assassinated in Dallas, I sat in a makeup room in New York with Richard Nixon while that same Frances Arvold was doing his makeup for an appearance on a JFK memorial broadcast and said to him: "You know, Mr. Nixon, if you had let Franny make you up at the first debate, you might have been president now." Quick as a wink, without a moment's hesitation, he said: "Yes, and I might be dead now, too."

Did he believe that the assassin who killed Kennedy was not after JFK in particular, but any president he could get in the crosshairs? No, I don't think he believed it, but I do believe he wanted me to.

Postscript two came in 1964 at the Cow Palace in San Francisco where once again I was sitting with Nixon in a makeup room and the same Frances Arvold was making him up—this time just before he was to go out to the rostrum to introduce the Republican nominee for president, Barry Goldwater. I couldn't resist pointing out the irony: "If you had let Franny make you up four years ago," I said, "Barry Goldwater would be going out there now to introduce you."

He thought about that for a couple of seconds while he stared at himself in the mirror, then turned toward me and said: "You know, you're probably right."

Yet another postscript was his settling on homes in San Clemente, California, and Key Biscayne, Florida. I can't prove it, but I always thought he settled on those two homes after I told him, "You know, Mr. Nixon, if you had a tan, you wouldn't need makeup."

And finally, a postscript that stunned me. Forty years after that first debate, Ted Sorensen, who was with Kennedy in Chicago as an aide and speechwriter, told me something I never suspected—that behind closed doors and out of sight, Kennedy also got a coat of makeup—a light coat, to be sure, but makeup nonetheless—that night before he went out to meet his opponent.

Whoever did it was a lot better at it than whoever smeared that shavestick on Richard Nixon.

The next time I saw JFK, Fred Friendly and I (he as producer, and I as director) were working on the first of what was to be a series of conversations with a sitting president to be aired simultaneously on ABC, CBS, and NBC. We arrived at the White House on a Sunday morning not long after he was inaugurated, which was my first time in the Oval Office. What I remember most was Jack Kennedy arriving back from Mass and poking his head in while we were setting up the cameras and lights. After introducing him to the crew, I told him we were being extra careful not to bang into anything and had put down drop cloths to protect the floor.

"Don't worry about the floor," he said. "Let me show you something." With that, he bent down and peeled back one of the drop cloths to reveal a section of the floor that looked like it had been attacked by termites.

"Look what that sonofabitch did with his golf cleats," he said. The minute he said "golf cleats," I knew who the "sonofabitch" was. It could only be Dwight Eisenhower, who had preceded him in that office and, golf nut that he was, apparently brought his putter to work and while wearing his golf cleats in the Oval Office had torn up the floor between his desk and the putting green just outside his office.

Even though he laughed when my associate director, Fred Stollmack, said, "I guess you can say Ike really left his mark on the Oval Office," I think Jack Kennedy was more pissed off about what Ike had done to the floor than he let on—at least to us.

The year 1962 was a time of tremendous upheaval in my personal and professional life. Even as I was meeting with the president of the United States and participating in the highest-level decisions at the world's best television news organization, I wasn't happy. My marriage was falling apart.

What I didn't know when I married Mary Weaver back in 1945 was that she drank. And try as she did to conquer it, the hundreds of Alcoholics Anonymous meetings I went to with her never did the trick. I stuck around and tried to keep the marriage intact for the sake of our sons, Jeff and Steve—two great kids who deserved better. After seventeen years of it, I finally threw in the towel. "Fellers," I told them, "I hate to tell you this, but I'm going to get a divorce."

"Jesus Christ," the kids said almost in unison, "we wondered how long it was going to take before you came to your senses."

I moved out of our apartment in New York's Greenwich Village and into one on the Upper East Side. It was about that time that I met Frankie Childers, who had been the first woman to run a Senate committee when she ran the committee on juvenile delinquency for Senator Tom Dodd of Connecticut. It wasn't long after my Mexican divorce from Mary that Frankie and I got married and soon had Lisa, the world's greatest daughter, who would grow to become the world's greatest mother.

And as I was sorting out my personal life and trying to start over at the age of nearly forty, the executives at CBS News chose this moment to shake up the evening news. *Douglas Edwards with the News* was no match for the *Huntley-Brinkley Report*, and CBS replaced Doug with Walter Cronkite, who was right out of central casting. Cronkite was irresistible. He had anchorman written all over him. Paley and Stanton only had to take one look at this former United Press war correspondent and they were ready to make a major commitment to television news. And at least for a while, they seemed happy to have me aboard as his sidekick.

CBS News was in transition, having a midlife crisis of sorts itself. My friend David Schoenbrun, our longtime man in Paris, for one, began to sink under the weight of his own foolishness. As we moved into the television age, David became convinced that everyone at CBS was out to get him, which they weren't, but one day someone at CBS did—David himself. In 1963, not long after he left Paris to become our Washington bureau chief, he got sacked. His version of why it happened and CBS's version don't square with each other, but suffice it to say that CBS's version was not unrelated to foolishness like this: When Frankie and I got engaged, she told President Kennedy that she was going to marry someone at CBS. The president asked, "Is he a pygmy?"

"A pygmy?" Frankie said. "What do you mean, 'Is he a pygmy?'"

"I don't know," the president said. "Schoenbrun says that over at CBS he's surrounded by pygmies."

The tragedy was that Schoenbrun had so much going for him and was the only one who didn't know it. He went from being CBS's Washington bureau chief to being Metromedia's chief European correspondent, and then just faded away.

One thing that Walter Cronkite brought to the job of anchoring the evening news was a palpable enthusiasm for a great story. And the greatest story of the 1960s, he was convinced, was the space program. Even before President Kennedy vowed to put a man on the moon, Cronkite was an unapologetic cheerleader for the seven Mercury astronauts, and he would be just as supportive of the Gemini and Apollo programs that came later in the decade.

Nobody ever said it because nobody had to say it, but I always figured that there was an understanding between television and NASA—never spelled out, never even whispered, never even hinted at, but they knew and we knew. If we continued to help the space agency get its appropriations from Congress, they would in turn give us, free of charge, the most spectacular television shows anyone had ever seen. Those of us who produced the television coverage of space soon found out that what we were getting was a lot more than free television shows. What we were getting as well was a chance to show the American people that we were team players, and that if television brought you distasteful things like race riots and a war we couldn't win, it also brought you the astronauts. It was a chance for television to show that it, too, had the right stuff.

There was no practitioner of the art better than Cronkite, who was known during those first manned flights as "the eighth astronaut." Nobody seemed to mind that at times he was their cheerleader. In fact, the public loved it. When John Glenn's mother first came to Cape Canaveral and was asked what she wanted to see, she said, "Walter Cronkite." During the weeks leading up to each space shot we all hung out at the Holiday Inn in Cocoa Beach—we and our kids and the astronauts and their kids. Although the astronauts didn't live at the Holiday Inn, that's where they hung out and sometimes dropped in for breakfast on their way out to the Cape. They may have been American heroes, but they were also the guys we had bacon and eggs with in the morning.

Did they mind us hanging around? I don't think so. We kind of came with the territory. The air force officer who was assigned to look after them, Colonel John E. "Shorty" Powers, managed to get his face on television more often than the astronauts did. Once, a couple of us decided we'd had enough of Cocoa Beach and drove to Miami. We ended up in a joint called the Bonfire, where Shorty, who fancied himself something of a ladies' man (didn't we all?), turned to a wicked-looking brunette sitting next to him at the bar and introduced himself. "I'm Colonel John E. Powers; I'm in charge of the astronauts." She looked back and introduced herself. "Fifty bucks," she said.

It was just before John Glenn's orbital flight in 1962 that I noticed that what we were missing from our coverage was any sense of a shared experience. Wouldn't it be good, I thought, if we could make every viewer feel he was truly part of the day's excitement? That's when I got the idea of putting a large television screen in Grand Central Terminal, where I knew it would draw a crowd. I also knew that by putting cameras in Grand Central, we could show the viewers at home that a lot of other people were watching the same thing they were at the same time. What I didn't know was just how big a crowd we would draw. During Glenn's reentry into Earth's atmosphere — those minutes when the ground stations lost contact with him and no one knew whether he was dead or alive — the crowd in Grand Central swelled to thousands. The cheer that went up when Cronkite said Glenn was safe and sound and back from space was deafening. It was just what I was after, and I'll bet some of the people watching all alone in their own living rooms joined in when the crowd cheered.

Cronkite was the consummate professional. He took nothing for granted. He picked up the phone and checked with people he knew would give him a straight answer and, at the same time, throw in a couple of facts that made his reporting better than anyone else's. I can't think of anyone, including the president, who wouldn't take a phone call from Walter Cronkite. He was as good a practitioner of disseminating information as anybody I ever worked with. Murrow's boys, I always thought, were jealous of the exalted place Walter occupied in broadcasting. Did that trouble him? I always had a sneaking suspicion that it did. But he was so big, so important, and so in demand that at worst, it was a small annoyance.

When it was first proposed in 1963 that we would expand our fifteen-minute nightly newscast to thirty minutes, I'm ashamed to say I thought it wasn't such a good idea. I wondered if fifteen minutes of news was as much as anyone wanted from their television set that they bought primarily to be entertained by and not informed by. Was I wrong. The half-hour newscast, on all three networks, is now one of the few constants that television can point to in a medium famous for going off like a Roman candle every time someone comes up with a new concept.

To inaugurate the first thirty minute broadcast in September of 1963, President Kennedy agreed to answer questions from Cronkite, principally about what he was going to do about Vietnam. During the course of the interview, one of the answers came off as (and was meant to be) a warning to the present South Vietnamese government to, in effect, shape up or ship out. When Cronkite and I decided not to use that particular exchange in our edited piece, Pierre Salinger, JFK's press secretary, said that if we didn't use it, he was going to call attention to it by releasing it as a separate statement that would make us look foolish. How did we deal with it? Sorry to say, we caved, reedited our piece, and included the president's warning to the South Vietnamese. News management by the White House? More accurately, strong-arm tactics by a White House press secretary who, to please his boss, was willing to break the agreed-to rules and release to other news organizations something that was in our outtakes.

On Friday, November 22, 1963, I was preparing to go out to lunch when the chatter of the AP teletype was interrupted by alarm bells that meant that something had happened somewhere in the world that editors should immediately take note of. The alarm bells that went off that afternoon signaled the biggest story I ever remember having a hand in—and that includes the D-Day landing. Were we under attack? Had an enemy decided that the best way to go to war with us was to knock out not a naval base (as the Japanese had in 1941) but the president of the United States? Until Lyndon Johnson raised his right hand on Air Force One and took the oath of office, no one was sure that government as we knew it was still intact.

We went into our fire alarm mode and crashed our way onto the air with a bulletin. However, Sig Mickelson, the vice president who ran CBS News, was already on his way to lunch, and I needed some guidance on how long to let Cronkite go on holding the air, so I picked up the phone and called the president of CBS, Frank Stanton, who at that moment was in a meeting so important, he told his secretary, that he was not to be interrupted.

"Sorry, Mr. Hewitt," she said. "I have instructions not to interrupt him. You'll have to call back."

"Tell him the president's been shot," I said, "and he might be dead before I can call back."

"Hold on," she said.

A second or so later Stanton was on the line. "Keep Walter on the air," he said, "until you know whether the president's dead or alive."

A few seconds later he called back and said to forget what he had just said and that even if the president survives don't go back to regular programming. "I'm on my way to your office," he said, "and we'll run the network from there," which we did.

Televisions across America went on as one, as people everywhere looked for *someone* to tell them that we were going to be all right, that our nation would survive. And that job fell to Walter Cronkite. That day, that weekend, Cronkite, who already was everybody's uncle, became everybody's priest, minister, and rabbi, too. He was the glue that held America together.

Dan Rather, new to CBS and our correspondent on the scene,

phoned me from Dallas and told me that a guy named Zapruder was supposed to have film of the assassination and was going to put it up for sale. In fact, he eventually did, sold it to *Life* magazine for a reputed $600,000. In my desire to get a hold of what was probably the most dramatic piece of news footage ever shot, I told Rather to go to Zapruder's house, sock him in the jaw, take his film to our affiliate in Dallas, copy it onto videotape, and let the CBS lawyers decide whether it could be sold or whether it was in the public domain. And then take the film back to Zapruder's house and give it back to him. That way, the only thing they could get him for was assault because he would have returned Zapruder's property. Rather said, "Great idea. I'll do it." I hadn't hung up the phone maybe ten seconds when it hit me: What in the hell did you just do? Are you out of your mind? So I called Rather back. Luckily, he was still there, and I said to him, "For Christ's sake, don't do what I just told you to. I think this day has gotten to me and thank God I caught you before you left." Knowing Dan to be as competitive as I am, I had the feeling that he wished he'd left before the second phone call. The things you do in the heat of battle!

Because I had had a hand in the so-called debate that helped catapult him into the White House, I felt, in a strange way, bonded to Kennedy as I never had to another president, and when an assassin's bullet ended his life I mourned his loss about as keenly as I remember mourning the loss of Franklin Roosevelt.

The plain honest-to-goodness truth about JFK was that, despite his potential for greatness, he realized very little of it between the time of his "Ask not what your country can do for you" inaugural speech and the motorcade that took him through Dallas's Dealey Plaza and to the emergency room at Parkland Hospital, where he was pronounced dead.

Assassinating John F. Kennedy made even less sense than the

Warren Commission's report about who did it and why. I always believed that the commission held something back and that there was more to the story than we were allowed to be privy to.

That's why one morning, while sitting with Bobby Kennedy in the backyard of his house at Hickory Hill, just the two of us, drinking iced tea and talking about a broadcast I wanted him to be a part of, I decided—with more guts than brains—to ask him the big one, the million-dollar question: "Bobby, do you really believe Lee Harvey Oswald, all by himself, killed your brother?"

He dismissed the question with an almost studied indifference. "What difference does it make?" he said. "It won't bring him back."

I never believed that Bobby believed "What difference does it make?" and have always believed that he knew something he didn't want to share with me or anyone else and that whatever was still being kept in the dark about that fateful day, he preferred it stay there.

In the fall of 2000, I had occasion to be in Chicago with Ted Sorensen, who had been President Kennedy's counsel, and I told him about my conversation over thirty years ago with Bobby. Ted responded that it wasn't just Bobby, that all of those who were close to JFK felt more or less the same: "What difference does it make? It won't bring him back." However, he did express the opinion (and I've gotten his permission to paraphrase it) that while it would surprise him to learn that Oswald had had accomplices, it would not dismay him, should it someday surface that he had, because it would lend some badly needed rhyme and reason to an act of insanity that up to now has had neither.

Be that as it may, I am still not satisfied that there isn't a lot more to the Lee Harvey Oswald story, especially since one of the most respected Republicans who ever held office said to me, in front of witnesses, that he had once asked Richard Nixon, "What do you know about the Kennedy assassination?" and that Nixon had told him, "You don't want to know."

But one of the things that sticks with me most about that November weekend was a typical television moment on the day of the funeral. No matter how serious and important an event is, in a television control room there are always light moments (as I imagine there are in operating rooms)—even funny ones. One of them came that day when a cameraman whose camera was focused on the White house gates saw them swing open to reveal a couple of dozen crowned heads of Europe and assorted pooh-bahs from every corner of the earth about to march out of the White House driveway and follow on foot as the casket made its way from the White House to the Capitol, shouted excitedly in his intercom: "Jesus Christ, will you look at this? Here come a whole bunch of kings!"

CHAPTER FIVE

The Battle of the TV Executives

Stories about Lyndon B. Johnson, who succeeded Kennedy in the White House, are legion at CBS. For instance, there was the time a railroad strike ended abruptly and the president decided to go on television to announce it. Trouble was, it was CBS's turn to provide the pool feed for the other networks and CBS's makeup woman was out of town. So into the breach we threw a youngster who did odd jobs around the Washington bureau, but makeup was hardly his forte.

Nevertheless, on the spur of the moment, he got tapped for the job and, on the air, made up by an amateur, LBJ looked atrocious. The broadcast wasn't over but a minute or so when a Secret Service agent appeared in the CBS remote truck parked in the White House driveway.

"You," he said to the makeup man, "the president wants to see you."

"Me?" the kid said.

"You!" the agent barked.

Once inside the Oval Office, he said, he was led up to the president's desk, where he stood more or less at attention while LBJ finished signing some correspondence. Finally, he said, his voice quavering, "D-d-d-did you want to see me, Mr. President?"

"Boy," the president said, "you trying to fuck me?"

At that, the kid said, his knees began to knock. "N-n-n-no, sir," he said.

After what seemed like an eternity of the president glaring at him, LBJ told one of the Secret Service agents, "Get him out of here."

He was sure LBJ was going to say: "Shoot him!"

Walking down the driveway and out of the White House gate, he said all he could think of was: "They'd never shoot me on the White House grounds. I know how they'll get me. I'll probably be found in a day or two run over by a U.S. mail truck."

Another time, shortly after LBJ took office, Martin Agronsky (who was assigned to the CBS Washington bureau) and I went to the White House to keep a date at nine o'clock in the evening with George Christian, LBJ's press secretary, to talk about doing a live broadcast of LBJ answering questions about Vietnam to be posed by the governors, who were coming to Washington to have dinner at the White House. To kill time, Agronsky had driven a friend to the airport and I had stopped at the Madison Hotel for dinner. After dinner I wandered slowly over to the White House so as not to get there before our nine o'clock appointment.

As I meandered up the driveway toward the press office entrance a nervous aide was waiting in the doorway. "Where's Agronsky?" he asked.

"He went to the airport," I said.

"What do you mean, 'he went to the airport'?"

"What do you mean, 'what do I mean'? He went to the airport. What's so difficult to understand about that?"

"The president," the aide said, "Is waiting upstairs for the two of you for dinner."

Jesus, I thought.

Sure enough, the president was waiting for us for dinner, and he was hungry, even if I wasn't. Agronsky, who had also had dinner, arrived a short time later.

We talked about what we wanted him to do on the broadcast, and then he picked up the phone alongside him at the table and told the White House operator to get him Bess Abell, the White House social secretary.

"Bess," he told her, "you're going to have to cancel the performance of *Hello, Dolly!* that we scheduled for the governors' dinner." The next thing I knew, he was saying, "Calm down, Bess. Hewitt says he can't do what he wants to do with all those sets and actors in the East Room." With that, he handed me the phone.

The White House social secretary was furious.

"What do you think you're doing?" she asked.

"I'm not doing anything, Bess. The president is. Canceling *Hello, Dolly!* is his idea, not mine."

After a few minutes of Bess's tongue-lashing, I told the president that she wanted to speak to him again. He told me he had nothing to tell her and that I should handle it. I didn't know how to handle it, so I hung up.

The only other eventful thing that happened brought me out of my chair. All of a sudden a buzzer went off. My God, it's the hotline; it's World War III, I thought. You know what it was? The president's battery-operated pepper mill. You say you've never seen a battery-operated pepper mill? Neither had I. And I've never seen one since.

That was just before the president noticed it was time for the eleven o'clock news. A White House butler rolled in a television set and turned it to one of the local channels just as the newscaster proclaimed, "The president said today that he would make an important speech tomorrow."

"I did not," Johnson said, talking back to the TV. "Never said it was important." And then for the next few minutes he carried on a conversation with the television set as if the newscaster were there with us at the table. It was some performance. Every time the newscaster paused, the president interjected a comment. It would have made a great skit on *Saturday Night Live.*

Around midnight, as Agronsky and I were strolling down the

driveway toward the guardhouse to leave the White House grounds, I told him, "This broadcast is never going to happen."

"Are you nuts?" Agronsky said. "Would he have spent all this time with us if it weren't going to happen?"

"It's not going to happen," I said.

"How do you figure that?" Martin asked.

"When Mrs. Johnson hears that he wants to turn *Hello, Dolly!* into *Hello, Lyndon!*, she'll nix it. Asking the governors to sing for their supper is a lousy idea."

Agronsky looked at me as if I had lost my mind, but sure enough, the next morning I got a call from George Christian.

"It's off," he said.

"Why?" I asked.

"Mrs. Johnson thought it was a lousy idea."

With Lyndon Johnson, I always wondered how much of the bluster was real and how much was staged for our benefit. But sometimes LBJ's theatricality got the better of him. In 1965, Johnson had agreed to sit for a three-network "Conversation with the President" in the Oval Office following in the tradition that John F. Kennedy had set. Once again, I was chosen to direct the broadcast, with Fred Friendly as producer, and the questioners were an all-star team of network reporters: Eric Sevareid of CBS, David Brinkley of NBC, and Bill Lawrence of ABC. At the conclusion of the taping, Friendly and I were anxious to get to New York to start editing the videotape for broadcast. It was touch-and-go whether we could get to the airport in time to make the three o'clock Eastern Airlines shuttle.

LBJ, aware of our predicament, told Bill Moyers, then his aide, to get a White House car to take us to the airport and to tell Eastern Airlines he wanted them to hold the plane for us.

"Yes, sir," Moyers told the president. Wow! I thought, this is big stuff.

Sure enough, as we left the White House there was a car waiting with the motor running. Friendly and I got in the back, Moyers up front with the driver. As the driver gunned the engine and we roared out of the White House grounds into the traffic, Moyers got on the radio and had a conversation with the Secret Service that went more or less as follows (I may have the code words wrong but the gist of what happened is still crystal clear):

"Red Fox to Mountain Squirrel. Red Fox to Mountain Squirrel."

"Mountain Squirrel here. Go ahead, Red Fox."

"Mountain Squirrel, the president would like you to call Eastern Airlines and tell them to hold the three o'clock shuttle for two important guests from the White House."

"Roger, Red Fox. Roger, Red Fox."

As we continued to weave our way through traffic at speeds that would have landed us in the pokey if we weren't in a White House car, over the radio came Eastern Airlines' answer to the request from the president of the United States to hold the shuttle.

"Mountain Squirrel to Red Fox," crackled the radio. "They say they won't do it!"

Moyers looked a little sheepish, but I was in heaven. We may have missed the plane, but I wouldn't have missed for the world the car ride—the exchange between Red Fox and Mountain Squirrel— and what was, in effect, the airline's "who do you think you are?" response to the leader of the free world.

Covering the president—any president—was always an adventure, and often came with unexpected surprises. On one of LBJ's foreign trips, Mike Wallace, who was on general assignment covering the president's trip, and I were in the Philippines when I came face to face with a legend from my childhood.

I was at the Manila airport waiting for a shipment of videotape to come from Bangkok when a skycap called my attention to a small plane flying overhead.

"Guess who's flying that plane?" the skycap asked.

"Beats the shit out of me," I told him.

"Lindbergh," he said.

"Lindbergh?" I said. "Colonel Charles A. Lindbergh?"

"No," he said. "General Charles A. Lindbergh."

On the crazy chance that it was the "Lone Eagle" himself, I went to the nearest phone booth and called Wallace in the hotel room where he was sleeping off his jet lag.

"Mike," I said. "I found Lindbergh."

"You did what?" Mike said.

"I found Lindbergh."

"What are you smoking?" Mike said.

"Jesus," I said, "don't you understand? Lindbergh is here in the Philippines and I'm going to see if he won't do a piece with you that we can satellite to New York for tonight's Cronkite news."

"You go ahead and do that," Mike said, "and while you're at it, stay out of the sun."

I couldn't blame him. It even seemed wacky to me. By that time, the plane that was supposed to be piloted by Lindbergh was taxiing to the gate, and you know who was flying it? Lindbergh.

The plane looked, for all the world, like what I remembered pictures of his *Spirit of St. Louis* looking like when it touched down at Le Bourget Airport in Paris one rainy night in 1927 after the first solo flight anyone had ever made across the Atlantic. Lindbergh, boyishly handsome in his coveralls and looking almost exactly like he did in all the pictures I'd seen of him over the years, was holding on to the strut and talking with a mechanic when I walked up to him and couldn't resist sticking out my hand and saying, "Welcome to Le Bourget."

"Hi," he said. "I'm General Lindbergh."

"I kinda figured that," I said. "I'm with CBS News. Mike Wallace and I are here on the LBJ trip and we would be honored if you let Mike interview you for tonight's Cronkite News."

That made *some* impression on a man who had withdrawn from the world and was in the Philippines on a hunt for an all but extinct white buffalo. I'm not sure Lindbergh knew or cared who Mike Wallace and Walter Cronkite were. Instead, he said:

"Why don't you and your colleague—what's his name?—come and have dinner with me at the Army Navy Club. But leave your camera at home."

We never did make it to the Army Navy Club, but that brief encounter made me aware as never before that there are people in the world who would just as soon the press left them alone, and in their case, we should, which makes me wonder if we, the press, have an exaggerated idea of what the Founding Fathers had in mind when they gave us the First Amendment.

I thought back to that editorial I had written in the seventh grade—"Press Drives Lindbergh to Self-Exile"—and I began to realize that he was as much a victim of the times in which he lived as he was an icon of those times. Though he had been driven into seclusion and left with a bad taste in his mouth about how the press had hounded him when his son was kidnapped, he handled my inquiry with admirable tact.

And about my hunch that Charles Lindbergh didn't know who Mike Wallace was, let alone that he didn't know who Walter Cronkite was, try this for a postscript to that story.

Having been invited to a small dinner party at Cape Canaveral on the eve of the first moon landing, two of the best-known names in America—Charles Lindbergh and Walter Cronkite—were huddled in a corner, with Cronkite regaling Lindbergh with stories about

Lindbergh's son, with whom Walter had done some deep-sea diving for his broadcast, *The Twentieth Century*. Hearing the glowing things Cronkite was saying about his son, Lindbergh asked Cronkite if he would mind telling some of those things to Mrs. Lindbergh.

"Nothing would give me greater pleasure," Walter said. "As a matter of fact," he added, "I've never met Anne Lindbergh."

"Well, let me introduce you," Lindbergh said.

With that, Lindbergh steered Cronkite through the room and up to Anne Morrow Lindbergh, pausing just long enough for Charles Lindbergh to whisper to Walter: "Now, what's your name again?"

True story? Cronkite says it is.

As for Lindbergh's sympathy for Nazi causes, they were more or less forgotten, or at least ignored, the night of the moon-landing dinner party.

But some years later, while doing a story for *60 Minutes*, Morley Safer got an incredible confession out of Anne Morrow Lindbergh when he asked how she felt about her husband saying, three months after Pearl Harbor, that the British, FDR, and the Jews were trying to get us into a war.

"I was horrified," she said. "Had he read Goebbels and Hitler, he would have known that people who are really anti-Semitic start with statements like that."

"Did you love him less for it?" Morley asked her.

"I can't say I did," she said, "but I pitied him."

The fun part of covering the president, though, was to cover presidential politics. And at political conventions, we sometimes created our own fun, to keep from being bored to death. In 1964 I was working on my fifth presidential campaign as the director of CBS's coverage of the two political conventions that year. Even though I knew that the conventions were becoming cut-and-dried affairs, I still occasionally went off the deep end in trying to get a leg up on NBC, and I never tried harder than I did at the Republican convention that year in San Francisco.

In the CBS contingent were the future president of CBS, Bob Wussler (who always seemed to be there when the devil got the better of me), and Bill Leonard, who was in charge of our political coverage. In the row in front of us at a preliminary meeting with the Republican National Committee was the NBC contingent. At one point I glanced down and noticed that the NBC man in front of me had accidentally kicked back under his seat a book titled *NBC Convention Plans*, which was practically resting on my shoe. I gulped. In that book had to be gold. I poked Leonard and gestured toward the floor. He gulped and whispered, "Take it." Pretending to tie my shoe, I bent down and stole it. Now the trick was to get it out of the room without attracting any attention. That turned out to be so easy that I got overconfident. Instead of taking it to a library to read or mailing it to myself in New York like any felon worth his salt would have done, I took it back to my room at the Fairmont Hotel. A few minutes later Wussler arrived. While the two of us were poring over it, trying to make head or tail of what NBC was up to, there was a knock at the door.

It was Scotty Connal, a former hockey player who was now a unit manager for NBC. "Where's my book?" he demanded.

"What book?" I asked.

"You know what book," Scotty replied.

"Okay," I said to Wussler, "we've been caught so let's give him his book"—as if we had a choice. After all, Scotty had played hockey and he was big. Ready for the punch in the mouth that never came, I heaved a sigh of relief when Scotty said, "Thank you. You don't know how desperate I was. If I hadn't found it, I probably would have been fired." (Letting an NBC book fall into CBS hands was like letting the D-Day plans fall into the hands of the German High Command. You could get shot.) He added that he had been so desperate to get it that he would have thrown me out the window if I hadn't handed it over. We all laughed at that, shook hands, parted friends, and I dismissed the incident as no more than a shenanigan gone awry. The next morning I had forgotten all about it until I opened my hotel room door and picked up the *San Francisco Chronicle*. There, on page one, was an eight-column banner headline shouting: THE BATTLE OF THE TV EXECUTIVES. "Hot damn," I thought, "Aubrey's in trouble again." (Jim Aubrey was the top man at CBS Television and had the same low opinion of news people that we had of him.) This, I thought, was going to be good. It was, but it wasn't about Aubrey. It was about me. And it began: "An NBC unit manager yesterday threatened to throw a CBS director out the tenth-floor window of the Fairmont Hotel."

But the fun and games stopped when Fred Friendly was promoted in 1964 to become president of CBS News. A barrel of laughs he wasn't. Fred was now my boss and acted like nothing good had ever happened in television until he got there. He wasn't what you'd call a team player, even when they gave him the team. He always appeared to me to believe that he was the starting pitcher, the cleanup hitter, and the manager all rolled into one and that the rest of us weren't worth much to him.

Fred Friendly's reign wasn't the happiest time for me. Nothing about either of us rubbed off on the other. The problem was that he didn't really approve of me. After all, Fred was not the kind of man who would sully himself brawling with another network. He was the kind of man who would hold your coat while you did. ("You hit 'em, kid. I'll be around the corner looking out for the cops.")

Within a year, he felt that he had to make a change, but I was the last one to know. Fred often would not confront someone directly, relying on the message to get through in other ways. Even his office was built to avoid confrontation; it contained an escape hatch—a secret door through which he could depart surreptitiously if there was someone in his waiting room he didn't want to see. I had never seen this before and have never seen it since. That day in 1965, however, there was someone he did want to see—me.

Fred put his arm around me and said, "Don, you know I've been thinking, the Cronkite evening news isn't big enough for you and your talents. You practically invented this business and I'm going to set up a special unit just for you. Your unit will have its own camera crews and film editors. Your assignment will be the world, and anything that breaks anywhere, you won't have to check with anyone— you just get up and go."

Fred laid it on pretty good, so I was feeling okay when I left his office. I immediately darted next door to see my all-time favorite CBS News vice president, Bill Leonard, and started babbling. "Guess what, Bill, Friendly says the Cronkite news isn't big enough for me and that he wants me to move up to a special unit he's creating just for me."

Leonard looked up, with wisdom and sympathy in his eyes. "Don, you just got fired."

"No, Bill," I said, "you don't understand. I'm moving up."

"No, you're not, Don," he replied. "You're being fired."

Finally, the light dawned: "Holy shit, you're right," I said. But for all our fights, Friendly taught me more about broadcasting than anyone else—about the craft of writing and especially about writing for the ear—and getting canned by him turned out to be the best thing that every happened to me. But at that moment, I was filled with despair.

It was devastating, the end of my short, happy career. I figured my life was over. I'd had this great run, and now what? Here I was, one of the golden boys, and suddenly I felt as if I'd been banished to Nielsen hell. The go-anywhere, do-anything job wasn't as swashbuckling as it sounded: Instead of becoming the poobah of breaking news, I ended up doing public-affairs shows and making holier-than-thou documentaries that no one watched, or not many people anyway. The truth was that all the documentaries got about the same share of audience—maybe 8 percent, which wasn't much—regardless of whether they were on CBS, NBC, or ABC. People don't like reading documents. Why would they want to watch something called a documentary?

Not everybody snoozed through documentaries. Most of the viewing public didn't even turn them on in the first place, although they said they did because they thought it gave them a certain cachet. In the '50s, when I was directing *See It Now* and bits and pieces of that other prestige broadcast, *Omnibus*, people used to say to me, "Those are the only things we watch," but I knew it wasn't true. I knew they also watched *Gunsmoke* and *Wagon Train* and *I Love Lucy*.

And even though some documentaries won awards and were credited with raising public consciousness—I'm thinking primarily of a 1971 *CBS Reports* program called "The Selling of the Pentagon," which was produced under the supervision of Perry Wolf, one of television's best documentarians—I couldn't help thinking that they would have even more impact if we could make the information more palatable and feed it in shorter and more digestible bites.

But in the meantime, I was spending my time on programs like *Town Meeting of the World*, in which prominent figures sat for discussions and interviews. People like Harold Macmillan, who was one of the many forgettable prime ministers the Brits squeezed in between Winston Churchill and Margaret Thatcher. Who in America wanted to listen to an hour with Harold Macmillan? I know I didn't.

This was back in the days when the Federal Communications Commission demanded a certain amount of public service in return for use of the airwaves. The idea was to give the FCC what it demanded, and no one thought much about attracting an audience.

I often thought that with CBS having most of the top-ranked entertainment shows at the time, many of the top executives believed we were in the news business only because of the FCC. If you wanted a license for a local owned-and-operated station, you had to demonstrate a certain amount of public service. Jim Aubrey, the president of CBS Television, was careful in public, but he would slip every now and then. Once, he was quoted as saying about CBS's coverage of a Republican convention: "This damn thing is going to cost us ten million dollars. Who wants to listen to news? If I had my way, we'd have some guy come on at 11 P.M. and say, 'the following six guys made horses' asses of themselves at the Republican convention,' and he'd give the six names and that would be it."

Once, in the days when I was still doing the evening news, Democratic Senator Warren Magnuson of the state of Washington was making a speech at the Waldorf-Astoria Hotel in New York. Magnuson chaired an important Senate committee, the one with oversight responsibilities for broadcasting. Word came down from the CBS executive offices that they would like us to cover his speech—but that they didn't much care whether there was any film in the camera. They just wanted Magnuson to know that we were there.

We did manage some bright spots on *Town Meeting of the World*. A German-accented Harvard professor named Kissinger and a fledgling politician named Reagan both showed some promise on one of our programs and might have made a great anchor team, but they got sidetracked.

One day, with the pace of my life slowed to a crawl, I went to see

Friendly and asked: "Why don't we see if Frank Sinatra would agree to open up to us? After all, he's one of the Americans other Americans are curious about."

"Well, see if you can get him," Friendly said.

So I called a guy named Jim Mahoney who I was told was Sinatra's press agent, and made my pitch.

"Well, we'll think about it. But I don't think he's gonna do anything like that." The next thing you know, I get a call from Mahoney saying he wants to come to New York with an attorney named Mickey Rudin, who was a lawyer for Desilu, the company owned by Desi Arnaz and Lucille Ball. Rudin had done a lot of work with CBS on Lucy's show. And he also represented Sinatra.

The two of them wanted to have lunch with Friendly and me. So we ate in the CBS cafeteria, and Rudin said: "He'll do it, but on certain conditions. No questions about Cal-Neva Lodge," a gambling casino from which Sinatra had been barred. "No questions about gambling. And no questions about the Mafia."

"Forget it," we told him. "No ground rules. Either he does it or he doesn't do it. But we have no interest in doing Frank Sinatra with ground rules." Rudin and Mahoney left, and I figured that was the end of it.

Three days later, Mahoney called me and said, "Come on out here. Sinatra would like to meet you." So I did. I went with Mahoney to Warner Brothers and the biggest office I'd ever seen in my life. Sinatra was in there alone, waiting for his tailor to come measure him for a couple of suits. Some of the measuring that went on while I was there was Sinatra trying to measure me.

"Frank, this is Don Hewitt," Mahoney said.

"Hello, Don, what's on your mind?" Sinatra said.

"I want to do a documentary on you."

"Why?"

"Because, like Jonas Salk and Hubert Humphrey and Willie Mays, you are part of the times in which we live." God, how I was selling. "You're part of the fabric of the fifties and sixties. People I grew up with remember who they were with and where they were by which Frank Sinatra song was popular at the time." Andy Rooney gave me that line, which was then and still is one of the best that anyone ever gave me. Rooney, whose principal job was to write essays for Harry Reasoner for *CBS Reports*, was tapped to write the Sinatra documentary. This was the first time Andy and I had worked together. We were never what you would call close, but I was, and remain to this day, an ardent admirer and have heard through the grapevine that Andy feels the same about me.

After giving him Rooney's line, Sinatra warmed up a little. I thought I was doing great until he asked, "What's in it for me?"

"Let's face it," I said. "You haven't got enough money to buy a CBS News documentary on yourself and CBS News doesn't have enough money to pay you what you're worth. Let's call it a wash."

"How do I know I can trust you?" came next.

"Frank," I said, "I'm going to ask you to sit in a seat opposite Walter Cronkite. That's the same seat that Dwight Eisenhower, Jack Kennedy, and Lyndon Johnson sat in. If you don't think you're big enough to sit in that seat, I wouldn't do it if I were you."

He thought about that for a moment and said, "I'm recording tomorrow night. Want to start then?"

We did. It was the night he recorded "It Was a Very Good Year" for his *September of My Years* album.

I'd heard he was difficult, but that night he couldn't have been more cooperative. He arrived at the recording studio with his coat over one shoulder and his hat on the back of his head, Frank Sinatra was playing "Frank Sinatra"—the man on the album cover. I wish the rest had been as easy. It turned out to be a bitch.

Glimpses of Sinatra the tough guy appeared as we began to prepare for the big interview at his Palm Springs house. Once, the New York media went wild trying to get pictures of Frank and his then-fiancée, Mia Farrow, when they were on a yacht anchored in the Hudson River. Sinatra wanted none of it. One who tried to get aboard but didn't was a local reporter for WCBS-TV named Jeanne Parr, who ended her story about Frank and Mia by noting indignantly: "They're not even married."

The next morning, the CBS operator called me at home and said, "I have Frank Sinatra on the line."

"Put him through," I said.

Without even a hello, the voice that purred to millions "I've Got a Crush on You, Sweetie Pie," purred to me: "You got a cunt named Jeanne Parr working for you?"

"Doesn't work for me, Frank," I said. "She's with the local station, WCBS."

"You tell that no-good whore that she's a broad with a bad complexion and dirty hair," he said, which I thought was kind of strange even given his cleanliness fetish. "If I ever see her, I'm gonna punch her teeth down her throat."

Oh my God, I thought, we've been getting along fine and now this happens. If Jeanne ever found out about this, she'd ring his doorbell and say, "Okay, Frank, here I am. Go ahead and punch my teeth down my throat." She'd be made for the rest of her life—and I'd be finished with Sinatra.

So I had to change the subject fast. "Hey, Frank," I said, "you know what I heard yesterday? I heard NBC wants you for a musical special."

"Yeah?" he said. "They got a million dollars?"

"I hear they got five hundred thousand."

"I got more than that on me," he said.

He might have had. As Cronkite would say on our broadcast, "The proceeds from the ballad 'Young at Heart' alone would provide a luxurious life income for most men." Arguable, but remember, this was 1965. What you can't argue with, even today, is as Cronkite also said, "people who know music hear sounds no one else makes when Sinatra sings."

The Jeanne Parr episode was nothing compared with the scene that would follow in Palm Springs. When Cronkite asked Sinatra about gambling, the Mafia, and the Cal-Neva Lodge, he went ballistic.

"Come inside," he said, pointing at me, "I want to talk to you." So we went into his bedroom.

"You broke all of Mickey's rules," he fumed.

"No, Frank," I said. "We never agreed to those rules."

"I ought to kill you," he said.

"With anyone else, that's a figure of speech," I said. "But you probably mean it."

"I mean it," he said.

"If I have a choice, I'd rather you didn't," I said, and scurried out of his house and back to my hotel. After that, Sinatra never talked to me again. Although his daughter Tina did. She thought that the hour that Cronkite, Rooney, and I had done on her father was a monument to him. In fact, the morning after his funeral in 1998, she called me to tell me that after the service she went home and played my tape.

Thirty-five years later I would finally get a fill-in from the horse's mouth—or more accurately, from the horse's daughter's mouth—about why the mention of gambling, the Mafia, and the Cal-Neva Lodge had thrown Sinatra into such a cold fury, and why his attorney, Mickey Rudin, had come all the way to New York to make sure we didn't mention those three things in front of him.

In September of 2000, Sinatra's daughter Tina had just published her autobiography and was the subject of a *60 Minutes* story by Steve Kroft. She told Kroft that her father had told her during JFK's campaign for the presidency in 1960 that he had been "summoned" by Joseph P. Kennedy, the patriarch of the Kennedy family, to ask for his help in lining up the mob boss Sam Giancana to make sure mob-controlled unions in West Virginia and Illinois delivered their vote to Kennedy and not Hubert Humphrey during the 1960 primaries in those states. Joe Kennedy's enlisting Frank Sinatra, who in turn enlisted Sam Giancana, to help his son Jack was, she said, no more than an exercise in "power turning to power."

After John F. Kennedy became president, his administration—most specifically his brother Bobby, the attorney general—started a series of congressional hearings designed to cut the mob's "power" down to size. The mob, in turn, according to Tina, saw this as biting the hand that fed them, and they let her father know why they felt they had been "had."

To make restitution, Sinatra (according to Tina) agreed to play sixteen dates for free at Giancana's Villa Venice Club in Chicago and bring the "Rat Pack" with him, something Sinatra denied ever happened when he appeared before a Nevada state hearing to apply for a gambling license at the Cal-Neva Lodge in Lake Tahoe. During the hearing, under oath, Sinatra was asked about his connections to Giancana and about his playing the Villa Venice for free as a payback for the mob's help in getting Jack Kennedy elected. He said he didn't do it; his daughter Tina said, "He lied."

In that short exchange between Kroft and Tina Sinatra were the seeds of why her father had gone around the bend that night at his house in Palm Springs and why Mickey Rudin had been so insistent that we stay away from that subject—and why Frank Sinatra felt compelled to say he ought to kill me.

*

As if Frank Sinatra telling you he ought to kill you isn't enough adventure for one trip to Palm Springs, what occurred the next day added an eerie chapter to the story. It was early evening and I was sitting on the diving board of the pool at a place called Howard Manor trying to figure out what happened to make Old Blue Eyes turn on me. That's when I realized that Rudin had lied to Sinatra and told him that we had agreed to his ground rules. No matter, I thought, I'm now on Sinatra's shit list, and that ain't a good place to be.

A good place to be was sitting on that diving board when three of the best-looking women I'd ever seen came traipsing by. It went like this:

"Hello," I said.

"Hello," they said.

"What's your name?"

"What's *your* name?"

They let it be known that they had dates with three major league ballplayers who were training near Palm Springs and, as luck would have it, the women couldn't get a room and had no place to change for the evening.

"Why not use my room?" I said.

"Hey, why not? Could we?" they asked.

"Sure," I said, and they did.

So I'm lying on the bed browsing *Playboy*—coals to Newcastle when you consider that the most spectacular of the three women has just come out of the bathroom wearing bikini panties and no bra, and the view in the mirror as she stands there combing her hair beats anything in the magazine.

To make conversation, I ask her, "What do you do?"

"You wouldn't believe me if I told you," she says.

"Try me," I say.

"No," she says, "I won't tell you, I'll show you."

With that, she walks over to the bed carrying her handbag, reaches inside and takes out a Smith and Wesson .38-caliber pistol.

Oh, shit, I think, if I'm lucky, I'm gonna get robbed. If I'm unlucky, I'm gonna get killed.

Killed? Oh, my God, I think, they were sent by Sinatra. Before I can shake myself of that possibility, she puts the gun away and takes out a can of mace.

Bullets can be traced, I think. She's going to mace me to death.

Next thing I know, she throws the can of mace on the bed, reaches once more into her handbag and takes out her badge. She's a lieutenant in the Long Beach Police Department; the other two are a couple of cops who work with her.

After they finish dressing, combing their hair, and putting on their makeup, they pick up their suitcases, kiss me goodnight, and head off to meet those lucky ballplayers.

If Sinatra meant it when he said, "I ought to kill you," he just missed the best chance he was ever going to get.

CHAPTER SIX

60 Minutes of Prime Time

By 1966 and 1967, I was already starting to think about a new type of personal journalism. The documentaries—*CBS Reports*, *NBC White Paper*, and *ABC Close Up*—all seemed to be the voice of the corporation, and I didn't believe people were interested in hearing from a corporation. They were like newspaper editorials, I thought. Do people really care about the "voice of the newspaper"? They want to read the reporting and the columnists, not the editorials.

There was the one-hour format for what amounted to the long form in broadcast journalism, and an hour seemed too long for the personal journalism that was beginning to form in my mind—journalism that might be both compelling *and* entertaining.

Entertaining? Wasn't that a dirty word when used in connection with the news? Not to me.

I had entered the television age in the era of news as a public service and spent my TV adolescence serving that cause. But I had begun to realize in the '60s that TV news was going to have to pay its own way. Otherwise, it was going to disappear into the sinkhole called The Sunday Afternoon Ghetto, where documentaries and discussion shows could do no harm to the Jackie Gleasons and Lucille Balls who paid the bills and made CBS Television the entertainment conglomerate it had become.

At the same time, Ed Murrow was beginning to realize the same thing—that his and Fred Friendly's *See It Now* program was not getting the respect from the corporate brass they thought it deserved and that in some markets it was being preempted by *Amos 'n Andy*.

What to do about it? The only way Murrow could give them a

show that could hold its own against the best the other networks could throw at it would be to get into the ratings game—a game he had roundly condemned as beneath serious journalists. But if we were going to please the corporation—and that was something he knew quite a bit about because he was a member of the CBS hierarchy for a while—it meant playing the game.

Going with the flow was what it was, but it was the only way to "make it" with the people he worked for and the only way to put the kind of money in his pocket that would take care of his wife, Janet, and their son Casey after he was gone. The broadcast he agreed to do was called *Person to Person*, and it concerned itself each week with visiting the homes of famous people.

We who worked on Ed's prestigious Sunday afternoon broadcast, *See It Now*, soon saw the public gravitating to *Person to Person* in the kind of numbers that frequently put it in the top ten while we languished in the cellar.

It was John Lardner, the television critic of *The New Yorker*, who coined the phrases "high Murrow" and "low Murrow" to distinguish between the two broadcasts.

Oh my God, I thought. That's the answer. Why not put them together in one broadcast and reap the benefits of being *both* prestigious and popular? For the first time, there could be a way for a television show to feed the network's soul and, simultaneously, its pocketbook. We could look into Marilyn Monroe's closet so long as we looked into Robert Oppenheimer's laboratory, too. We could make the news entertaining without compromising our integrity.

That, in essence, was the genesis of *60 Minutes*.

It could be like the old *Life* magazine, I thought—a family friend in the home of millions of Americans each week, serious and lighthearted in the same issue. The ads didn't interrupt the stories in *Life*: You'd have a story for a few pages, then some ads, then another story.

We could do the same thing on television, each reporter telling a complete story without interruption, then the commercial break. If we split the public-affairs hours into three parts to deal with the viewers' short attention span—not to mention my own—and made it personal journalism in which a reporter takes the viewer along with him on the story, I was willing to bet that we could take informational programming out of the ratings cellar.

I began to tell people at the network about my notion of an hour-long program combining "high Murrow" and "low Murrow." Fred Friendly thought it was a terrible idea, but I was undeterred and kept working on refining and improving the concept. A short time later, Friendly had a run-in with the top network management over their reluctance to preempt afternoon soap operas to carry the Fulbright hearings, in which the Senate probed the conduct of and the whys and wherefores of our presence in Vietnam. Following Friendly's resignation as president of CBS News, Richard S. Salant, who came from the legal department, took over. So I wrote a note to him, asking him why in the hundreds of prime-time minutes of make-believe that CBS beamed into American living rooms each week, the network couldn't find "60 minutes" of prime time to air some reality, produced with the same flair that the entertainment division had become famous for.

Salant, hardly overwhelmed by or even vaguely interested in what I had proposed, told CBS News Vice President Bill Leonard that it was a lousy idea. "That's funny," Leonard said. "That's exactly what Friendly said." Believe it or not, that is how *60 Minutes* got born. Because anything Friendly was against, Salant was for—even if it meant turning over a prime time hour each week to me, about whom he felt, at best, lukewarm.

In early 1968, Salant reluctantly put his seal of approval on my proposed broadcast, which took its title from the phrase in my memo, "60 minutes of prime time."

"What kind of stories do you want to do?" he asked me.

"Good stories, interesting and arresting stories," I told him. I couldn't come up with anything more specific than that, except to say that we would do three a week, with style and wit, each edited down to a manageable twelve to fifteen minutes to deal with the viewers' attention span.

We still had to make a pilot, but Salant initially balked at the cost—$25,000, which was a paltry sum in television even then. But a savvy woman named Ellen McCloy intervened. She was the daughter of John J. McCloy, one of the "wise men" who helped to shape the post–World War II order, and she had recently started work at CBS as an assistant to Salant. Ellen called, told me she loved the idea, and said she would talk Salant into going along with the money. And she did.

In the early days of television, there was an hour-long weekly series called *Four Star Playhouse*, in which Dick Powell, Ida Lupino, David Niven, and Charles Boyer formed a repertory company and each week played different parts. Any one of them could play anything. It gave me the idea that maybe I could do the same thing with reporters and cover the world that way. In effect, they would be a repertory company of freelance journalists, each dedicated to his or her story, but there would be no star out front, no master of ceremonies, no Ed Sullivan introducing the acts.

But my rep company started with a cast of only one—Harry Reasoner. He was a superb writer, personable, one of CBS's most accomplished correspondents who, I thought, could sort of publish his notes on air and take people along on his story. He had for a long while been on the *CBS Morning News* and was now on general assignment, not doing anything very exciting, just covering stories the way he had done for the *CBS Evening News* back when I was producing it. I approached him and he agreed to give the pilot a shot. As he recalled: "When Hewitt told me about this idea he had for a television magazine, I figured what the hell, I wasn't doing anything very exciting at the time and even if it didn't get on the air—and it probably wouldn't—I didn't have anything to lose. Besides, I owed him one for our early days together on the Doug Edwards news. It wasn't going to have much effect on my career one way or the other to do a pilot, so I said yes."

With so little money for the pilot, all I could do was to cannibalize existing film from documentaries that were in the CBS library. For instance, a ten-minute piece on Bobby Kennedy taking his kids skiing was taken from an hour we had done on him. Another story we called "Two Faces of Black America" (Ed Brooke, then a Republican senator from Massachusetts, and Stokely Carmichael, one of the founders of the Student Non-Violent Coordinating Committee, or SNCC) were taken from an hour broadcast we had done on the two of them.

When the lights came up in the screening room after Salant, Leonard, and Bob Chandler, Leonard's assistant, had viewed the pilot, Salant and Leonard seemed pleased. Chandler had a feeling it wasn't quite right.

"Wouldn't it be a better broadcast," he asked, "if you paired Reasoner with another correspondent, à la Huntley and Brinkley?"

"Like who," I said belligerently, guarding my turf.

"Like Mike Wallace," Chandler said.

Holy shit, I thought, *what an idea*. They could be the real start of my rep company. Reasoner and Wallace were made for each other.

Were they ever! Good guy, bad guy. The guy you love, the guy who makes you quake. Wallace had developed a tough-guy reputation over the years, going back to a show called *Night Beat*, in which he would take on anyone and ask the questions no one else had the guts to ask. He was someone I *knew* people would be interested in hearing from.

Mike is, quite frankly, the best thing that ever happened to a television set—certainly the best thing that every happened to *my* television set. He's a tiger, the kind of journalist who comes along once in a lifetime, and he hasn't lost a step along the way. He also brings out the best of everyone who works with him, which is a rare quality, especially in the television business.

Like every other genius, he can sometimes be his own worst enemy, although there are moments when it's clear he thinks that honor belongs to me. Almost twenty years after we started working together, I would learn what a rough time Mike was going through, fighting depression. At *60 Minutes* today, he is affectionately known as the Depression Poster Boy. But Mike Wallace not only licked his debilitating depression, he also devoted a good portion of his life to helping others lick it.

I'd better stop right now before someone accuses me of ass-kissing, but it's hard for me to say enough about Mike Wallace. He's the tough-as-nails newsman who is a soft touch when it comes to helping colleagues and perfect strangers cope with a disease he fought successfully. There's a Yiddish word for what Mike is. Mike's a mensch.

Back in the late '60s, though, I didn't know for sure whether Mike really took the offer to be on *60 Minutes* seriously. He was so sure he was going to be CBS's next White House correspondent that he figured he could tell me anything because he could always get out of it later when his glamour job came through. So he told me yes. Mike got into the act as an afterthought—probably the most fortuitous afterthought that ever came my way or his.

For more than three decades, Mike and I have had the same conversation. He'll record a narration and invariably ask: How was it,

kid? (Mike calls everybody "kid." I think he called his father "kid.")
For more than three decades, I've given him the same answer: "I'll
give you an A. Want to try again and see if you can get an A-plus?"
He always does—and he always gets an A-plus.

Reasoner set the tone on our first broadcast, September 24, 1968, letting our audience know that this was a new form for television. "The
symphony of the real world is not a monotone and while this does
not mean you have to mix it all up in one broadcast, it seems to us
that the idea of a flexible attitude has its attractions," Harry began.
"All art is the rearrangement of previous perceptions, and we don't
claim this is anything more than that, or even that journalism is an
art, for that matter. But we do think this is sort of a new approach."

The new approach intentionally abjured music. If there was a
forerunner to the TV newsmagazine format, it was the old newsreel,
The March of Time, which ran in movie theaters during the 1930s
and '40s. But the clips were done with music, which can be used to
make editorial points as effectively as words, or they can convey a
mood: When *CBS Reports*, the famed documentary series, used
Aaron Copland's "Appalachian Spring" as its theme music, it said to
the audience that this is very serious business indeed. It was the
series trademark.

We didn't want to editorialize, but we did want some sound,
arresting enough to bring people in from the kitchen. And how to do
it came at the end of our first broadcast in the form of a ticking stopwatch. I said, "Wait a minute, why are we wasting the ticking clock
at the end?" After that, we put it at the beginning and it became our
trademark.

We began in the 10–11 P.M. time slot, every other Tuesday, alter-
nating with documentaries and opposite the top-rated ABC series

Marcus Welby, M.D. Normally, if you didn't make it with the audience, it was thirteen weeks and out, never to return. But because Tuesday night at ten had been put aside for news and documentaries, and you could survive in that spot if you got good press, even though you got lousy numbers—which we did—could this kind of program keep its head above water in a sea of Jackie Gleasons, Lucille Balls, and Arthur Godfreys? No one really thought it could, but us. And there were times when even we had our doubts. What I wanted as much as to be good was to be different, to take viewers to places they hadn't been before and never would have had a chance to go to if it weren't for us—like Richard Nixon's hotel suite the night he watched himself being nominated the Republican candidate for president. What I remember most about that story was that when the voting was over and Nixon had the nomination and he and his cronies were congratulating one another, Pat Nixon sat in the corner completely ignored. Nobody said a word to her. Nixon never went up to her, kissed her, or put his arm around her.

I happened to mention the Pat Nixon incident to Hubert Humphrey a couple of weeks later, before we filmed him on his nomination night. The night Humphrey got the Democratic nomination, his wife, Muriel, was at the convention hall and not in the room with him. The moment Hubert became the nominee, he got up from his seat, walked to the television set and kissed Muriel's picture on the screen. Do I think that what I told him about the Nixon was why he did it? I don't have a doubt about it.

Within a few weeks of our premiere, I could start to breathe easier, because right off the bat we were a critical success. Even though our share of the audience was pitifully low, *60 Minutes* was something the right people liked, and that was something the network brass liked. As long as we stayed in the Tuesday 10–11 spot and in effect stayed out of their hair, we were good for at least a year.

I faced my first crisis less than two months later, soon after the presidential election. Nixon had defeated Humphrey—the kiss proved not to be a decisive issue—and the new president-elect offered Mike Wallace the job of White House press secretary. Mike was intrigued and flattered, as anyone would be, but I told him, "That doesn't make any sense. You don't want to go from being Mike Wallace to being a press secretary, even a White House press secretary. It's the kind of job a nobody takes so he can become a somebody." I don't know if that's what convinced Mike to stick with 60 Minutes, but shortly after that conversation he told the Nixon people thanks but no thanks.

I was so glad he did, and 60 Minutes was on its way.

How 60 Minutes went from just another horse in the stable to being Secretariat is something I have never been able to explain. I have said on occasion that we were successful because we generated a lot of psychic energy rubbing off on each other. And for reasons I can't explain, we are able to transmit that psychic energy through the tube every week. Is that really it? Or is that a lot of mumbo jumbo to answer a question that none of us really knows the answer to. I don't know the answer to that one, either. What I do know is that without Palmer Williams at my side as my number two during the early years and Phil Scheffler at my side now as my number two, I think this ship may have foundered. (You mean the horse is now a ship?) Palmer Williams was the good steady hand on the tiller who got us out of the harbor, and Phil Scheffler is the steady hand who keeps us on course. Palmer knew more about more things than anyone I ever knew in my life—a virtual walking encyclopedia.

He was the guy Murrow and Friendly had depended on to keep his cool when things were falling apart—film that got lost en route to the editing room, a temperamental correspondent blowing his top, keeping Murrow from taking a swing at Friendly and vice-versa.

In essence, he was part our play doctor and part our resident psychiatrist. The roof's caving in? Call Palmer; he can fix anything.

Every enterprise needs a Palmer Williams—someone who knows where all the bodies are buried, who knows how to convince you that what you're about to do is something you're going to regret later, and actually points you in the right direction when you lose your way. I can't recount all of the many times Palmer saved us from ourselves, but it's safe to say that without him there, we wouldn't still be here, thirty-three years later.

CHAPTER SEVEN

What Makes a Great Story

One of my favorite segments from those early seasons was Harry Reasoner revisiting my favorite movie. I knew Harry was onto something good when he sat down in my office one day and said, "Do you know what's still in Hollywood, intact? The whole set of *Casablanca*."

"Wow," I said. And the story Harry did about what is on everybody's list of the ten best movies is now on everybody's list of the ten best *60 Minutes* segments. It was "low Murrow" at its highest. Harry sat at the piano and said, "Remember when Dooley Wilson sat at this piano?" And then we dissolved into the scene from *Casablanca*. It was a thrill to see the piano still sitting there, and the "Rick's American Café" sign. And how could you do *Casablanca* without talking to Ingrid Bergman about it? That's when she told Harry, "We planned two endings. One, I would go with Paul Henreid and leave Bogart standing at the airport. Or, I would let him get on the plane alone and I would stay with Bogart.

"We shot the first one," she said, "and it was so good, we never did shoot the second one."

But for all of Harry's joyfulness on the air, in private he was looking for greener pastures, and in the fall of 1970 he was offered a great opportunity at ABC, to be the anchor of their evening news program (with another former CBS newsman, Howard K. Smith), and go head-to-head with Walter Cronkite. It didn't do very well, prompting ABC to bring in Barbara Walters, a choice Reasoner disapproved of and made painfully clear, on the air, that he did. I knew Harry would be back, but I knew that whether he came back or not, there was a spectacular piece of talent in the wings. Morley Safer, CBS's London bureau chief, in the 1960s had been the network's main man in South Vietnam, and his reports from the war were consistently on-target and provocative. The most provocative of which was his reporting that marines had burned down a Vietnamese village with their cigarette lighters.

When Bill Leonard picked up the phone and called Morley Safer in Paris, where he was preparing to cover Charles de Gaulle's funeral, he told Safer: "Reasoner's leaving Monday. Come to New York tomorrow."

"Can't come tomorrow," Safer said. "Tomorrow I'm burying de Gaulle."

"How about the day after?" Leonard said.

"Okay, but on one condition," Safer shot back. "When 60 Minutes folds, I go back to London." That was over thirty years ago, and neither of us has regretted a moment of it. Morley has a great eye for stories, both the hard-edged and the softhearted, and certainly the offbeat. Can you imagine anyone else doing the 60 Minutes piece on the cool and remote Finns and their love affair with the hot tango? It's stories like that that give 60 Minutes its flavor.

Just a few months later, in March 1971, Morley showed his versatility by reporting a groundbreaking story I consider to be as good a piece of reporting as any I have been associated with in my fifty-three years at CBS.

The story, reported by Morley and his producer, Joe Wershba, was about the incident in the Gulf of Tonkin, off the coast of North Vietnam, that had occurred on August 4, 1964, and had brought about America's entry into the Vietnam War. On that day, Morley said early in his broadcast, "the U.S. destroyers Maddox and Turner Joy were attacked by Communist torpedo boats. Or were they?"

Was what happened really a trumped up excuse to go to war—a

war that would end up costing 58,000 Americans their lives? A war that tore apart a nation, undermined confidence in government—a war that casts a lingering shadow even into the twenty-first century?

What Morley and Joe reported was that the incident almost certainly did not happen the way President Lyndon Johnson told the American people it did. Johnson already had a resolution of support from Congress to "take any action to repel aggression and save South Vietnam," but he needed an incident, some provocation, to implement it. An attack on two American destroyers, if it really happened, was made to order. But if you examine in detail, as Joe and Morley did, the cable traffic between Seventh Fleet headquarters and Captain John Herrick on the *Maddox*, it was quite clear that although the president was sure an attack had taken place, others in the chain of command were not. The Pentagon was pressing Admiral Ulysses S. Grant Sharp, the commander in chief of the Pacific fleet, to press Captain Herrick to verify that the destroyers had come under fire.

The two American ships reported that they were ambushed early in the evening by perhaps a half-dozen torpedo boats, but the "entire action leaves many doubts" about what actually happened, Herrick said in an early cable to Sharp. Other Herrick cables in the early morning hours suggested even more confusion. One said: "Review of action makes many recorded contacts and torpedoes fired appear doubtful. Freak weather effects, and overeager sonar men may have accounted for many reports. No actual visual sightings by *Maddox*. Suggest complete evaluation before any further actions."

By 6 P.M. Washington time, a half-day behind the time in the waters off Vietnam, President Johnson had given the final go-ahead to bomb North Vietnam. And yet, the Pentagon was still leaning on Admiral Sharp to "make damn sure," in Defense Secretary Robert McNamara's words, "there had been an attack."

What Safer and Wershba reported next was the last cable traffic between Sharp and Herrick:

Admiral Sharp to Captain Herrick: "(1) Can you confirm absolutely that you were attacked? (2) Can you confirm sinking of PT boats? (3) Desire reply directly with supporting evidence."

Captain Herrick's final report to Admiral Sharp still reflected his doubts: "*Maddox* scored no known hits and never positively identified a boat. No known damage or personnel casualties to either ship...the first boat to close *Maddox* probably fired torpedoes at *Maddox*, which was heard but not seen. All subsequent *Maddox* torpedo reports were doubtful in that it is supposed that (my) sonar man was hearing (our) ship's own propeller beat."

Two days later, Congress approved the Gulf of Tonkin Resolution that Lyndon Johnson would use to justify his actions in Vietnam.

Some twenty-four years after Safer and Wershba filed that story, McNamara rhetorically asked (in his book *In Retrospect: The Tragedy and Lessons of Vietnam*) whether the Johnson administration that he served so loyally was justified in basing its future military actions in Vietnam—including an enormous expansion of force levels—on the Tonkin Gulf Resolution. "Answer: Absolutely not. Although the resolution granted sufficiently broad authority to support the escalation that followed, as I said, Congress never intended it to be used as a basis for such action and still less did the country see it so," McNamara wrote.

And to think the whole senseless adventure was justified by what was called the Domino Theory—the notion that if South Vietnam fell, the rest of Southeast Asia would fall with it. Well, South Vietnam fell and nothing else, absolutely nothing else, fell with it.

For our story, Safer got the Pentagon to give him permission to board the *Maddox* and talk to Captain Herrick. It wasn't easy: Morley was no favorite of the Pentagon, dating back to that story he reported from Vietnam in August 1965 of U.S. Marines using their cigarette lighters to set fire to the homes of South Vietnamese civilians in the village of Cam Ne. In fact, the night the Cam Ne story ran on the *CBS Evening News*, LBJ was watching and, in a cold fury, called CBS president Frank Stanton. Stanton wasn't home and hadn't seen the story so you can imagine his surprise when his phone rang early the next morning and a voice said, "Frank, are you trying to fuck me?"

"Who is this?" Stanton asked, groggily.

"Frank, this is your president, and yesterday your boys shat on the American flag!"

The truth about the Vietnam War was that someone had indeed "shat" on the American flag. But it wasn't Frank Stanton and it wasn't Morley Safer.

But if former President Johnson was angry about our Tonkin Gulf story in 1971, it didn't stop him from playing host to Mike Wallace and me a few weeks later in Austin, Texas. We were there to videotape for *60 Minutes* a tour of the about-to-be-opened Lyndon Baines Johnson Memorial Library on the campus of the University of Texas. Our tour guide was to be LBJ himself.

On arrival, we were prepared to take a taxi to the hotel we had booked in downtown Austin, when who did we find waiting at the gate to greet us but LBJ and Lady Bird. "Forget the hotel," the former president said. "We canceled it. We want you to stay at the ranch." And we did, in what I knew from all the westerns I'd seen was a "bunkhouse" — better suited, I might add, to providing a good night's sleep to cowboys than to city boys. If it weren't for the honor, I would just as soon have stayed at the hotel. It didn't have bunk beds, but it did have a generator that never shut down or shut up the whole night through.

About 6 A.M., I heard a rooster crow and a knock on the door. It was LBJ himself, ready to take Mike and me on a tour of his "spread." Sure enough, parked outside was that big white Lincoln convertible that had become as much identified with him as the Stetson he wore.

As we piled in—Mike in the front, me in the back—he reached into the glove compartment and took out a candy bar. Remember, it was 6 A.M., but the thirty-sixth president of the United States wanted a candy bar. Then, I guess to let this young whippersnapper from New York know who was boss on his ranch, he stopped the car near a trash can, turned to me in the back, handed me the wrapper and said: "Throw it in the can."

"Sir?" I said.

"Throw the wrapper in the garbage," he said impatiently.

"Yes, sir," I said.

Was it demeaning? Not as demeaning as his driving off and leaving me to run after the car.

I caught up with my colleague and my former president parked near a shack that looked as if it had seen better days. That's when Johnson got out of the car and pressed a button on a tree so we could hear from a loudspeaker hidden among the branches, a story about the shack. Imagine, two guys and a former president of the United States sitting in a white Lincoln convertible, not long after sunup, parked on a lonely road in Texas, with the top down, listening to a tree tell them a story.

This, as best I can remember, was the story the tree told us.

"The little old black lady who lived here was a midwife, and one night she got on her mule and rode ten miles down the road through the thunder and lightning to deliver a little baby." As the tree moved through the story and approached the punch line, LBJ was all ears and I do mean "all ears"—even at rest, they were his trademark but now they were positively vibrating as the tree said, "And that little baby's name was Lyndon Baines Johnson!"

I was nonplussed. Mike, cool customer that he is, said, "Mr. President, that's the loveliest story I ever heard." Mike said it. Honest to God, he actually said "that's the loveliest story I ever heard." How I kept a straight face I'll never know.

After breakfast—bacon, eggs, toast, coffee, no candy bar—we went to LBJ's television station in Austin to wait for the former president and first lady to take us to the library. While we were waiting, over the paging system came: "Now hear this, now hear this. The president has arrived and eggs are in the waiting room."

"What in the hell is that all about?" I asked one of the cameramen.

"Oh," he said. "Whenever the Johnsons come in from the ranch, they bring us fresh eggs."

"Isn't that nice?" I said.

"Nice, hell," he said. "They sell 'em to us."

Next stop was the LBJ library where, while waiting for the tour to begin, Mike and I sat on a low stone wall that circled the mezzanine twenty feet or so above the marble entry hall and plotted our strategy to get LBJ to level with us about the Vietnam War. "Just spring it on him," I said.

"No," Mike said, "I want him to know it's coming so he can think about it and give us a cogent answer."

What we completely forgot was that Mike was wearing a microphone and that it had been hooked up and that Lady Bird and her friend, aide, and confidante Liz Carpenter were in the control room, listening to our every word. So when the president, apparently forewarned by Lady Bird, arrived, his first words were: "Goddammit, Mike, I've said all I'm going to say about the war so forget it."

"You're wrong, Mr. President," Mike said. "You can't avoid it."

"I can't avoid it?" he said. "I can avoid any goddamned thing I want to avoid, and I don't *want to* and I'm not *going to* talk about the Vietnam War."

"You're wrong," Mike said again. And this time I could see the veins beginning to bulge in LBJ's neck. Jesus, I thought, if Mike doesn't shut up, he's going to push both of us over this wall and down onto that marble floor twenty feet below. I knew—and so did Mike—that LBJ bitterly resented being tagged with a senseless war that had begun under his predecessor, Jack Kennedy. What he wanted to be remembered for was his "Great Society" and not a war from which we had turned tail and run away.

Having all but given up on his relenting and talking about the war, we began the interview. It was kind of dull until, out of the blue and apropos of nothing, he stunned us by volunteering, "You will recall the War of 1812 was branded Mr. Madison's war.... The Mexican War was Mr. Polk's war.... The Civil War was Mr. Lincoln's war.... World War I was Mr. Wilson's war.... World War II was Mr. Roosevelt's war.... Korea was Mr. Truman's war. But Kennedy was spared that. Vietnam was Mr. McNamara's war and then it became Mr. Johnson's war."

At that, he stopped dead and looked at Mike for a second. Mike gave him a playful shove and said, "Goddammit, Mr. President, that was great!" And a grinning LBJ said, "Is that what you were after?"

"Damn right, Mr. President," Mike said.

I don't remember what the pictures from the LBJ Library looked like, but I'll never forget Johnson's words. The truth is, that while most people think of the eye when they think about television, I think of the ear. There are no hard and fast rules in writing for the ear, but after more than fifty years of working at it, I believe in some rough guidelines.

Two of them are: Short is usually better than long and don't waste words. The bank robber Willie Sutton got it right when he was asked why he robbed banks. "That's where the money is," he replied. Have you ever heard three words that convey a message better than "stick 'em up," or "I've had it!" or "I'm outta here"? Have you ever heard anyone express himself better, faster, or more to the point than the judge who had the following exchange with a defendant in his courtroom: "As God is my judge," the defendant said, "I am not guilty." To which the magistrate answered: "He's not! I am! You are!"

Now that's good writing. No unnecessary adverbs or adjectives, just telling it like it is. Don't be afraid to write the way people talk.

My writing heroes are too numerous to list here. But certainly when I think about good writing, I think about Abe Lincoln delivering, from scribbled notes, the Gettysburg Address. Or touching a nerve in his second inaugural address that ended with an appeal to both sides in the Civil War: "With malice toward none, with charity for all, with firmness in the right as God gives us to see the right, let us strive on to finish the work we are in, to bind up the nation's wounds, to care for him who shall have borne the battle and for his widow and his orphan, to do all which may achieve and cherish a just and lasting peace among ourselves and with all nations."

I also think of President Franklin Roosevelt, applying a tourniquet to a country hemorrhaging away its life's blood during the Great Depression of the 1930s—and I'm old enough to remember hearing on the radio his telling his countrymen that "the only thing we have to fear is fear itself." Short, sweet. In this case, bittersweet and to the point.

And Winston Churchill rallying his people against Nazi Germany during the early days of World War II by telling them: "Conquer we must as conquer we shall." But until we do, he cautioned, "all I can offer you is blood, tears, toil, and sweat." Nothing about Churchill ever impressed me more than what Ed Murrow said about him: "He mobilized the English language and sent it into battle."

I'm in awe of Shakespeare and Dickens, but that's easy: Who in his right mind isn't? Think, though, of the wisdom in the lyrics of some Broadway musicals. *The King and I*, by Richard Rodgers and Oscar Hammerstein, includes this stunning admission by the otherwise egomaniacal King of Siam: "Sometimes, I am not sure of what I absolutely know is so!" Now that's not just a lyric, that's insight.

A whole carload of twentieth-century social significance was summed up by Stephen Sondheim's lyrics in *West Side Story*, when a gang member tells Officer Krupke, "I'm depraved because I'm deprived." Shakespeare couldn't have said it better.

And could anyone have said better what the great black baseball player Satchel Paige said when he asked a friend: "How old would you be if you didn't know how old you was?"

Pictures are, of course, essential to television, but a picture is not *always* worth a thousand words. Sometimes, often, in fact, it's the other way around.

To be sure, an out-of-focus picture leaves a lot to be desired—but out-of-focus sound? That's a catastrophe. If you don't know how to communicate with words in broadcast journalism, you're in the wrong business. And I fear there are too many people today in my business who *are* in the wrong business.

I'm a bit of a fanatic on content and audio and delivery. When one of the *60 Minutes* correspondents records a soundtrack, I turn my back to the screen and listen. Sometimes, I'll whirl around and say, "That pause is too long! That inflection is not right. That sentence doesn't belong there." I listen to the way words hit my ear, how the story sounds, not how it looks. I know that if we can get the sound right, we can make the pictures work. To prove it, *60 Minutes* works almost as well on radio as it does on television.

It's the writing, the spoken words, that gets people hooked and keeps people hooked. Fred Friendly and I had a lot of disagreements—hell, the bastard fired me from the evening news—but he taught me how to tell stories. And it isn't easy. You don't talk down to people but you also don't assume they know as much as you do about your subject. A rough rule of thumb is from the great publisher Roy Howard: "Never *under*estimate the public's intelligence and never *over*estimate its knowledge." Don't be too clever at the cost of making yourself clear. I sometimes call it the "Hey, Mildred" rule—i.e., don't let a husband turn to his wife during your story and say, "Hey, Mildred, do you know what this guy's talking about? No? Me neither. Hand me the remote."

At *60 Minutes*, we are intensely aware of our competition, which isn't other TV newsmagazines or even what's up against us in our time slot. Our competitors are the distractions of the household. Walking out of a television show is the easiest thing in the world. After all, you've made no commitment to stay. You didn't book a seat, you didn't have to find a baby-sitter, you didn't search for a parking space, you didn't wait in line, you didn't buy a ticket, you didn't even have to get dressed. It's not like going to the movies or a sports event—how many of those have you actually walked out of? Television is a different beast. When someone says, "This is terrible," it's automatic exit—so easy that most of us walk out of as many as a dozen TV shows every night.

The best way I know to keep people from walking out is to catch their ear even more than their eye. That's what has made *60 Minutes* different from the gaggle of newsmagazines that have followed in our wake, and it's what has kept us in television's top ten for nearly a quarter-century. It is our conviction that, although it is television, what we tell people rather than what we show them is what they tune in for every Sunday.

Actually, the proposition that what you hear is every bit as important as what you see—and frequently more important—hit me between the eyes (or more accurately between the ears) at the coronation of Pope John XXIII in 1958. It was before satellites, back when space was nothing more than something you never had enough of.

Having rigged up a Rube Goldberg contraption to convert European television to the American standard and having shipped the film on one of the new Pan Am 707 jets to get it across the Atlantic in what was in those days an astounding seven hours, we could— miracle of miracles—show Americans on the other side of the pond an event in Rome that happened that very same day.

The only problem was that the picture quality was atrocious: It didn't matter: The sound echoing off the Bernini columns—*sic transit gloria mundi*—was so magnificent it made you forget that what you were looking at was all but unwatchable.

It's that preoccupation with audio that causes me to tell journalism students who want to go into television not to get hung up only on pictures. And to do themselves a huge favor and get hold of Fred Friendly and Ed Murrow's *I Can Hear It Now* record album, an adjunct to their *Hear It Now* radio program. And to take note of how writing for the ear has a different cadence than writing for the eye.

When the writing is crisp and sharp and imaginative, it's lyrical. As an example, listen to the priceless bit of prose Friendly penned and Murrow voiced to evoke what it was like in the South Pacific during World War II: "If you've ever been to the jungle at night, you know that when a howitzer screams, the jungle screams back." Learn to write like that, I tell the students, and you can't miss becoming another Fred Friendly—and if you're as lucky as he was, hooking up with another Ed Murrow. Men and women with a way with words don't need pictures. They draw their own with words.

Too many people in television forget this. They rely too often on

meaningless phrases that keep showing up like clockwork on everybody's newscast—for instance, unless you're talking about the NFL,
"team coverage"; unless you're talking about Jacques Cousteau, "in-
depth"; and unless you're talking about Bob Dole, "hard news."

Liza Doolittle, being made over in Lerner and Loewe's *My Fair
Lady*, said: "Words, words, words, I'm so sick of words." She might
have been. I'm not.

Consider the following examples of priceless prose—wonderful
phrase-making in perfect pitch and context.

> My wife Marilyn's answer when her mother, Celia Cher-
> nowsky, called to say that she'd read that Elizabeth Taylor had
> been dating a second or third cousin of my wife's. "Do you
> realize," her mother said, "someday we may be related to
> Elizabeth Taylor?"
>
> "Mother," Marilyn said, "someday everybody may be."

> My former secretary Petey Baird, who became Mrs. Charles
> Kuralt, sizing up another secretary at CBS: "She's the kind of
> girl who would use clichés…if she knew any."

> The definition of an "English gentleman" by Sir Howard
> Stringer, who used to run CBS and now runs Sony: "Some-
> one who knows how to play the bagpipes but doesn't."

> The songwriter Tom Lehrer saying that when he was a kid,
> there were certain four-letter words you couldn't say to a girl.
> And now that you can say them, you can't say "girl."

> Paul Loewenwarter, a former *60 Minutes* producer, a few days
> after he came to work at CBS as a "gofer" on the news desk,

being asked by a friend: "You work at CBS, what's Walter Cronkite really like?"

"Two sugars," he said.

Broadway and Hollywood writer Peter Stone, toasting Peter Jennings at his fiftieth birthday party: "Peter is Canadian so he can't say 'house.' What he says is 'hoose,' but that's all right, Barbara Walters can't say 'Barbara Walters.' "

The comeuppance I got from one of the best writers in America, Molly Ivins, after I had taken a blue pencil to a commentary she had written for 60 *Minutes*, to wit: "The strongest human emotion is neither love nor hate. It is one person's desire to fuck with another person's copy."

The father of David Schoenbrun, CBS's longtime man in Paris, watching television in Schoenbrun's apartment during a visit from the States, even though he neither spoke nor understood French. "What are you looking at, Pop?" David asked.

"I don't know," his father said. "It goes in one eye and out the other."

Sir David Frost's secretary on her first visit to Texas, excusing herself to go to the ladies' room, only to return a few seconds later to ask: "David, am I a steer or a heifer?"

But the best is a story about Fred Friendly, who became a professor at the Columbia School of Journalism after leaving CBS News in 1966. The first day he showed up, one of his students came to class wearing a button that said, "Make Love, Not War."

Fred said to her, "I don't think that's an appropriate button to wear to class."

"Oh, Mr. Friendly," she said, "you're so square you think making love is making out."

That day at lunch, Friendly told Walter Lippmann about the student who had told him, "You're so square you think making love is making out," to which Lippmann replied, "What the hell is 'making out'?"

The next day Fred told his class he'd had lunch with Lippmann, who asked him, "What the hell is 'making out'?" Friendly thought that pretty well summed up the generation gap until a student got up and said, "Who the hell is Walter Lippmann?"

I always thought nobody could top that until I told the story a few years ago to a group of journalism students. When I got to the punch line—"Who the hell is Walter Lippmann?"—one of them stood up and said, "Who the hell is Fred Friendly?"

CHAPTER EIGHT

Hitting Our Stride

*I*n 1972, CBS moved *60 Minutes* from Tuesdays at ten to Sundays at six, which meant we now would be seen every week, except during football season. It was a better slot than the one opposite *Marcus Welby, M.D.*, and because six o'clock was an hour before prime time there was no way we could cause much trouble. Then in 1975, Oscar Katz, a vice president in the entertainment division, proposed that we move to seven o'clock, an hour of prime time designated for public affairs or family programming. Instead of *Marcus Welby*, we were up against *The Wonderful World of Disney*, and that's when we took off. That's when our percentage of the audience, which had been creeping up, began to impress the brass.

Now that we were on every week and attracting a bigger audience, it had become apparent that the story load was too heavy for Mike and Morley to carry alone. We needed a third correspondent, and one name stood head and shoulders above the rest: Dan Rather.

Dan was one of the stars of CBS News, having just completed the Johnson and Nixon years as CBS's White House correspondent. If Dan thought his career had come to a full stop after he traded barbs with Richard Nixon, he was the only one who did. He was just too good to go down for the count over a silly exchange like the one he and President Nixon had had at a televised news conference during a National Association of Broadcasters convention in Houston, Texas. Rather, a Texan who had made it big in the big time, was applauded when he was called on by the president, only to be asked by a miffed Richard Nixon, "Are you running for something?" To which Dan responded, "No, sir. Are you?" Those four little words had done it. Rather was now persona non grata with the Nixon White House, but he hung on until Nixon left office and then came to New York to be the principal broadcaster/reporter on *CBS Reports*, but not for long.

As Dan recalls, Mike Wallace called him and said, "Listen, my friend, we are going to have a third correspondent. We all want it to be you. There is no second choice."

To which Rather said, "I just don't know."

"Whadda you mean you don't know?" Wallace said.

"I mean it sounds good and all that," Rather said. "But I'm just beginning to really feel good about *CBS Reports*."

That prompted a typical Wallace response: "Are you out of your mind? If you were a KGB agent looking for a place to hide, you couldn't find a better place than *CBS Reports*. Dan, Dan, Dan! Even Ed Murrow couldn't make *CBS Reports* fly. Come on. Don't be an idiot."

"Mike, I'll think about it. Really think about it. And talk to Jean [his wife]."

"Atta boy," Mike said. "Call me as soon as she tells you to say yes."

Nothing has demonstrated to me the hold that people like Rather have on the public than what happened after a small-town mayor brought a defamation suit against both him and CBS a couple of years after he joined *60 Minutes*. When the mayor lost the suit, which was for several million dollars, he called Rather and said, "At least can I have your autograph?"

About a year or two after Rather came on the broadcast, we inaugurated "Point-Counterpoint," Jack Kilpatrick and Shana Alexander's weekly catfight (or dogfight—take your choice) at the end of each *60 Minutes* broadcast. Jack and Shana—for want of a better description, our house conservative and our house liberal—would debate a contentious issue of the day as the closing segment of the show. (Before Shana, our house liberal was Nicholas von Hoffman, who I reluctantly had to let go when he insisted on referring to the president of the United States, Richard Nixon, as "a dead mouse on the kitchen floor that everyone was afraid to touch and throw in the garbage." Granted, it was a difficult time and the description was not that far off target, but it wasn't the kind of thing I wanted someone to say about the president of the United States on 60 Minutes.)

It never seemed to amaze me how downright sappy TV critics can be when a columnist wrote that I had taken Jack and Shana off the air because Saturday Night Live was satirizing them with such bits as Jack calling Shana "you ignorant slut." What the silly son of a bitch didn't know and should have known was that the satirizing of "Point-Counterpoint" on Saturday Night Live was what had been keeping them on the air, even though the segment had run its course.

My problem now was, What to replace it with? I knew that Andy Rooney, who had written essays for Harry Reasoner, was a hell of a writer. What I didn't know was whether he could cut it as an on-air personality. So my first thought was to do an animated comic strip each week that Andy would write and somebody else would voice. What I had in mind was an animated, Rooney-written television version of Andy Capp, the newspaper comic strip starring a Cockney that everybody could identify with. Then, I thought, that's not half as good an idea as letting Rooney appear in person, reading his own copy, and I was willing to bet that Rooney, just sitting at a desk and talking to our audience, would strike a responsive chord. And because I gave him his head — let's face it, I don't know anybody brave enough not to give Andy Rooney his head — he came through with flying colors.

Oh yeah, one more thing. Did you ever wonder why Rooney's 60 Minutes trademark is "Did you ever wonder why…"? He has, because he's never said it. As Casey Stengel liked to say, "You could look it up." I have, and Andy's right. He's never said it. Where did it come from? Joe Piscopo, playing Andy Rooney on *Saturday Night Live*, used it as his catchphrase — never Andy.

Over and above Rooney's nonexistent line, there was a word that did become identified with *60 Minutes*. It was "gotcha" — often accomplished with the help of a hidden camera that competitors mistakenly thought was the secret of our success. It not only wasn't, we abandoned that technique as a tired stunt early in the game, mostly because those who were trying to produce another *60 Minutes* were using it not to show how crooks and con men operated, but to show off that anything *60 Minutes* could do, they could do — if not better, at least more often. In short, they ran it into the ground.

One of the two times we used a hidden camera most effectively was in 1976 when we demonstrated, in a story we called "The Clinic on Morse Avenue," how labs in Illinois that examined blood and billed Medicaid for their work "kicked back" money to clinics that sent their blood work to those labs. Such kickbacks are illegal under both Illinois and federal law.

The producer, Barry Lando, working with the Better Government Association of Chicago, rented a store on Chicago's South Side and opened a bogus clinic equipped with a camera that was installed behind a one-way mirror, then announced we were open for business. With a BGA employee playing the role of the clinic's doctor, we were able to capture on film lab owners who came to the clinic offering to kick back money to the clinic if it would send its blood work to their lab.

The climactic moment came when Mike Wallace, who was standing in the back behind the one-way mirror, stepped out and confronted the lab owners with the illegality of the kickbacks he had just heard them offer.

What is the morality, the ethics, of that kind of journalism? I, for one, have no trouble with it. Although I am a great believer in everyone's right not to be snooped on, I don't think the Constitution guarantees anyone the right of privacy while he or she is committing a crime.

However, Gene Patterson, late of *The Washington Post* and one of my all-time favorite newspapermen, took issue with me. "They hadn't been charged with a crime and certainly hadn't been indicted for one when you showed them 'in the act,' " he said. At least, he went on, wait until law enforcement charges them with something before exposing them to the public as criminals. His argument was that we were overstepping our role as journalists and denying those lab owners a fair trial.

"Okay, Gene," I said, "Have you, as a newspaper editor, ever run a picture taken from a hidden bank camera of someone holding up a bank?"

"Of course, I have," he said. "Who hasn't?"

"You don't really believe, do you, Gene, that television does not have a right to run pictures taken by a hidden camera of a crook robbing a clinic and newspapers do have a right to run pictures taken by a hidden camera of a crook robbing a bank?"

My point was that newspapermen, even ones as good as Gene Patterson, look at what television does differently from the way they look at what they do, and I think that extends to what the television stations owned by their newspapers do, as opposed to what the newspapers that own them do.

Along that line, I was never prouder of a *60 Minutes* story than I was of the one Marion Goldin conceived and produced in 1978 called "This Year at Murietta"—a play on the title of a movie that was popular at the time called *Last Year at Marienbad*. Both the movie and our story were about a health resort. Theirs was in Ger-

many. Ours was in California and was in business solely to bilk
unsuspecting Americans out of their life savings while claiming to
cure their incurable cancers.

Mike Wallace introduced the story by saying: "60 *Minutes* cameraman Greg Cook, 60 *Minutes* soundman James Camery, and 60
Minutes producer Marion Goldin spent nine days at a spa at Murietta Hot Springs, California. Because we'd been told the bottom line
at the spa was dollars, we told them that our soundman James
Camery, whom we dubbed 'the Colonel,' was a wealthy, semiretired
investment counselor who had just learned he had leukemia. Our
cameraman Greg Cook, we told them, was a traveling photographer
and the Colonel's concerned nephew. And producer Goldin? She
was the Colonel's longtime secretary."

What better way to arrive than in a Rolls-Royce? Before we knew
it and had even handed over the $1,200 they charged for "the cure,"
the Colonel was enrolled in a program that consisted, in its entirety,
of living on distilled water and lemon juice and having his urine
analyzed at regular moments—which they used as opportunities to
report remarkable progress in curing his leukemia. What we didn't
tell them was that on two occasions we had substituted cameraman
Cook's urine for soundman Camery's, and on another gave them
producer Goldin's.

Soon, it was time for Mike Wallace to arrive with another film
crew and face R. J. Rudd, the Baptist minister who ran the phony spa
and had no idea that Mike was in any way related to or in league
with Camery, Cook, and Goldin. By the time Mike got through with
R. J. Rudd, he was splattered all over the California countryside, and
it wasn't long before the state of California moved in and shut the
place down.

Now, what about the ethics of that one? Didn't we lie to get in
and lie at every turn while we were there? Sure we did. Did that

trouble me? Not for a moment, and it still doesn't. I'd do it again tomorrow if we found another phony spa selling a phony cancer treatment and "taking" cancer patients as R. J. Rudd's spa did until Mike Wallace and Marion Goldin put him out of business.

That isn't the only place and the only time we threw the rules out the window and did what we thought was the right thing. The time I remember best was the Sunday in 1979 when Mike Wallace got to Iran's Ayatollah Khomeini right after his followers seized the American embassy in Tehran and took dozens of Americans hostage. Wallace was the only newsman the Ayatollah agreed to see and so, at that moment, he was the only link our State Department had to something that had never happened before and that had them completely flummoxed about what to do.

With the interview Mike conducted with the Ayatollah in the holy city of Qom, unedited and in its entirety, about to be fed by satellite to the control room of Studio 41 at the CBS Broadcast Center on New York's West Fifty-seventh Street, I got a call on the control-room phone from Assistant Secretary of State Hodding Carter, asking if Secretary of State Cyrus Vance could listen in. Of course, I said.

There are times, although some colleagues of mine are shocked by the thought, that being an American takes precedence over being a journalist. And if ever there was one of those times, this was one of them!

I wouldn't have it any other way. Nor would I back off covering what are called investigative stories. Although the people we investigate almost invariably claim that we're out to get them and that we have little regard for fair play.

Businesspeople, otherwise some of the smartest folks on the planet, seem particularly susceptible to crying foul when we say anything about them that doesn't jibe with the corporate image they are trying to project. Does that make us antibusiness?

Easy question: The answer is no. I run *60 Minutes* and I'm about as pro–free enterprise as you can get. And after all, we're a business, too, and a very successful one at that—successful because we're supported by some of America's biggest and best companies.

Don't get me wrong: I can understand why some companies may resent us. It has been my experience that most businesses, including the one I work for, like only two things said about them— what their own public relations people say about them and what their advertising agencies say about them. The PR and ad images often present, to be generous about it, a somewhat blurred vision of reality. Covering business as a journalist means covering business, warts and all. It means the bad along with the good. It means balance and evenhandedness.

Our job is to get beyond and behind the slogans and reveal what's actually happening. Critics ask us why we don't report the good things that businesses do. Sometimes we have done just that. For instance, we reported the extraordinary way Johnson & Johnson responded when bottles of its Tylenol product that had been tampered with began showing up on drugstore and supermarket shelves. Recently, the Ford Motor Company invited us to watch and report just how the company was going about trying to clean up its image after the trouble it had with defective Firestone tires and the rollovers that ensued with the Ford Explorer.

But for the most part, there's a very good reason why we don't report the good things companies do: It's because that's not news. If a company advertises a product and tells the consumer what that product will do, and by God, it turns out the product does exactly what the company said it would do, the public and that company are even steven. I don't know why anyone thinks *that* deserves milk and cookies. If the company doesn't deliver what its ads say it will deliver, then you might have a gripe and *60 Minutes* might have a story. But if you get a fair shake, which is how it's supposed to work, and the store get its money, what's news about that?

If, as the old saw goes, the scariest words in the English language are "Mike Wallace and a *60 Minutes* crew are in the waiting room," you can bet they're there for a good reason. Usually, it's because some company or organization is keeping to itself something it should be sharing with the public. Is that enough for a sponsor to blackball *60 Minutes*? Not if it's big enough to admit when it's wrong.

For example, when Mike reported in the 1970s that the gas tank on the Ford Pinto, a product that was advertised on *60 Minutes*, had a tendency to explode, Ford canceled their commercials on *60 Minutes* for all their cars—but for one week! The next week, their ads were back. Apparently, Ford thought a news broadcast that told it like it was and leveled with the public, even at Ford's expense, was the kind of broadcast they wanted to be associated with.

Have we made mistakes along the way? Sure, though never out of malice or deliberate disregard for the truth. One of the most glaring became a kind of totem for the company involved. It was a 1979 story on Illinois Power's new nuclear plant at Clinton, which was approved by the Illinois Public Service Commission at an estimated cost of $350 million but was headed much, much higher when we got there—not double or even triple the cost, but more like $2 billion and beyond. The company was so nervous about being interviewed by *60 Minutes* that they had their own camera in the room alongside ours. Did they have a right to do that? Of course they did. It was their office, their executives, and their nuclear plant.

While human error is inevitable in our business or any business, we, like just about everybody else, take pains to avoid making mistakes, but we did make some factual errors in reporting the Illinois Power story. Among other things, we failed to report that one of the critics of Illinois Power—a man we interviewed for the story—had falsified his credentials and we knew it. Inexcusable, no question about it, but we tried to make restitution by reporting a correction on a later broadcast. One thing about *60 Minutes* and any good news organization is that we let it be known when we've made an error.

An unflattering videotape that Illinois Power made about *60 Minutes* played before sympathetic audiences for years and became a bible for those who thought we were antibusiness and especially antinuclear. Although we were right on the facts—the plant was years behind schedule and the cost overruns were huge—we made some mistakes and frankly admitted that we had.

When we do investigative stories, why do the bad guys let us in the door? Good question. Morley Safer's answer was a gem: "A crook doesn't believe he's made it as a crook until he's been on *60 Minutes*." The real answer is that anyone who has made a living conning the public can't believe he can't also con a reporter. Con men never believe they're going to be unmasked and never come to grips with the fact that someone may know more about them than they know about themselves.

Which raises the next question: Don't we ambush unsuspecting people? That depends on what you mean by "unsuspecting people." The people we confront on camera know damn well why we are there and, in many cases, have been trying to duck us for months. What they usually don't know is how much we know about them.

Okay, but what about the right to privacy? Until someone has been indicted of something, what right do you have to put him in the spotlight? Chances are, whoever he is, he did something or other to put himself in the spotlight.

One subject of a *60 Minutes* piece didn't mind being put in the spotlight. After Mike Wallace's story about "ghost surgery"—the story of surgeons who charge big bucks, then allow interns or residents to perform the actual operation on an anesthetized patient while they are, many times, on a golf course or a tennis court—Mike ran into one of the ghost surgeons cited in the story. Mike tried to duck him but he was trapped. What do you say to a guy you embarrassed in front of the entire country? Well, Mike didn't have to say a thing. The doctor spotted him, stuck out his hand and said, "Mike, I can't thank you enough. I've gotten seventeen new patients since I was on *60 Minutes*." Go figure.

We at *60 Minutes* also are in the business of making reasonable assumptions, as we did in the case of Dr. Carl Galloway. The Galloway story caused something of a ruckus—not least of all because it wound up with Rather on a witness stand testifying that we had done nothing improper in reporting about accident mills that "manufactured" auto accidents and clinics that fabricated medical reports as part of the scam. Dr. Galloway was related by marriage to a man who owned one of the clinics, and it was his name that had appeared on a fictitious medical report. Galloway claimed that although his name appeared, the signature wasn't his. We had made the assumption that if a doctor is the only doctor working at a clinic and his name is displayed on the wall, then he is indeed the doctor who signs the clinic's reports. As Dan put it: "If it looks like a duck, walks like a duck, and quacks like a duck, it's a duck."

Only in this case it wasn't, and Dr. Galloway claimed his reputation had been damaged by his association with that phony clinic. But a jury refused to award him a penny and acquitted us of any wrongdoing. Shortly after the verdict, a reporter rang my doorbell and asked if he could talk to me about the Galloway case. Sure, I said, come on in. The conversation then went something like this:

REPORTER: "You just made the assumption that it was, indeed, Dr. Galloway whose signature was on that fraudulent accident form."

HEWITT: "It was a pretty good assumption. He was the only doctor at the clinic and his name was on the door, so it never dawned on me that the signature Carl Galloway had been signed by someone else."

REPORTER: "But you just made the assumption that he himself had actually signed it."

HEWITT: "Yes. We all make assumptions. And this was one we had very little reason to doubt. All of us go through life making assumptions. For instance, I make the assumption that you're going to publish this interview."

REPORTER: "Of course I am. Why not?"

HEWITT: "Well, for openers, how do you know it's me?"

REPORTER: "What do you mean, how do I know it's you? I knocked on the door and said, 'Mr. Hewitt?' and you said 'yes.' "

HEWITT: "See? You made the assumption that I'm Mr. Hewitt. Maybe I'm not. Maybe I'm just some guy who said he was Mr. Hewitt."

By far the most important thing that happened to me during this period—even more important than Harry Reasoner's return to *60 Minutes* from ABC—was that I got married to Marilyn Berger in 1979. My second marriage, to Frankie Childers, had gone the way of my first a few years earlier, but this time I was the one left and not the one leaving. After twelve years of what was hardly marital bliss, Frankie decided that she would rather run Washington, D.C.'s Ford's Theater than be married to me, and just up and left. It was hard to start over yet again in my fifties, but meeting Marilyn made everything a lot easier.

It was all Mike Wallace's doing. He had run into Marilyn in 1977 at some party in New York and said I ought to get together with her.

"Who the hell is Marilyn Berger?" I asked him.

Shows how much I know. Marilyn had been the diplomatic correspondent for *The Washington Post* when Henry Kissinger was flying high and she was flying with him on his shuttle all over the Middle East. Marilyn had since moved into television. "She's NBC's White House correspondent," Mike said.

"Oh, shit," I said, "that's all I need in my life, a journalist." As it turned out, this particular one was irresistible, and I fell in love with her. We lived together the better part of two years (she remembers it as three) before getting married in a storybook wedding by the captain of *La Belle Simone*, the storybook yacht of Simone and Bill Levitt, of Levittown fame.

Not long after the wedding, Marilyn and I were strolling along one Saturday morning on the main street of Southampton, one of the famous Hamptons on Long Island that New Yorkers use for summer weekends along the Atlantic Ocean. We were window-shopping and minding our own business, when we came face-to-face with another man and woman strolling along, window shopping and minding their own business. Damned if the man wasn't William S. Paley and the woman, Happy Rockefeller, the recently widowed wife of Nelson A. Rockefeller, four-time governor of New York and one-time vice president of the United States.

I wasn't sure what to say to him. I was like a parish priest and he was the pope. Even though I had worked at CBS for thirty-one years, I wasn't sure Paley knew who I was.

I said good morning, a bit hesitatingly, and added, "My name is Don Hewitt and I work for you. At least, I work for CBS, and this is my wife, Marilyn."

"Oh," he said, "Do you have a house out here?"

*All of twenty years old and a war correspondent covering the
U.S. merchant marine in the waters of the North Sea in 1943.*

In the early 1950s, before anybody had ever heard of videotape, Douglas Edwards and I are about to look at a film that was planned for that evening's newscast.

With Edward R. Murrow in the control room of Studio 41, above Grand Central Terminal in New York City, getting ready to go on the air with another edition of his and Fred Friendly's famous broadcast, See It Now.

Walter Cronkite and me with our boss, Sig Mickelson, going over last-minute details before they rapped the gavel at the 1956 Democratic National Convention in Chicago.

How far would I go to get a story? When Nikita Khrushchev visited a farm in Iowa in 1959, I managed to get myself sworn in as a deputy sheriff to go places that were off-limits to journalists. On the right is a guy who seems most amused by it, a young Charles Kuralt.

In a hangar at Chicago's Midway Airport in September 1960, briefing Senator John F. Kennedy and his communications adviser, Leonard Reinsch, on what the rules would be at the first televised presidential debate.

On the set of the presidential debate, giving Vice President Richard Nixon a last-minute briefing on what was expected of him.

At the end of the debate, both candidates agreed to pose with me for posterity, in a picture that always struck me as looking like three mannequins in a clothing-store window.

With former president Dwight Eisenhower at his home in Palm Desert, California, just before he and Walter Cronkite, in the background, sat down for one of their famous one-on-one conversations.

Showing Jack Kennedy how he looked on a television monitor before Fred Friendly, kneeling by his side, and I began taping a "Conversation with the President" in 1961.

I wish I could remember what the joke was that got LBJ, me, and two CBS colleagues to break into gales of laughter. We were at the White House in 1964 to tape a "Conversation with the President" that ran not only on CBS but on NBC and ABC as well.

Going over a script with Walter Cronkite in the early 1960s, during the time I was the executive producer of the CBS Evening News.

Frank Sinatra and me with Sinatra's bodyguard, Ed Pucci, backstage at a benefit performance in St. Louis in 1965, during the time we were taping the hour-long CBS broadcast on him called "Sinatra."

Waiting for General William Westmoreland to arrive during the time I was in Vietnam producing a CBS documentary on him.

Mike Wallace and Harry Reasoner in the first publicity photo for
60 Minutes *in 1968.*

At the blackboard we still use today at 60 Minutes to list the stories that are in the works. The only change is that Dan Rather has moved on to another job.

My wife, Marilyn Berger, and me at a state dinner at the White House, with Ronald and Nancy Reagan.

With William S. Paley, the founder of CBS, at a dinner in 1987, not long after we had become close friends.

With Laurence Tisch during the time he was chairman of CBS. Despite the tensions that existed between us, we could still manage a smile — or at least he could.

With three television legends—Barbara Walters, Roone Arledge, and Joan Ganz Cooney—the night in 1990 when the four of us were inducted into the Television Academy's Hall of Fame.

No, I wasn't about to slug them; I was commiserating with Bill and Hillary Clinton after a light fell down and almost hit them during the taping of their famous "Gennifer Flowers" interview at the Ritz-Carlton Hotel in Boston in 1992—before practically anyone had ever heard of either of them.

On Boris Yeltsin's tennis court at his dacha outside of Moscow, shaking hands and in effect making up after he accused me of doctoring a video-tape to make him look inebriated.

The current team at 60 Minutes: *(standing, left to right) Steve Kroft, Ed Bradley, Morley Safer, and me; (seated, left to right) Andy Rooney, Lesley Stahl, and Mike Wallace.*

"We do," I said. "We just moved in."

"You got a phone?" Paley asked.

"Yes," Marilyn chimed in, "but we don't give out the number."

Leave it to Bill Paley to know when he's being flirted with and to know how to flirt back. Breaking into that infectious grin of his, he came right back at her and said, "Bet you'd give it to me."

"Bet you're right," Marilyn said.

From that moment on, they adored each other.

I'm not given to hero worship, but I make an exception for Bill Paley. He was what I wanted to be more than anything else in the world, what is known as a gentleman of the old school—something I fear I am not suited by temperament to be. That Bill Paley and I became close friends meant more to me than just about anything else that happened to me in more than half a century at CBS.

His affection for Marilyn made me *kvell*. That's Yiddish for feeling thrilled, not a term he would have used, and not one I use very often. But in this case, I can't think of anything more appropriate.

Back behind Paley's house in Southampton, there was a bench supported by two iron swans that overlooked a little lake. That's where he and Marilyn used to sit and reminisce about their mothers. One Christmas, not too long after Bill Paley died, a truck showed up in our driveway in Bridgehampton, and in the back was the bench, with a note from Bill's daughter, Kate, that said simply: "Daddy would have wanted Marilyn to have this. Love, Kate."

Being a friend of Bill Paley's was rewarding in all the ways you would imagine being a friend of Bill Paley's would be rewarding. But being a student of Bill Paley was the real payoff. To this day, I still try to get into his head, fascinated by how he and his sidekick, the good doctor Frank Stanton, would have dealt with the strange twists and turns broadcasting has taken from what they envisioned broadcasting should be.

In the winter of 1980–81, the question on everyone's lips at CBS News was, "Who is going to replace Walter Cronkite?" Uncle Walter, America's favorite newscaster and my comrade in arms from the political conventions of the '50s to the space race of the '60s, had announced his retirement, and all of CBS, it seemed, was abuzz with whether Dan Rather or Roger Mudd would be the next anchorman of the *CBS Evening News*.

Ed Bradley, who everybody at CBS knew was destined for big things, eyed the deal that Roger Mudd got as a consolation prize when Rather got the nod to replace Cronkite—as much time off as he wanted *with pay* to think about his future. Bradley said, "If I don't get the nod to replace Rather on *60 Minutes*, can I get the same great deal Mudd got?" He got an even better one: He became Rather's replacement.

The day I got the news that CBS had agreed with me that Bradley should replace Rather, I was scheduled to address the company's Black Employees' Association. And among the things I told them was that Bradley would be the latest addition to *60 Minutes*. The second I said it, the audience broke into applause. Wait a minute, I said, you don't understand. I would have hired Bradley if he were white. In fact, years later I would introduce Bradley when he received the Paul White Award (for distinguished service to broadcast journalism) at the convention of the Radio and Television News Directors Association. I figured there was only one way to introduce him. I said, "I hired Ed Bradley because he's a member of a minority. He's a great reporter and a great gentleman, and if that's not a minority, I've never heard of one."

Not long after Ed signed on, my secretary, Beverly Morgan, came into my office and said, "You're not going to believe this." What she had in her hand was a memo from Ed to the personnel office at CBS informing them that he was changing his name to "Shaheeb Sha Hab."

All I could think was: "I'm Mike Wallace. I'm Morley Safer. I'm

Harry Reasoner. I'm Shaheeb Sha Hab. Those stories and Andy Rooney tonight on *60 Minutes*."

"Is he kidding?" I asked Beverly.

"I don't think so," she said. "The memo has already gone to personnel."

What I could do about it I didn't have the slightest idea. How can you tell a guy he can't change his name to anything he wants it to be? But on the off chance that it wasn't true (and God, I hoped it wasn't), I went to Bradley's office, figuring that maybe I could smoke him out.

I respect what you're doing, I told him, and suggested that one of us should call Kay Gardella at the *Daily News* and let her break the story.

"Good idea," Ed said. "Do you want to call her or do you want me to?"

"Why don't I do it?"

"Fine and dandy," he said. "You do it."

My God, I thought, he isn't bluffing. I picked up the phone and started dialing.

"Hello," I said when Kay answered, "I've got a good item for you."

"Tell me about it," she said.

That's when Bradley cracked. "Hang up," he said. "Tell her you'll call her back." And he burst out laughing. Shaheeb Sha Hab indeed.

If Bradley had really wanted to change his name, I would have had no choice but to live with it. What I can't live with is the idea that we are giving a politician or world figure the *60 Minutes* stamp of approval just because we interview him. For example, Mike Wallace's interview with the Ayatollah Khomeini during the hostage crisis hardly conferred our blessing on Iran's spiritual leader. But that didn't stop some viewers and *The New York Times*, which had requested but was refused a Khomeini interview, from saying the next day that our broadcast only served Iran's propaganda aims. And mind you, this was the same *New York Times* that day after day published pictures of Iranian students waving signs castigating the United States. But what the hell, it just proves the *New York Times* has its share of muttonheads just like everyone else.

But, dammit, they're good. The reason it's so much fun to beat up on the *Times* is because it's so hard to do. Morley Safer put it best when I once asked him which he'd consider the bigger hardship, a television strike or a newspaper strike. His answer said it all: "First you have to tell me what city I'm living in."

While the *New York Times* has no comics, no horoscope, no advice to the lovelorn to lighten the load, it does have, God bless 'em, a daily corrections column with bits of minutiae that frequently become "collectors' items," like the one on December 12, 2001, that informed me that a Russian novelist named Viktor Zastafayev was not, as they had told me nine days before, "working on" a novel at the time of his death but had finished it six years before he died. Then I was told that two more of his books "were published in the 1990's, not in the mid 70's," as they had said they were, and, in case anyone cared, that it was the government of "Mikhail S. Gorbachev, not Leonid I. Brezhnev," which was in power when he wrote yet another of his books. End of correction? No, not yet, not until the *Times* told me, "References to the death of the author's parents were also incorrect. His mother died in 1931, his father in 1979. They did not die of hunger in the early Soviet years."

If that doesn't do it, how about this, which honest-to-God ran in the *New York Times* on June 6, 1988:

A report in the Metropolitan Diary column on May 25 about a nun who bought a package of cookies at an airport was published in error. The incident—in which the nun thought a man was helping himself to her cookies when in fact she was helping herself to his—did not occur recently at Kennedy International Airport. It is current myth and has been recounted by a folklorist, Jan Harold Brunvand, in a variety of renditions in two books, *The Choking Doberman* and *The Mexican Pet.*

Enough for now about All the News That's Fit to ... Correct.

We also took heat when we interviewed South African Prime Minister P. W. Botha during the bad old days of apartheid. One viewer, who equated the broadcast with support for the terrible policies of the white government, said, "Surely, you wouldn't have interviewed Adolf Hitler in the midst of the Holocaust." To which I replied: "Boy are you wrong." Hitler was as despicable a human being as ever walked the earth, but he was also as big a newsmaker as ever walked the earth. And I don't know a newsman on earth who would have passed up an opportunity to have interviewed him.

It's easier when you interview celebrities. In late 1982, Ed Bradley interviewed one of my all-time favorites. At the time, he was finishing up a dangerous assignment in Israel, and after a rough day on the West Bank, he found a message in his hotel room to call Jeanne Solomon, a *60 Minutes* producer, who worked with him out of London.

"Ed," she said when Bradley reached her, "how do you feel about stopping in London on your way home?"

"Do I have to?" Ed asked. He was beat and just wanted to finish up in Israel and get back to New York. "What do you want me for?"

"Laurence Olivier," Jeanne said.

Ed and Jeanne has been trying to land an Olivier interview for more than two years. Eventually, his agents even stopped returning their phone calls. But Britain's greatest actor had just completed his autobiography and the requirements of publicity-seeking publishers sometimes trump a celebrity's desire for privacy. "Sir Larry" had agreed to sit for an interview.

Bradley fretted that he wouldn't have time to prepare, but Jeanne had thought of everything. She had amassed stacks of briefing material and arranged for a VCR to be in Ed's hotel room so he could watch some of Olivier's best performances.

The interview was set for Friday. Ed arrived in London on Wednesday and for forty-eight hours, interrupted only by the room-service waiter, he boned up on Olivier. On Friday morning Jeanne picked him up and they went to Claridge's, where Jeanne had taken a suite to film the interview. Norman Langley, her husband and as good a cameraman as any in the world, was waiting, camera and lights at the ready. It got later and later. Just as Ed and Jeanne began to think Olivier had chickened out, the door opened and in tottered a frail, elderly gentleman wearing a red-and-blue sports jacket. He looked around the room bewildered, as if he had never seen a film camera before.

Oh, Jesus, Jeanne thought. It's not going to work. She knew he had recently been ill—but could this really be the great Laurence Olivier? Jeanne knew he had just finished a television film of *King Lear*. Could Lear have finished him off? Olivier sat down and Ed began the interview—very gently. He had only gotten as far as Olivier's eighteenth birthday and some obscure story about a long-lost brother when Olivier leaned forward and said to Ed in cowboy lingo, "I'm getting tired, pardner."

Ed assured him that we were almost through. The fact is that we hadn't even begun. He agreed to stay a while longer. Gradually, prodded by Ed's questions, the frail old man who had tottered into the room became Laurence Olivier, the actor. The interview went on for another hour and a half, and Olivier and Bradley jousted with each other. When Jeanne finally said "cut," neither had fallen off his horse, and 60 *Minutes* had wrapped up one of its more memorable interviews, punctuated by such Laurence Olivier lines as his take on acting:

It's a game of make-believe. I mean, originally. It's just like a nursery game of make-believe. In a way, the essence of it is that. I'm going to pretend I'm a fellow called Hamlet. I'm going to pretend I'm a fellow called King Lear. Lear is—I'm sorry, it's regrettably easy for me because now in my crusty old age I'm almost like him. I haven't the majesty, of course, but I—I have every other characteristic of Lear: unreasonable, impossible, stupid, stubborn. And I'm sorry, that's me. In Hamlet's time, I was much more like Hamlet. I had all those qualities, all the weaknesses particularly. And I think if you can recognize that, I think that's a little secret for the actor. Use your weaknesses. Aspire to the strengths.

Olivier had had such a good time with 60 *Minutes* that he and Ed carried on their conversation as they left the suite, went down in the elevator with their cameraman in tow, and walked through the lobby of Claridge's. It ended only when the hotel manager said to Jeanne, "Madam, please remember this is a hotel, not a film set." Hotels are always nervous about film cameras. Who knows when someone might inadvertently get a shot of a gentleman checking in with a lady not his wife?

Ed and Jeanne saw Olivier off in the Rolls-Royce we had hired to bring him to and from the interview, and went back upstairs to thank the crew for its patience, but not before telling the driver to please come back for them. This is one time they thought they deserved to arrive at the CBS London office in style. The Rolls came back, but as they were getting in, the car unaccountably shot forward and ricocheted off a parked Mercedes into the path of an oncoming Ford. No damage done, except to the driver's frazzled nerves. "Gor, blimey," he said, "it's never done that before."

Had it done that before—only a half hour before—60 Minutes might have been Olivier's last performance.

It was always the offbeat things like Olivier's near-accident that stick with me, like the time Mike Wallace and I went to see Yasir Arafat at his headquarters in Tunis. While Mike was having dinner with Arafat upstairs, Barry Lando, the producer of that story, the crew, and I had dinner down in the basement along with a dozen or so of Arafat's bodyguards who sat around playing cards or watching television with their Uzis on their laps. They seemed like nice enough guys, and I didn't pay them much mind until Yasir himself came downstairs with a stunning young brunette in tow and told me she was the daughter of one of his fallen comrades and was an aspiring journalist. He said he hoped I could help her get into the Columbia Journalism School and asked me to talk to her about it. That didn't seem like an unpleasant task, so I did. And as she was telling me about her desire to be a journalist, I noticed out of the corner of my eye one of the bodyguards beginning to pat his Uzi and glare at me.

"Does he resent all Americans," I asked her, "or just me?"

"Don't pay any attention to him," she said. "He's my boyfriend and sometimes when he gets jealous he acts crazy."

"Uh-oh," I thought. This is either for real or Wallace (who was still upstairs in the dining room) was working one of his famous practical jokes. If it's for real, as valuable as it would have been to do a favor for the chairman of the PLO, I didn't think it was worth getting shot by a crazed jealous lover in Yasir Arafat's basement.

When Diane Sawyer became available, she was irresistible. She had been CBS's State Department correspondent and had been on the *CBS Morning News*. That she was great looking everybody knew. That she was a great reporter we all surmised but weren't sure of it until she proved it on *60 Minutes*.

One argument I didn't accept was the one that said it was time to put a woman on *60 Minutes*. Baloney. It was time to put Diane Sawyer on *60 Minutes*—as far as I was concerned, she could have been named Tom Sawyer. Gender didn't have a damn thing to do with it, any more than Ed Bradley's hiring had to do with race. My wife, Marilyn, said it best. When she was NBC's White House correspondent, someone said to her: "You're a woman on television. Don't you think there ought to be more women on television?"

"You're wrong," Marilyn said. "I'm not a woman on television. I'm a woman when I'm *not* on television. When I'm on television, I'm a reporter."

Actually, Sawyer and I had discussed her career and *60 Minutes* once before. Here's how she remembers that earlier conversation:

In the spring of 1970, fresh from a local television station in Louisville, I came to New York and asked the executive producer of *60 Minutes* if I could join the broadcast. After all, I reasoned, I had covered everything from local fires to local fires. I had proven myself in the intellectual crucible of reading the local weather. I had sprayed my hair and memorized the record high and low temperatures in fifty states. *I was ready*. It would take nerve, as I saw it, for Hewitt to tell me no.

He found the nerve.

Fourteen years later, Diane found out about her imminent posting to 60 Minutes from an assistant, who had heard me mention it at
a CBS seminar. But it still wasn't official by summer when we all
packed up and shipped out to San Francisco for the 1984 Democratic Convention. She and I found ourselves at an elegant dinner party
given for Chuck Manatt, then-chairman of the Democratic
National Committee, at the home of Gordon and Ann Getty. All the
talk, it turned out, was about Manatt himself: Rumor had it that
Walter Mondale, the party's presidential nominee, in a tough election against Ronald Reagan, had decided to fire our host.

At one point, between courses, I got up and walked over to
Diane's table, tugged on her satin sleeve and whispered, "Hey, we've
got a hell of a story here." She made her excuses, and we headed for
Manatt's table. We asked him to step outside.

After we peppered him with questions, Manatt not only confirmed the story but also tossed in an acid quote or two.

With that, I commandeered a phone in the Getty library and
called in the story to an overnight radio crew in New York, who
were stunned that the executive producer of 60 Minutes and his
newest star correspondent were acting like a couple of rookie wire-
service reporters. Suddenly, Diane Sawyer was broadcasting live on
CBS Radio—to anyone listening at one-thirty in the morning, eastern time.

Diane was working so hard to impress me that she was the one for
60 Minutes that she didn't notice I was working just as hard to
impress her that 60 Minutes was the one for her.

As everyone knows, Diane eventually left CBS for ABC, and
came back only once, the day she interviewed me for a profile she
was doing of Lesley Stahl. During the course of that interview she
asked me the obligatory male-chauvinist-pig question: "You talked to
Lesley about her hair. Would you have done that with a man?" As so

often happens, the answer didn't come to me until after she left, but I couldn't resist phoning her and saying, "Diane, you asked me if I would be as concerned with a man's hair as I was with a woman's. The answer is, I would be, if the man were Sam Donaldson." I've always wondered if she would have had the guts to use that line if I had thought of it while the cameras were rolling.

CHAPTER NINE

Corporate Politics and Holy Wars

The early and mid-1980s were not a happy time. Don't get me wrong: *60 Minutes* was going great, and we were well into our run as the most successful program in television history. But CBS itself was a mess. Bill Paley was one of the great benevolent despots and businessmen, but he had his share of blind spots and he made some mistakes. As he hung on to the job of chairman past the time he should have given it up and let someone else fill it, mistakes were beginning to accumulate to the detriment of the network he founded.

One of the things that got out of hand was who his successor would be. Frank Stanton, the company's longtime CEO, was Paley's logical successor. Stanton had been with CBS since the 1930s and had played a comparable role to Paley's in the company's triumphs over the years. In fact, Paley depended on him to run CBS day-to-day but he could never bring himself to reward him with the chairmanship of the company. In the end, Stanton retired at age sixty-five in March 1973 after nearly four decades at the company, most of them as president. Was Paley afraid that Stanton would replace him as the grand old man of CBS? That's certainly not out of the realm of possibility.

The old-timers at CBS News—and many "young-timers," too—were stung by Paley's rejection of Stanton and by the fact that he was followed by a succession of short-time CEOs. When, in 1980, Paley hired Tom Wyman as his CEO, Wyman had had no background in television, coming to CBS from the Pillsbury Company, where he'd been vice chairman, and the Nestle Company and Polaroid Corporation before that. The absence of television experience wouldn't have been disqualifying by itself. But in my view, and as it turned out, the view of many others, he also wasn't much of a broadcast-company CEO. His entire focus seemed to be on CBS's stock price, and to help bolster it, he sold off the company's book and record divisions. Before he got through with us (or we got through with him), the Tiffany Network was no longer what it had once been. But then again, tell me something that is.

During the time Wyman was CEO, Van Gordon Sauter was president of CBS News, although he eventually moved over to CBS corporate. One of Sauter's favorite lines to us was, "You're not in news, you're in television." I never thought it was a choice; I thought you could be in both, which is exactly what 60 Minutes is. At any rate, Sauter and Ed Joyce, who replaced Van as CBS News president in 1983, thought I wielded too much power, and they worried about how close I was to Paley. Joyce also thought I was out to get him, which was untrue. In fact, I always thought Ed should have had Sauter's job.

One night in early October 1985, I was sitting in my office watching Dan Rather broadcast from the site of an earthquake in Mexico, from a hotel room, via a satellite dish stuck in his window. The dish sent a signal to a satellite, the satellite sent it to New York and, boom, just like that, Dan was on the air. That's when it hit me: With a satellite dish, you're a television network. Put one on the Potamkin Cadillac garage across from my office, and with no trouble at all, Potamkin would be a network.

That was the easy part. What would you put on your network? What if my colleagues at CBS could form a cooperative of the top names in television news and go into business for ourselves? It was, after all, a time when CBS was selling its record division, its magazine division, and other less-than-wildly profitable parts of the company. Maybe they might consider "unloading" the less-than-wildly profitable CBS News—and if they would, why not to us?

This could be a way, I thought, for my colleagues and me to protect ourselves against the possibility that a new owner would play even faster and looser with one of America's gems than the current management of CBS was playing. A news division that was once the envy of the world was being "cut down to size," subjected to massive cutbacks, and being pushed around and getting the "who do you guys think you are? treatment from Ed Joyce and Van Gordon Sauter, who I felt was more interested in moving up the corporate ladder than in keeping the news division at the top of the ladder.

I stewed about it all evening, got a few hours' sleep, then started working the phones about 7 A.M. the next morning. Among others, I called Mike Wallace, Morley Safer, Dan Rather, Bill Moyers, and Diane Sawyer—waking up several of them—to explain my idea and ask whether I could count them in. Everyone said yes.

I was pumped up later that morning as I headed for Black Rock, the CBS corporate headquarters at Fifty-second Street and Sixth Avenue. First stop: Gene Jankowski's office. Jankowski was president of the CBS Broadcast Group, essentially the top network executive, but he wasn't around.

I did manage to locate Jim Rosenfield, Jankowski's top assistant, and explained to him what I wanted to discuss with Gene. Before the day was out, I had a lunch date with Jankowski for the following Tuesday.

Over lunch, bursting with enthusiasm, I laid out for Jankowski what I had in mind. "You're crazy," he said. "Nobody's going to sell you CBS News."

"Why not?"

"Because it's a valuable part of the company, and we're not about to give it up," Gene said. "Forget it. No one is going to sell you CBS News."

"Sell us CBS News? We *are* CBS News," I said, more brazenly than I should have, because Jankowski was a friend, and we had apparently embarrassed him with both Wyman and Paley.

A day later, I had lunch with Lew Wasserman, chairman of MCA, a friend of many years, and gave him my pitch about buying CBS News. This prompted an initial one-word reaction: "Dumb," followed by "You're fooling yourself. No one's going to sell you CBS News."

Out on the sidewalk after lunch, he reiterated how crazy the whole idea was, then paused and said, "If they say yes, call me." That was not the worst thing he could have said. After all, Lew Wasserman and MCA had the money we would have needed to pull off a deal like that.

A few days later, I found myself in the CBS Paris bureau to do some final editing on a 60 *Minutes* story and who should walk in but Van Gordon Sauter. By now, the story of how I and a handful of other malcontents wanted to hijack the news division had traveled through every corridor and office of CBS and had found its way into various press accounts. The story was moving almost as fast as the satellite feed that had inspired my idea in the first place.

Van was not happy, and he made clear what he thought of me. "You've embarrassed everyone, including me and Ed Joyce," he said. "You're nothing but a destructive asshole." It was plain I was on his shit list, but then again, I can't remember a time when I wasn't.

One of the stories going around was that the dust storm I had kicked up was really a ploy to force a renegotiation of my contract. Another was that it was a cover to get Sauter and Joyce fired; that was later reduced to my targeting Joyce alone. All of it was nonsense, and I said so in a memo to Jankowski shortly after I returned to New York from Paris. Copies went to Joyce, Sauter, and Rosenfield, as well as the colleagues I had originally contacted—Wallace, Moyers, Safer, Sawyer, and Rather. "What started out as an effort to let you know that six of us who helped build CBS News were interested in buying it if it ever came on the market has degenerated into what is being perceived as a 'get Ed Joyce movement.' I, for one, want to go on the record as disassociating myself from that."

I went on to say that I intended to confine myself to what CBS paid me to do—be the executive producer of *60 Minutes*—and would consider the rest of CBS News "none of my business." I said it and I meant it.

The entire episode was a one-week wonder. As I look back on it, that they said "no" may be the best thing that ever happened to me. Instead of working on the most successful news broadcast in the history of broadcasting, and enjoying every minute of it, I would today be saddled with the minutiae that go with being a corporate executive. More prosperous? Maybe, maybe not. Happier? No, no, a thousand times no.

In late summer 1986, I was at the U.S. Open tennis matches near Shea Stadium. CBS had a box, and Tom Wyman was sitting in the first row. Dan Rather, Mike Wallace, and I were right behind him in the second row. *Newsweek* had just done a real job on CBS with a cover story detailing how bad it had become. Making conversation, Wyman turned and asked me whether I'd heard about the piece coming out in *Newsweek*. I had received an advance copy of the story earlier in the day and had it with me.

"Sure," I said, "you want to see it?"

There was this fantastic match on the stadium court, everybody glued to the action, and here were the three of us, peering over Wyman's shoulder as he read the *Newsweek* piece. The cover line was "Civil War at CBS—The Struggle for the Soul of a Legendary Network," and the story detailed the multiplying problems at the company—from a wave of layoffs to Sauter's announcement that the network was scrapping the *CBS Morning News.*

Wyman finished and, without a word, folded the magazine, put it in his pocket, walked over to Bill Paley's box and resigned. At least I thought he did. Whether he did it then or later on, it was not long after that CBS issued an announcement that the CBS board had requested and accepted Wyman's resignation. A day later, Sauter was canned. His replacement, Howard Stringer, was named in October. Howard was, is, and remains to this day a good friend and one who was very helpful in smoothing over the ruffled feathers we had left in the wake of our trying to buy CBS News.

If Paley had a hand in Wyman's sacking, he hadn't acted alone. The Tisch brothers—Laurence and Preston Robert—had acquired nearly 10 percent of CBS stock by August 1985. A few months later, they had increased their stake to 25 percent, and Larry Tisch had himself a seat on the CBS board. What happened next was inevitable, I suppose: Wyman was history and two months later, the board reappointed Paley, then eighty-five, as chairman. The new president and chief executive officer of CBS would be Laurence Tisch.

The thought that Bill Paley selling CBS to Laurence Tisch would make the Paley era go on was among the most naive thoughts I ever had. But it did seem for a moment or two to be a marriage made in heaven. I remember the night I heard about it.

We were all at designer Molly Parnis's apartment—the Cronkites, the Wallaces, the Tisches, "tout New York," as they say. I even got Paley on the phone and told him to come over to the party and help us celebrate the wonderful thing he had done. He declined, but you could tell how delighted he was to see how delighted we were. To us, he had picked the perfect successor, a self-made billionaire who eventually would be memorialized in broadcasting lore as a worthy successor to Bill Paley.

As head of Loews Corporation, which had tobacco, hotel, theater, and many other interests, Larry Tisch had all the money anyone could want. I believed that all a man that rich could possibly crave was a place in the history books. I miscalculated badly. But then, so did Cronkite and Wallace.

The problem was that what we thought Tisch wanted out of life, and what Tisch himself wanted out of life, were at opposite ends of the spectrum. We soon learned that he was mainly interested not in achieving immortality but in maximizing the value of his investment.

Ben Bradlee, the legendary editor of *The Washington Post*, saw it coming. In his memoir, *A Good Life*, he wrote that "the best newspapers in America are those controlled by families to whom newspapering is a sacred trust." That was once true about broadcasting as well, but not since Bill Paley of CBS, David Sarnoff of NBC, and Leonard Goldenson of ABC passed from the scene has any owner— Tisch's Loews Corporation, Jack Welch's General Electric (NBC), Michael Eisner's Disney (ABC), Viacom's Mel Karmazin, and Sumner Redstone (CBS now)—taken that attitude about the news organization it controls.

Why aren't we broadcast journalists hollering about it? Because we want it both ways. We want the companies we work for to put back the wall the pioneers erected to separate news from entertainment, but we are not above climbing over the rubble each week to take an entertainment-size paycheck for broadcasting news.

Since I stayed at CBS taking a large salary from Larry Tisch, it would be hypocritical of me to criticize him for his cost cutting, which resulted in the elimination of several key jobs in the news division. Those of us who signed and re-signed during the Tisch era are in no position to join the chorus. Be that as it may, what really disturbed me, and I told it to him, was that he was, in addition to our chairman, our publisher. And with that position came an obligation to put one's personal political views aside for the sake of fair and unbiased coverage. Tisch never understood this concept, particularly when it came to the Middle East. He was an ardent supporter of Israel and had close ties to its political leaders. Tom Wyman had reportedly warned about this on his way out the door, saying "Okay, now try to cover Israel."

I would find out very quickly that as long as Tisch was weighted down with ideological baggage about Israel, we were in danger of shortchanging the public. But we never caved in.

Case in point: the Temple Mount massacre. Tisch's anger at Mike Wallace and me for reporting it truthfully and objectively was the low point of my more than fifty years at CBS. Here's the background: On October 8, 1990, a tragic incident occurred in Jerusalem that would paralyze relations between Palestinian Arabs and Israeli Jews. The incident, which took place in the third year of the so-called *intifada*, or uprising, of Palestinians against Israel's presence in East Jerusalem and its occupation of the West Bank, was called the Battle of the Temple Mount. It came at a particularly difficult time in a particularly dangerous neighborhood, since Iraq's Saddam Hussein had invaded Kuwait just two months earlier in what would become the precursor to the Persian Gulf War.

The Temple Mount, called *Haram al-Sharif* by the Arabs, is an elevated area of thirty-five acres that is the site of the Dome of the Rock and the Al-Aqsa mosque, two of Islam's holiest sites; one side of the compound is held up by part of the ancient temple called the Western Wall, Judaism's holiest shrine. At this intersection of two great religions, a place dedicated to peace and understanding, Israeli police and Palestinian demonstrators clashed. When it was over, seventeen Palestinians were dead and dozens of others on both sides were injured.

The commission appointed by Israeli Prime Minister Yitzhak

Shamir to investigate the shooting essentially supported the police, concluding that the circumstances justified the use of deadly force by the Israelis. But we were hearing different accounts of what happened, and Mike Wallace and producer Barry Lando were dispatched to investigate the Temple Mount killings. Their resulting story led our broadcast on December 2, 1990, less than two months after the event that inspired it.

Did the police fire more bullets at those Palestinian kids than were necessary to restore the peace? That's what we went there to find out. And what we found out—that that excessive force was indeed used—did not sit well with the Jewish community in America.

The written and verbal bazookas fired at *60 Minutes*, Wallace, and me began that Sunday night and continued for months. Mike and I were called Palestinian sympathizers and self-hating Jews. We were said to have played fast and loose with the truth by putting an anti-Israeli spin on the story and ignoring the white-hot tension that existed between Arabs and Jews as a result of the *intifada*, not to mention Saddam Hussein's designs on the entire Persian Gulf that one month later would produce a war in which Iraqi Scud missiles would be fired at Israel.

The Jewish-American organizations that objected to the way we told that story found a soulmate in Laurence Tisch. Among those organizations was the Anti-Defamation League, which criticized us for what they characterized as less-than-objective reporting.

It would have been difficult for Tisch to take punitive action against a program as popular and critically acclaimed as *60 Minutes* or to openly repudiate our story, and he didn't. Instead, he pretended we didn't exist. Shortly after the piece aired, there was a party at River House, a very expensive and exclusive cooperative apartment building on the East Side of Manhattan, to honor Brad Bradshaw, the new chairman of NBC. I walked in and spotted Larry.

"Hi, boss," I said.

"Don't you 'hi boss' me," was what I got in return. He then spun on his heels and walked away.

The contrast with Bill Paley was stunning. Paley, for example, had been openly supportive of Dwight Eisenhower in the 1950s, but nobody ever heard a word from him about CBS's political or presidential-campaign coverage, which had a decidedly pro-Stevenson tinge about it. Or, for that matter, about any other news coverage.

The encounter with Tisch was so disturbing that I couldn't let it pass. Right then and there, I parked Marilyn with a couple of friends, hailed a taxi, and went across town to the CBS Broadcast Center to see David Burke, the president of CBS News at the time. I walked into his office and said, "David, I'd like to resign."

"Why?" Burke asked.

I recounted the incident that had just happened, and said, "If this is what I get from the top guy at CBS because of honest reporting in Israel, then I probably shouldn't be working here."

Burke convinced me to cool it. It would pass. But it didn't. Anytime I walked into a room full of people that included Larry Tisch, he would give me his back to avoid any chance of conversation — behavior that continued even after reports out of Israel that were beginning to surface that we had told the story almost exactly the way it had happened.

As it turned out, an Israeli judge, Ezra Kama, had been taking testimony for months, testimony in which two police officers had testified that they had emptied their assault rifles at Palestinian demonstrators, in violation of Israeli police rules, who they said were attacking them with stones and iron bars. That incident apparently was over in a matter of minutes, but officers testified that shooting continued "all over the Mount," as one put it, and that many of the deaths probably occurred well after the initial Palestinian charge and far from the Western Wall.

After learning of the Israeli inquiry, I called Abraham H. Foxman, national director of the Anti-Defamation League of B'nai Brith, and followed up with a letter. Here's what I wrote:

Dear Abe:

The vilification Mike and I suffered at the hands of our fellow Jews was touched off by the reaction of Jewish leaders to what *60 Minutes* said about the "Temple Mount Incident."

Now that a Jerusalem judge has said ostensibly the same thing, is it unreasonable to think that some of those Jewish leaders will so inform their congregations and that maybe, just maybe, some of those who wrote such vile, nasty letters might want to take this opportunity to say they were wrong?

Sincerely,

Don Hewitt

Foxman responded, at somewhat greater length, six days later. Here is all of it, lest someone accuse me of taking something out of context:

Dear Don:

This responds to your recent telephone call and letter asking Jewish leaders who criticized your segment on the Temple Mount to say that they were wrong in light of new evidence in Jerusalem.

At the outset, one must bear in mind that the investigation underway by Judge Kama is not yet completed. Media reports in *The Washington Post* and *Los Angeles Times* were based on selected testimony from several police officers and do not represent either complete transcripts nor the final findings of the Jerusalem court. We are eager, as you are, to hear Judge Kama's final ruling.

Nevertheless, should the Jerusalem court contradict the findings of the Zamir Commission and find, for example, that Israeli police indeed used excessive live fire, we do not believe that we erred in our original critique and still stand by our findings that your segment "demonstrated clearly a bias and prejudicial attitude towards the incident."

If you reread our analysis, it will be evident that we did not blanketly accept the official Israeli version of events, nor did we state that Israeli police were not guilty of excessive use of live fire. In fact, we specifically noted that there were issues "open to further discussion and investigation" and that "*Sixty Minutes* and Mr. Wallace have every right to disagree with the findings of the inquiry."

No matter what Judge Kama finds, your segment still failed to give historical and political context for the incident and for the general environment in Jerusalem; accepted unambiguously Palestinian claims and allegations; used unobjective interviewing methods marked by leading questions and essentially telling subjects what to say and portrayed a deliberate Israeli cover-up. Indeed, the Jerusalem court's investigation demonstrates quite clearly the democratic mechanisms of Israeli society.

Finally, our critique of the *Sixty Minutes* segment was not a "vilification" of you and Mike Wallace, as your letter suggests. We reviewed the segment a number of times and were extremely careful in supporting our statements with examples from the broadcast. I hope that you will take the time to reread our assessment and find, as we have, that it remains valid.

Sincerely,

Abraham H. Foxman

Now it was my turn. Two days later, I wrote back to Foxman, a bit more succinctly than he had written to me:

Dear Abe:

I guess it's time to bring this dialogue to a close. It is now quite apparent that there is no way to dissuade you from the idiotic belief that this news organization would be party to "unobjective interviewing methods" and "telling subjects what to say" on any subject.

About what you term the failure "to give historical and political context" for the incident, that is more or less what the National Guard said about news coverage of the Kent State incident...what the U.S. Army said about the news coverage of the My Lai incident...and what the Chinese Anti-Defamation League (if there were one) would say about the news coverage of the Tiananmen Square incident.

If we were the dishonest reporters you say we are, I don't think we would be the most watched and most honored broadcast in the history of television, although "dishonored" would be a more appropriate term when it comes to the ADL.

Could it be that it's you, not us, who has that "prejudicial attitude" you write about?

Sincerely,

Don Hewitt

Abe Foxman is a good man who believes passionately in Israel's right to survival within safe and secure borders. He is also a mensch, as he demonstrated more than three months later, when the Israeli judge had concluded his proceedings and issued a final report, and Abe sent me the following:

Dear Don:

The facts are now in regarding the Temple Mount incident. Judge Kama rejects some of the claims the Israeli officials made and came closer to some of the conclusions reached by *60 Minutes*.

On that basis, while I still have some problems with the methodology *60 Minutes* used, I want to publicly apologize to you, Mike, and the staff of *60 Minutes*.

I hope we can put this long and difficult situation behind us.

Sincerely,

Abraham H. Foxman

cc: Mike Wallace
Eric Ober
Laurence Tisch

The P.S. said: "Feel free to release this however you wish, Abe."

I can't believe Larry Tisch never got his copy—and I can't believe either that Larry never acknowledged that *60 Minutes* had been right all along.

As I write this, in the fall of 2000, the Temple Mount and the matter of who has access to it has taken on an importance even greater than the importance Jews and Muslims attached to it when we covered the story for the first time. I am sometimes asked, in this context, whether the possibility that the state of Israel and the lives of its people could disappear in a new Holocaust awakens in me some of that Jewishness that has never played much of a part in my life. My answer is that of course it does. But while I feel there are some things worth dying for, I don't think that "sacred ground" is one of them. And it was "sacred ground" that caused some of the smartest people on earth to plunk themselves down in one of the most hostile places on earth. Why they came there and why it never worked out for them were summed up by the brilliant Israeli military tactician Moshe Dayan, an Israeli hero if there ever was one, in a piece on *60 Minutes* some thirty years ago:

"Things are happening now not the way that the beginners of the Zionist movement thought they would. They had a very pastoralic picture, a very idealistic picture. They thought that we would come to a country where nobody is here. They didn't realize that many Arabs were here and that everybody will be happy because we will bring money and property and development and all the Jews will be nice people and they will become farmers.... Well, it didn't work out that way. It didn't work out that way."

To those who think *60 Minutes* has been less than evenhanded in reporting from Israel, let me share a letter with you that I've had framed and sits on a bookshelf in my office:

Dear Mr. Hewitt:

Word has reached me from the Big Apple that you are currently celebrating your 70th birthday. Let me congratulate you on this occasion and extend my best wishes to you for many more years of good health and continued work at *60 Minutes*.

As you know, your program is critically acclaimed throughout the world and is held in high esteem by many of us in Israel.

I would also like to take this opportunity to express my personal gratitude to you for dedicating one of your *60 Minutes* segments to the tragic story of our Israeli Air Force navigator MIA Ron Arad. Both as a Jew and as a human being I was touched by your coverage of his plight and I am deeply grateful to you and *60 Minutes* for all your efforts.

As you enter your 25th year at *60 Minutes*, I wish you the best of luck and continued success in the future.

Sincerely,

Yitzhak Rabin
Prime Minister of Israel

Now that Larry Tisch no longer has anything to do with CBS, having sold the company to Westinghouse, when I see him now, which I frequently do on social occasions, everything is all peaches and cream, claps on the back and squeezed shoulders. His comments to me about *60 Minutes* are uniformly complimentary. We rarely talk about internal politics at CBS and never discuss the incident at the Temple Mount or our coverage of it.

CHAPTER TEN

Razzle Dazzle

By the time the 1990s came along, the cast of 60 Minutes had undergone a lot of changes, even if the essential character and tone of the broadcast remained constant. Mike Wallace, Morley Safer, and Ed Bradley were still at the top of their game, but some old friends had gone — with new talent rising to fill their spots.

Harry Reasoner retired shortly after Diane Sawyer had joined the staff. While I like Diane very much, and we got along famously, being a member of a repertory company was not her cup of tea. She had "star" written all over her, and Roone Arledge knew it when he wooed her and won her and installed her to be the eventual successor to Barbara Walters at ABC News (though both she and Barbara Walters would deny that intention).

After Diane flew the coop, David Burke, who was president of CBS News, with my concurrence, tapped Steve Kroft and Meredith Vieira to replace her. Steve and Meredith had been on a magazine show called West 57th, which had recently folded. And if you think they landed on their feet at 60 Minutes, think of what a great landing the producer of that failed show made; his name is Andy Lack, and today he's the president of NBC. At the time, Meredith had had a baby, was about to have another, and was in no position to give the job the attention it required. I have been criticized on many occasions for firing her. The truth is, I neither hired her nor fired her. David Burke did both — the latter, when I told him she was reluctant to turn out her share of stories and that the rest of the team was too exhausted to take up the slack. That's when he said that we had no alternative but to make a change. The change was Lesley Stahl, who for years had been the moderator of *Face the Nation* and before that, CBS's White House correspondent. She had all the credentials to be what she is today, a coeditor of what is considered to be the best newsmagazine in television. She is as good a reporter as any I've ever worked with.

Steve Kroft, who writes about as well as anybody in the business, and is a reporter who can hold his own with just about anybody in the business, made his reputation the night of the 1992 Super Bowl — about an hour and a half after the game was over. That's when Kroft presided over an abbreviated nine-minute edition of *60 Minutes* that would be remembered long after the game that preceded it.

An obscure governor by the name of Bill Clinton, who had left the state house in Little Rock, Arkansas, hoping to move into the White House in Washington, D.C., found himself at the center of a potentially career-ending scandal while he was one of five Democrats seeking his party's nomination for president. A woman named Gennifer Flowers claimed to have had a twelve-year romantic relationship with Clinton, and she said she had tape recordings of phone conversations to prove it. The story had broken just before the New Hampshire primary and hard on the heels of other revelations about Clinton's past, particularly involving his efforts to avoid the draft during the Vietnam War. Clinton was sinking in the polls and wanted a forum where he could address these scandals before the American people. He decided he needed to go on *60 Minutes,* and there wasn't a better time to do it than on the night of the Super Bowl broadcast.

We had gotten word that Clinton was looking for a forum to explain himself. I was on a flight coming back from California a few days before the big game, and was told during an in-flight phone call to my office that if I called a guy named George Stephanopoulos at a number my secretary had for him, he was anxious to talk to me about it. I did, and right there and then he made a commitment to show up in Boston with his candidate, and I made a commitment that we'd put him on *60 Minutes* that Sunday. What I didn't know at the time was that because of a lot of postgame shows, the network was planning to preempt *60 Minutes* that night. So my next phone call was to the program department, to beg, borrow, or steal at least fifteen minutes for a special edition of *60 Minutes*. But the verdict was that the best they could give me was nine minutes. That's how Steve Kroft, his producer Frank Devine, our studio producer Merri Lieberthal, our director Arthur Bloom, and I ended up in Boston the night of the Super Bowl. Before meeting Governor Clinton and his wife Hillary, Steve, Frank, Merri, Artie, and I had a meeting with two guys I'd never seen before. One of them was George Stephanopoulos, the young charmer I had talked to on the phone from the plane. The other was a strange-looking duck named James Carville. The woman who was with them, Mandy Grunwald, I knew. At least I knew her father, Henry Grunwald, who had been a longtime editor of *Time* magazine.

They kept insisting that we had obligated ourselves to allow time for Bill Clinton to give what they called "his view of America." I told them that because the broadcast had been whittled down to nine minutes, we'd have to see how forthcoming he was about the business at hand before determining how much time would be left over for anything else. And besides, I told them, he was one of five guys running for the Democratic nomination—he wasn't even the front-runner—and if he wanted to give his view of America, I was sure the network would be happy to sell him commercial time to do just that.

The Clintons arrived at the Ritz-Carlton in Boston that Sunday afternoon, and we began the taping early that evening. Kroft came at them every which way but Sunday, but they weaved and bobbed and ducked and left the ring, I thought, unbloodied. I think Bill Clinton thought he had faced down Kroft but that the real test was having to face down Hillary after they left the hotel room we had turned into a studio.

She, on the other hand, was in a snit, so much so that she told the Associated Press that the questions Kroft asked them on the air were not the ones he had actually asked in that room. I got her on the phone and told her that what she told the AP about us was libelous and defamatory. Her answer was that, as she watched it, it didn't seem that those were the same questions they were asked during the taping. I could only conclude that she was shell-shocked (who wouldn't be?) by the whole experience and couldn't come to terms with it.

Years later, after being elected and reelected president, Bill Clinton seemed to have put it all behind him. In fact, when we went there some years later—all of us, Wallace, Safer, Bradley, Kroft, and Stahl—to query him about Bosnia, I said jokingly to Mike McCurry, his press secretary, "I know why we're here, because she's out of town." Mike gave me a knowing grin and changed the subject.

Now why do I think Mrs. Clinton carried a grudge all those years? I think it goes back to an episode during the taping. Carville had plunked himself down in a chair at the back of the control room and, like an adoring groupie mesmerized by a couple of rock stars, begun nattering to himself and sobbing about how wonderful the Clintons were and how much he loved them. In the interest of a little quiet in the control room, I said to no one in particular and everybody in general: "Will someone please shut this guy the fuck up or get him the hell out of here!"

Did Carville hear it? He must have. Did he tattle—report to Hillary Clinton what I said? I think so, and I think that may be why, for the next eight years, I was on report and the name *60 Minutes* was mud in her wing of the White House.

I didn't realize it in January, but 1992 was destined to be a truly "screwy year" in American politics—at least the *Wall Street Journal* said so—and I especially didn't realize how my wife, Marilyn, and I would find ourselves seduced by Ross Perot, the eccentric billionaire who took it upon himself to run as a third-party candidate for president that year.

You would think that the executive producer of *60 Minutes* and his wife—herself a former diplomatic correspondent for the *Washington Post* and White House correspondent for NBC—would have been too knowledgeable, sophisticated, and "with it" to fall for Ross Perot. But, God help us, we both did, although it was at best a short-lived romance. For a brief time, Marilyn even gave Perot foreign-policy advice, although she'll probably kill me for reminding her of it. It was a role she was encouraged to play by our good friend Lloyd Cutler, the former White House counsel to Jimmy Carter (and later, Bill Clinton)—and who will also probably kill me for reminding *him* of it.

To the credit of all three of us, it didn't take us long to fall out of love with Perot and drop out even before Perot quit the race in June, only to change his mind and drop back in again in September.

While I know why Marilyn, Lloyd, and I dropped out, no one knew why Perot had until Lesley Stahl got him to come clean about it in a story that aired in October. It became not only a *60 Minutes* classic, but Perot was convinced that it also kept him from becoming the forty-second president of the United States.

"You said that you heard that there was a plan about your daughter," Lesley began. "Was it the Bush-Quayle people?"

Yes, Perot replied, "Everybody up there panicked in May and June when I was leading in the polls, and they went crazy."

Then he volunteered that he had received a call from a person who said that the Bush-Quayle campaign had manufactured "a computer-created false photo" of his daughter (presumably in a compromising position) that they were going to hand out to the press shortly before her wedding that summer to embarrass her and her father.

He also told Stahl that "they're trying to wiretap my office," which prompted her to ask him, "What would you say if I told you the FBI told us there was no evidence there was any plan to wiretap you?"

Perot's answer? "Sounds like politics to me. Can't talk to me, but can talk to *60 Minutes*? Don't you find that interesting?"

Needless to say, Ross Perot did not get elected president that year, and told David Frost, Britain's best-known television interviewer, that I and *60 Minutes* cost him the election.

When Bill and Hillary Clinton appeared on *60 Minutes* in 1992 to try to save his candidacy from charges of marital infidelity, who could have imagined that we hadn't seen the end of Bill Clinton and marital infidelity, and that a woman named Kathleen Willey would appear on our doorstep six years later, in the midst of the Monica Lewinsky scandal.

When we got wind of Willey's story in 1998, the one she told to the grand jury about Bill Clinton "hitting" on her when she went to see him about a job, Michael Radutsky, a producer who works with Bradley, suggested to me that we try to make contact with her and see if she would tell Bradley the same story she told the grand jury. Radutsky went to see her, and she agreed that she'd do it.

Was she lying when she told Bradley about her encounter with Bill Clinton in the Oval Office? While Clinton himself might tell you, "It depends on what the meaning of 'was' was," I'll tell you, absolutely not, unless you believe she also lied under oath to members of a grand jury. Why? Because there was nothing she said to Bradley that she didn't say to them.

Were we especially careful in how we told the story? Damn right we were, because if there is anything we know about "taking on" the White House, it's that, if you're going to do it, you better be prepared to put up or shut up when they come gunning for you. Which in this case they did, big time!

Now remember what she told Ed: According to Willey, she had sought an appointment with Clinton, whom she had known from campaign days, to seek his help in getting a job. Instead, she said to Bradley, the president of the United States groped her. Actually touched her breasts.

Had her story never happened, had she made it up, they would have kissed it off, refused to dignify it with an answer, pooh-poohed it as nonsense. But they didn't. Instead, they went into full battle dress and came out with guns blazing. Over a little nooky in the Oval Office? Over a little nooky in the Oval Office.

For several weeks, prior to the story's running, I had several conversations with the president's attorney, Bob Bennett, imploring him to appear on 60 Minutes to offer the White House's take on Willey. His response was unmistakably clear: "You think I'm crazy?"

So we went ahead and prepared the story without him. The Saturday before it went on the air, I was in the office working with Bradley and Radutsky when my phone rang. It was White House Press Secretary Mike McCurry and the two lead lawyers on Clinton's legal team, Bruce Lindsey and Charles Ruff, requesting—no, not requesting, demanding—that we allow Bob Bennett a role in the story.

"Don't you know," I said, "that we've been trying to do just that for weeks and Bennett's answer was: 'You think I'm crazy?'"

"He's changed his mind," one of the lawyers said. "We'd like you to give Bennett twelve minutes of unedited airtime." How they arrived at twelve minutes I have no idea.

"You guys are out of your minds," I told them. "For one, I've tried until I'm blue in the face to get Bennett to be part of this story. And two, you know better than to ask for unedited airtime." That's when McCurry gave me the opening I was waiting for.

"You mean," he said, "two people were in that room and you only want one person's version of what happened?"

"No, Mike," I said, "I'd much rather have the other person's version, too. Bob Bennett was not in that room. Bill Clinton was. We won't give Bob Bennett twelve minutes to plead Clinton's case, but we'll give Bill Clinton sixty minutes to lay out his own case."

McCurry, who was the class act in that White House, knew he had just put his foot in it, but because we were too chicken to say no to the White House, we did agree to interview Bob Bennett and edit his answers down to whatever length we thought they warranted. When Bennett showed up for the taping that evening, he made a complete fool of himself. He had his notes on his lap, so he kept looking down and not at the camera. Clinton's people later criticized us, saying, "You made us look silly by having him look down." I said, "I didn't put the notes in his lap, for Christ's sake."

And about Bennett's question: "You think I'm crazy?" The answer is no, I don't think Bob Bennett is crazy, just very boring and not very straightforward—at least when talking to us.

Was that whole power play of McCurry, Ruff, Lindsey, and Bennett—hey, sounds like a law firm—because the president's approval rating was slipping? I think not. His job approval rating remained high during the entire mess.

Were they worried that independent prosecutor Ken Starr, by adding Kathleen to Monica, would have a stronger case? Maybe. But what I really think was on the president's mind when he unleashed his fearsome four was: How am I going to explain to Hillary having yet another go at yet another woman in the Oval Office?

To put a period on the Bill Clinton sex-in-the-Oval-Office story, if television is the powerful medium that people think it is, how come the televised impeachment hearings didn't knock him out of office? Simple. The Republicans on the other side—the Henry Hydes, the Bob Barrs, the Robert Livingstons—made bigger damn fools of themselves than he did. There they were in everybody's living room getting their rocks off on Capitol Hill about Clinton getting his rocks off in the Oval Office. Everybody should be so lucky as to have enemies like them.

And who could take seriously the sight of the Chief Justice of the United States in his ceremonial robe, replete with gold braid, sitting there looking like the Mikado ready to burst into Gilbert & Sullivan:

> *Our object all sublime.*
> *We shall achieve in time*
> *To make the punishment*
> *Fit the crime...*
> *The punishment fit the crime.*
> *And make each prisoner pent*
> *Unwillingly represent*
> *A source of innocent merriment*
> *Of innocent merriment.*

And innocent merriment it would have been if Kathleen Willey hadn't been hung out to dry by the White House. Why do you suppose, the day after the *60 Minutes* story ran, the White House released what some would call adoring letters she had written to the president?

Simple! If, as Dr. Samuel Johnson said, the last refuge of a scoundrel is patriotism, the last refuge of a guy trying to justify an affair or some hanky-panky is "she was asking for it."

How did he get away with it? No less a Clinton watcher than Dee Dee Myers, his first White House press secretary, told writer Richard Reeves in *Talk* magazine: "There's almost nobody he can't razzle dazzle."

CHAPTER ELEVEN

Big Tobacco

One morning in February 1994, Mike Wallace and Lowell Bergman, one of Mike's producers, walked into my office and said they had a hell of a story.

The story was that Jeffrey Wigand, a Ph.D. biochemist who had been vice president for research and development at the Brown & Williamson Tobacco Company, was willing to blow the whistle on how B&W and other tobacco companies had turned a blind eye to irrefutable evidence that their product contained harmful ingredients and that they now were lying when they said it didn't.

More than a year earlier, CBS had paid Wigand to be a consultant on a different tobacco story we had done, on the reluctance of tobacco companies to develop a safer cigarette when it came to the number of fires that were started by people smoking in bed. And now, Wigand was willing to tell us all he knew about the shenanigans that went on in the tobacco companies to keep from the public the truth about the harm they were doing to the health of the nation.

To me, the story had everything: an issue that touched almost every American and a lone voice in the wilderness ready to put his career on the line to be a good samaritan and "tell all"—all that he knew about the inner workings of the cigarette company he worked for. It never dawned on me that CBS, even though it was owned by a man who also owned a tobacco company, would put any roadblocks in the way of our doing this story. Boy, was I wrong.

Jeffrey Wigand had been hired by Brown & Williamson in January 1989 as vice president for research and development. He had been hired, Wigand was told, to help develop safer cigarettes. Eventually, he would earn a salary of $300,000 a year, oversee a multimillion-dollar department, and supervise hundreds of employees. But his work at the company didn't turn out as he expected, in more ways than one.

B&W, like all tobacco companies, was under heavy fire from consumers, regulatory agencies, and Congress for turning a blind eye to evidence of the harmful ingredients in tobacco products, and it tended to circle the wagons when the attacks got especially harsh. Wigand was, and certainly felt like, an outsider. He learned over time that the company wasn't much interested in safer cigarettes and he became, by his own admission, something of a disruptive force, particularly at odds with Thomas Sandefur, B&W's president.

In January 1993, Sandefur was made CEO of the company. On March 24, Wigand was fired. As part of his separation from B&W, and to retain his family's health benefits, he signed a confidentiality agreement that covered his work at the company and his severance package. Under the agreement's terms, he could say very little, if anything, about what was done and said inside the facilities of his previous employer, or about his severance contract. Later, under threat of a lawsuit for breach of contract because he had allegedly discussed his severance deal, Wigand signed a more stringent confidentiality agreement, prohibiting him from saying anything about his previous employer.

60 Minutes got involved in Wigand's life not long after he was fired, when Lowell Bergman found a carton of documents on the front stoop of his home in Berkeley, California. The papers were highly technical and clearly came from the Philip Morris Company. Bergman was an award-winning investigative reporter who had cut his teeth at the left-wing magazine *Ramparts* during the turbulent '60s and had produced a bunch of terrific stories for us in the '80s and '90s. Bergman was talented, but he needed help deciphering the meaning of the documents on his doorstep and called a friend who knew something about the tobacco business. Could the friend recommend a consultant? Yes, the friend said, call Jeff Wigand.

Bergman did, but it wasn't until February 1994 that they finally met in Louisville, Kentucky. Wigand said he couldn't talk about B&W, certainly not until his severance package ran its course a year or so later, though he said he would take a look at the Philip Morris documents. *60 Minutes* did not end up doing a Philip Morris story, but ABC did. Later that year, Wigand became an adviser to ABC in its defense against a $10 billion lawsuit that Philip Morris had brought in response to that story, which had alleged that the company was manipulating nicotine levels.

Meanwhile, Bergman continued trying to convince Wigand to sit for an on-air interview, and he and Mike kept me abreast of developments. In August 1995, Wigand finally agreed to come to New York. Time was of the essence, because some of the B&W documents we were interested in had shown up on the Internet. Things were moving quickly, and we were afraid that the story would get away from us.

But a funny thing happened to us on our way to reporting Wigand's account of the lengths his company, Brown & Williamson, was prepared to go to bamboozle smokers into continuing to keep puffing on cigarettes until they died.

The funny thing we bumped into was a piece of legal mumbo jumbo called "tortious interference," which in layman's language, refers to a party of the third part (in this case, CBS) inveigling a party of the second part (Wigand) to divulge information he promised a party of the first part (B&W) not to reveal. I had never heard this phrase in fifty years of journalism, but I would hear it a lot in the next few months.

CBS at the time was about to be taken over by Westinghouse, and everyone at the network was twitchy about anything that might queer the deal. B&W never actually made the threat of lawsuit. But CBS brass went to outside counsel, who convinced them of the definite possibility of legal action in Kentucky—friendly territory for tobacco, but not for us. The dollar amount the lawyers mentioned was $15 billion. If we lost, they said, Kentucky law stipulated that the defendant had to put up a 10-percent bond before registering an appeal. In other words, it would cost $1.5 billion just to appeal a lower court decision against us.

On September 12, Eric Ober, then the president of CBS News, asked me to come to his office to talk with the lawyers and hear them lay out the problem as they saw it. Wallace, Bergman, and Phil Scheffler, our executive editor, were there as well.

Ellen Kaden, the network's general counsel, explained that if Wigand broke his contract with B&W by appearing on 60 Minutes at our urging, we might be liable for aiding and abetting his violation of the severance agreement—and that, she told us, was "tortious interference." What she was urging, and what Ober endorsed, was that we pull the plug on the Wigand story, even though B&W had yet to raise the issue with CBS.

Because I am not a lawyer and had never heard of the phrase "tortious interference," I was in no position to tell the corporation that I thought it was making a big mistake in rolling over and playing dead for Brown & Williamson. At that point, the Philip Morris suit against ABC had been settled out of court, which meant that the network had written a check to the tobacco company and had apologized on the air.

I also was inclined to believe at the time that the decision had nothing to do with CBS Chairman Larry Tisch being in the tobacco business. (Loews Corp., which he and his brother controlled, owned

Lorillard Tobacco.) Did I know that for a fact? No. But I believed it was strictly a money decision—the possibility of having to put up $1.5 billion and upsetting the Westinghouse deal in the event we lost round one in Kentucky.

But it's still an open question: Did Tisch really call the tune? Kaden says no, she did. I have difficulty believing that a decision of this nature could have been made without the concurrence of the chairman of the board. It wasn't until several years later that I learned from Dick Scruggs, the lead outside counsel for the twenty-eight states that took on Big Tobacco, that while we were prohibited from broadcasting our interview with Wigand, Tisch's Lorillard may have been negotiating with B&W to purchase six of their discount brands—Montclair, Malibu, Riviera, Crowns, Special 10's, and Bull Durham. Scruggs himself said that he did not learn of those negotiations until March 1996, and that he was flabbergasted by the news.

Wallace argued against the company's decision to keep Wigand off the air and talked to several journalists who said that B&W would never sue. I kept saying, "Mike, they're not lawyers. I also think we ought to be doing it, but how are you going to do it if the lawyers aren't going to let you?" Finally, I said to him, "Look, the only way to get this story on the air is to go out and hire a bunch of guerrillas and take the transmitter at gunpoint." Failing that, what could we do about it? We could quit, of course. But I had spent too much of my life making 60 Minutes what it was. There were a hundred people who worked there and depended on me, and I wasn't about to let them down and neither was Mike. So while some of my colleagues were wringing their hands in despair and running off in every direction looking for sympathy and solace, Mike, Phil Scheffler, and I hit upon the idea of telling our audience not the story the CBS legal department wouldn't let us tell but the story *behind* the story—the story of the bind our own company had put us in.

The story contained all the salient facts we had learned about the chicanery of the tobacco companies. The only thing it didn't contain was the name of the tobacco scientist and the company he worked for. But we decided if we were going to tell the story without revealing the source, we owed it to our viewers at least to reveal how dismayed we were over CBS's behavior.

What we did broadcast on November 11, 1995, was considered a cop-out by our critics. At the time, we thought it was the best we could do under the circumstances.

After a brief windup in which Mike introduced the story and the existence of our tobacco "insider," he pitched the truth to our audience straight and hard. We wanted to be completely up-front: "We cannot broadcast," Mike said, "what critical information about tobacco, addiction, and public health he [Wigand, the unnamed insider] might be able to offer."

He then described the confidentiality agreement and added: "The management of CBS has told us that, knowing he had that agreement, if we were to broadcast an interview with him, CBS could be faced with a multibillion-dollar lawsuit. Fact is, we are not allowed even to mention his name or the name of the company he worked for. And, of course, we cannot show you his face." We didn't show Wigand, but viewers heard his voice after Mike had him confirm that his confidentiality agreement was still in force and asked whether his unnamed former employer would sue him for appearing on 60 Minutes even in shadows. "I would bet on it," Wigand said.

Mike took viewers through ABC's battle with Philip Morris and R. J. Reynolds, another tobacco giant, and we showed the file footage of Diane Sawyer's on-air apology. This wasn't much of a visual story—tape of cigarette manufacturing and knots of smokers aren't all that exciting—but as I said, it was a subject that touches almost everyone in the country. It was a terrific example of what I mean about the importance of the spoken story compared with the visual one. It was the words that mattered.

The next part of Mike's tale underscored the point. He set it up with a reference to the industry's hardball tactics, then raised the case of Merrell Williams, a paralegal in Louisville, Kentucky, who had worked in a firm that represented Brown & Williamson. Williams had walked off with 4,000 pages of B&W files, including some pretty revealing top-secret stuff, and the company had gone to court for a gag order to prevent him from talking to anyone about the documents. That really meant anyone, including his lawyer, Fox DeMoisey.

In Mike's "interview" with the two of them, Williams nodded once in answer to a question but said nothing. DeMoisey said his client could go to jail for six months if he talked. And even though B&W had filed a motion to hold Williams in criminal contempt, DeMoisey was prohibited from talking to him. "Oh, I can ask him about the Reds and what he thought of the World Series and things like that. And I can –"

"But you cannot–" Mike interjected.

No, DeMoisey said, he could not provide legal counsel to his client. "You know, Jeffrey Dahmer killed and ate people," he pointed out, "and he wasn't–he had counsel, complete access. Aldrich Ames had sold our country's national security secrets. He had counsel."

The lesson, DeMoisey went on, was that even the worst criminals imaginable are entitled to counsel, "but if you take Brown & Williamson documents, your rights are suspended."

The guts of the story came next, in Wallace's interview with Dr. Stanton Glantz, a medical-school professor from California who had obtained copies of these documents and had led a team of scientists who published an analysis of them in the *Journal of the American Medical Association.*

Glantz said the documents proved that the company knew nicotine was addictive and that it developed sophisticated legal strategies to keep the information from reaching the public. He also talked about the additives, flavorings, and other compounds that tobacco companies put in their products. One of them was Freon, the synthetic chemical used as the cooling agent in refrigerators. Another, reported in the *Wall Street Journal*, Wallace said, was ammonia—used as an "impact booster" for the nicotine in cigarettes.

The documents, Glantz said, repeatedly say the company is "in the business of selling nicotine"—"producing a nicotine-delivery service," in Mike's words.

> WALLACE: Am I taking this too seriously? I mean, it's like sticking something in your—in your arm.
>
> GLANTZ: Well, it is, except inhaling it gets it to your brain faster than sticking it in with a needle.... That's why crack cocaine is more addictive than snorted or injected cocaine.... It's absorbed very fast. And within a few seconds, it gets to your brain.

We ended the formal part of the story with that classic scene of the tobacco chiefs, including Larry Tisch's son Andrew, raising their right hands and swearing before a congressional committee that, by God, none of them believed nicotine was addictive.

But Mike wasn't finished. He reminded our audience of the confidentiality agreement and the potential liability to CBS. "All of this," Mike said, "speaks to a disturbing reality—that news organizations can be sued not for the truth or falsity of what they report, but instead just for seeking out information from insiders who have material important to the public health and welfare, but who have signed confidentiality agreements. I'll have a personal note about all this later in the broadcast."

Here is what Mike said in that unprecedented "personal note" at the end of the broadcast that night: "We at 60 Minutes—and that's about a hundred of us who turn out this broadcast each week—are proud of working here and at CBS News, and so we were dismayed that the management at CBS had seen fit to give in to perceived threats of legal action against us by a tobacco-industry giant. We've broadcast many such investigative pieces down the years, and we want to be able to continue. We lost out, only to some degree on this one, but we haven't the slightest doubt that we'll be able to continue the 60 Minutes tradition of reporting such pieces in the future without fear or favor."

That was a first—a network-news broadcast holding its own management's feet to the fire. And as it turned out, Mike's closing line in his "personal note" of the November broadcast was more prescient than any of us had any right to think at the time. In late January, everything went public when the Wall Street Journal published a long account of Wigand's testimony in a Mississippi court case—and of the Brown & Williamson campaign to undermine his credibility and, in the process, destroy his reputation. We quickly reviewed our Wigand interview, put together the story and broadcast it on February 4, 1996.

Once again, we needed to talk about ourselves to give our audience context for the story they were about to hear. Mike began with background—how a story we set out to report six months earlier had now turned into two stories. One was on cigarettes and their destructive power. The other was the saga of Jeff Wigand and how his former employer was trying to destroy his reputation. Mike alluded to CBS management, its worries over a lawsuit and that phrase I never want to hear again—"tortious interference"—and ended his introduction with this: "While a lawsuit is still a possibility, not putting Jeffrey Wigand's story on 60 Minutes no longer is."

The Wigand interview, this time with the man himself in living color, went through some of the material we had broadcast before, particularly the addictive qualities of cigarettes and the chemicals that tobacco companies use to manipulate taste and the impact on the central nervous system.

Wigand said that Brown & Williamson executives had told him categorically that the company had not done pharmacological studies on nicotine, even though those confidential documents we cited in our first broadcast proved otherwise. And one of his mandates—to work on safer cigarettes—had gone up in smoke. In fact, he said, a company lawyer, Kendrick Wells, had edited out discussions of safer cigarettes from a meeting of scientists who worked for British-American Tobacco, which owned B&W. From then on, Wigand said, lawyers regularly intervened to purge documents when there were references to "less hazardous" or "safer" cigarettes.

"As I dug deeper and deeper," he said, "I started getting a bodyguard." Wigand's bodyguard, he told Mike, was Kendrick Wells, who would accompany the scientist when he traveled to major scientific meetings. Wigand complained to Thomas Sandefur, who was then the president of B&W.

> WALLACE: What'd he say to you?
> WIGAND: I don't want to hear any more discussion about a safer cigarette.

Sandefur, Wigand said, was worried about legal exposure if it became known that the company was pursuing a safer cigarette. After all, he and the other tobacco executives had testified that cigarettes weren't addictive.

Wigand bit his tongue and kept quiet, switching his attention to the additives, flavorings, and other compounds in B&W tobacco products. One flavor-enhancing compound, coumarin, was known to cause tumors in the livers of mice. "I wanted it out immediately," he told Wallace, "and I was told that it would affect sales and I was to mind my own business." Instead, he complained to Sandefur in a memo and was again told to button his lip. Not much later, Sandefur, now the CEO, had him fired. The reasons? "Poor communication skills, just not cutting it, poor performance," Wigand said, although none of these criticisms had apparently been mentioned before.

But according to Wigand, B&W wasn't through with him. It sued him, claiming he had broken his confidentiality agreement, and they cut off his severance pay and health benefits—the latter critical because one of his children required daily health care. And, he said, there were personal threats on the lives of his kids: Once, "a male voice that was on the phone…said, 'Don't mess with tobacco anymore. How are your kids?' "

Mike reported that, three years after his firing, Wigand had become the star witness in a criminal investigation of the tobacco industry by the U.S. Justice Department, as well as in the huge lawsuit against Big Tobacco by more than two dozen state attorneys general. He had also become the focus of a massive campaign to impugn his integrity and discredit the scientist-turned-whistle-blower. "I think the word they've used, Mike, is a 'master of deceit,' " Wigand said.

B&W produced a 500-page dossier on Wigand and hired a public-relations hotshot in New York named John Scanlon to get the word to the media, Mike reported. Scanlon wouldn't sit down with Mike for an interview, but he did make a statement to a CBS News camera crew: "[Wigand is] running from cross examination. His victims have decided to respond and present evidence that he is, in fact, a habitual liar."

The dossier, Mike said, was given to the *Wall Street Journal*, whose reporters did their own investigation and found what they called "scant evidence" for B&W's charges. Mike confronted Gordon Smith, an attorney picked by B&W to talk to us. Smith claimed we were being misled, that there were no "material inaccuracies" in the dossier, and that we had, as he put it, "a vested interest in making this man [Wigand] credible."

WALLACE: Why do we have a vested interest?
SMITH: CBS has—has paid this guy $12,000.
WALLACE: For what?
SMITH: I believe for consulting.
WALLACE: Now wait just a moment. Let's get this straight. Paid him $12,000 for what?
SMITH: To consult on a story for CBS.

We had hired Wigand two years earlier, as Mike explained on the air, to act as our expert consultant on the highly technical Philip Morris documents regarding fire safety and cigarettes. At that time, Mike added, Wigand told us he would not talk with us about B&W—and he did not, until more than a year later.

Our broadcast, toward the end, included interviews with three state attorneys general—Minnesota's Hubert Humphrey III, son of the late vice president; Mississippi's Mike Moore, who would become the telegenic spokesman for the states in their suit against the tobacco companies; and Florida's Lieutenant Governor Bob Butterworth, who would gain a measure of national notoriety more than four years later during the struggle between Al Gore and George W. Bush for his state's twenty-five electoral votes.

Smith, the B&W-designated lawyer, defended cigarettes and the 50 million Americans who use them: "It's their choice," he told Mike. "It's a lawful product. It's marketed and manufactured lawfully."

Mike closed with an explanation. B&W kept insisting that we could not report the story objectively because we were indemnifying Wigand in the company's lawsuit against him, he said. We had indeed agreed two months earlier to indemnify Wigand. Why? A leak had disclosed Wigand's identity before he was prepared to go public. "Though still unaware of where that leak had come from," Mike told the audience, "CBS decided to take financial responsibility for the impact that leak had on Dr. Wigand because it exposed him to a lawsuit by Brown & Williamson."

A footnote: To defend Wigand against B&W, CBS assumed legal bills of more than a million dollars. In addition, CBS paid another several hundred thousand dollars in legal bills to keep B&W from getting its hands on confidential notes and documents pertinent to the CBS/Wigand matter and to keep me, Mike Wallace, Lowell Bergman, three CBS lawyers, the president of CBS News, as well as the president of CBS from being deposed.

Three months after the second story aired, Marie Brenner published a first-rate article on Wigand in *Vanity Fair*. Her piece, "The Man Who Knew Too Much," was tough but fair when it came to CBS and the decision to keep Wigand off the air in November 1995.

Brenner's article gave the whole affair a second life when it attracted the attention of director-producer-screenwriter Michael Mann. The result was *The Insider*, a commercial movie in 1999 starring Al Pacino as Bergman, which purported to tell the story behind the story. Bergman, of course, is portrayed as a heroic figure battling the CBS Evil Empire and quitting out of principle. Okay in Hollywood, not so okay in the real world. Why? Because Bergman never quit.

Let me tell you a story of my own: In the fall of 2000 I delivered the keynote address at the annual meeting of an international organization of journalists called News World, where I was asked what I thought of *The Insider*. In response I asked the reporters in the audience how many of them had seen the movie and how many of them knew who the reporter was who resigned from CBS in protest. A sizable number acknowledged that they had seen the movie and that the reporter was Lowell Bergman.

No, it wasn't, I said. The reporter who resigned from CBS News was Al Pacino, *playing* Lowell Bergman.

The fact is, Bergman did not resign. He was on the *60 Minutes* payroll for more than seven more months after the tobacco fracas and on the CBS News payroll as a freelancer for another two years.

Remember the sequence of events. First, in November 1995, we did the best we thought we could do, with Mike taking a shot at CBS management. Then, in February 1996, we did the full Wigand story, which also included Mike saying publicly what the company stopped us from doing. So we twice took on CBS on the air. How many news organizations do you know that would permit one of its own reporters to tell the world that the company he works for had turned chicken? Now Bergman says it was a disgrace. You know who produced those stories? Lowell Bergman.

After *The Insider* came out, Bergman seemed to be making a new career for himself touting the virtues of truth here, there, and everywhere and talking about the movie as a "kind of historical novel" that conveys a "higher truth." But it took John Darnton, the culture editor of *The New York Times*, to remind Lowell that there is no such thing as "higher truth" or "lower truth." There is only "truth" and "untruth." Protect us all from so-called journalists looking for higher truths.

In June 2000, the professional organization Investigative Reporters and Editors asked me to give a speech at their annual convention and address the controversy over *The Insider*. The day before I was to speak, Bergman got an advance copy of my written text and faxed to IRE what he hoped would be a preemptive strike. In his letter, he repeated his view of events—all of it "reported in the film." A couple days after my speech, I sent him a short note:

Dear Lowell:

What you had to say about me and Mike and *60 Minutes...in words uttered by an actor...*played in dimly lit movie houses all over the world to an audience of millions. My response...*in my own words...*came in a single fully lighted room to an audience of maybe 1200. Do the arithmetic and tell me what you're kvetching about.

Yours truly,

Don Hewitt

About Michael Mann, who touted the movie as the story of CBS "caving in" to the threat of a lawsuit by B&W, can this be the same Michael Mann who admitted that he himself "caved in" to the threat of a B&W lawsuit? That's what he told *DGA Magazine*, the publication of the Directors' Guild of America, because, as he said, Wigand "was being sued by Brown & Williamson for breaching his confidentiality agreement" and "we could not even be seen as potential recipients of confidential information or else we...could have been named in the suit." (The collective "we" includes Mann himself, cowriter Eric Roth, and the Disney Company.)

Sounds quite a bit like what he accused CBS of, no?

Anyway, according to Mann in the same article, the threat left him no choice but "to guess [Wigand's] motivation for [the] pivotal moment in the story." As it turned out, that wasn't his only "guess." So allow me, if you will, a guess of my own. I guess that had Mann opted to tell the story straight—as Marie Brenner wrote it—and not gone off on flights of fancy, he might have gone off with a couple of Oscars.

Oh, hell, it was only a movie. And if they had gotten Paul Newman or Robert Redford to play me, I would have forgiven them anything. As it was, when I found out I was going to be played by an actor named Philip Baker Hall, I said, "That's not an actor, that's a dormitory!"

Now, if a movie is a movie, a lie is a lie. And the ones Bergman told in an article he wrote for the July/August 2000 issue of the *Columbia Journalism Review* make me wonder whether the journalist I respected for several stunning contributions to *60 Minutes* had gone around the bend. Bergman subsequently wrote that during the CBS/B&W fracas, I had "conferred repeatedly and secretly with Brown and Williamson public relations executive John Scanlon, who initiated a smear campaign aimed at discrediting Jeffrey Wigand."

That lie is testimony to Bergman's complete and utter disregard for the truth. I not only never met secretly with Scanlon, I took pains to avoid him and on the odd occasion that I ran into him, made it a point to tell him I wanted no part of him and "to go peddle his papers." In fact, on receipt of some unsolicited documents he sent me about Wigand, I immediately took them to Wallace to show the lengths to which Scanlon was going to smear Wigand. Convinced the documents had been stolen, and were in Scanlon's possession illegally, Mike and I turned them over to the CBS legal department.

Then, not content with that lie about me and Scanlon, Bergman came up with one so big I didn't think even he was capable of telling it—the libelous and defamatory accusation that a story cannot be told honestly if it includes "a friend of the executive producer" and that network-news broadcasts have to pull back when it comes to reporting anything derogatory about events in which their network has a commercial interest.

If that's true, how does he think Bob Simon and Michael Gavshon used 60 *Minutes* to tell the world about the chicanery and the bribes that went into the awarding of the 1998 Winter Olympics to Nagano, Japan, at the same time CBS Sports was reaping millions from its arrangement with that same Olympic Committee to broadcast the events at Nagano?

If television news steers clear of stories about institutions that are "powerful," can someone explain to me how Mike Wallace went on 60 *Minutes* and took on one of 60 *Minutes*'s biggest sponsors—the "powerful" (I think it's fair to say) Ford Motor Company—with a devastating story about how unsafe the fuel tank was in the Ford Pinto and how irresponsible Ford was not to do something about it?

And how—at the same time CBS Sports was carrying the Final Four basketball tournament—does Bergman suppose Lesley Stahl and Rome Hartman were able to go on 60 *Minutes* and hold college basketball's feet to the fire about the behind-the-scenes wheeling and dealing that basketball coaches were involved in with companies like Nike and Adidas—which were then and continue to be clients of CBS?

And if 60 *Minutes* allegedly steers clear of doing stories about what Bergman calls "powerful institutions," can someone please explain to me why 60 *Minutes* is, has been, and continues to be *persona non grata* at the Pentagon, and why government agencies, almost to a man, treat us like a pariah and would rather eat razor blades than face a team from 60 *Minutes*?

Because we're patsies?

Because we're afraid to offend?

Anyone who has watched 60 *Minutes*—let alone worked for 60 *Minutes*—knows that that is foolishness, and if a journalist who worked for 60 Minutes for thirteen years doesn't know it, then the editors of the Columbia Journalism Review who published it should.

CBS finally had enough of Bergman. Is he telling the truth when he says he didn't ask Mike Wallace to help him get his job back? That happens to be one of the few true things he has said. What he asked Mike to do was help him get a job at 60 Minutes II, the magazine show that CBS started in 1999. Knowing Lowell, he'll probably deny that, too. So, on the one hand, Bergman implored Wallace to get him rehired at his old network and on the other hand went on the record in the Columbia Journalism Review saying that his "old network" doesn't measure up to his standards.

Why would I, in writing about a half century in broadcast journalism, devote so many pages to one broadcast journalist (and an insignificant one at that) who has trouble with the truth? I wouldn't have, if the magazine that allowed him to play fast and loose with the truth hadn't been the Columbia Journalism Review, which is published under the auspices of no less an institution than the Columbia University Graduate School of Journalism, whose dean, Tom Goldstein, just happened to be a friend and former colleague of Lowell Bergman. How, incidentally does a journalism school explain to aspiring journalists that a magazine published under its auspices made no effort to verify the truth or accuracy of an article it published, by a friend of the dean?

Of course, the nation's editorial writers and a slew of op-ed writers had a field day comparing the way CBS "folded" to the way the New York Times and The Washington Post "stood up" and, in effect, shouted, "Damn the torpedoes; full speed ahead" when they were confronted with legal action over the publishing of the Pentagon Papers.

The plain fact is that the principal business of The New York

Times and *The Washington Post* is making sure their newspapers continue to be their pride and joy. Acting and feeling the same about their news divisions was hardly a front-burner concern of Larry Tisch's CBS or Michael Eisner's ABC when the networks opted to make accommodations to Big Tobacco to avoid a lawsuit. ABC did it by forcing its news division onto the air and apologizing for saying Philip Morris had "spiked" its nicotine, and CBS did it by refusing to let *60 Minutes* broadcast a story, which—while true in every aspect—threatened them with a lawsuit.

Make no mistake about it, while journalism is the principal business of great newspapers, it is not the principal business of great television networks. It is a very small part of the corporate culture and thus a very small part of its concerns. Was it ever thus? No. Bill Paley wandered into uncharted waters when he put his stamp of approval on Ed Murrow taking on Joe McCarthy—something that could have brought down CBS faster and with more finality than a lawsuit by a tobacco company that, had it been brought, we probably could have won. And I remember something very few others do, that Frank Stanton was willing to go to jail to protect CBS's First Amendment right not to make available to the government outtakes of a 1971 broadcast called *The Selling of the Pentagon*, which was about the incestuous relationship between the Defense Department and the defense-contracting industry.

Be that as it may, by and large the CBS executives that followed in the wake of Paley and Stanton, Mel Karmazin and Les Moonves for example, who run the place now, and Andrew Heyward, who runs *CBS News*, have given *60 Minutes* the same kind of kid-gloved, hands-off treatment their predecessors gave Ed Murrow and Walter Cronkite. What delights all of us who work on this broadcast is that they don't expect anything of us other than to operate without fear or favor—either of the people we cover or the people we work for.

CHAPTER TWELVE

Striking the Right Balance

If *60 Minutes* is anything, it's a loose shop. I remember holding a meeting once back in the 1970s, but I can't remember one since—and that's not my age talking. We make it work not with meetings and memos, but with ideas and an open-door policy. Any member of our extended family—our on-air reporters, our executive editor Phil Scheffler, our off-air reporter-producers, the assistants and secretaries—can weigh in. When Mike gets an idea, he storms into my office with a "Hey, kid, why don't we..."

We have no assignment desk at *60 Minutes*; everyone's his own assignment editor. For reasons I can't explain, it dawned on me when I first thought about doing a television newsmagazine that the best way to do it would be to do what print magazines generally do: They rely on a stable of writers to pitch them ideas and once one of those ideas is approved, they give the writer his head to more or less act on his own and bring them a finished story. That is, in essence, how *60 Minutes* works. Each of the five correspondents has his own team of producers, and between them, they generate the stories that come to me for my approval.

Here's how it works: After talking over an idea with Phil or me, the correspondent or producer writes up an outline of the story—what we continue to call a "blue sheet" even though we switched to white paper years ago. We prize originality, but we don't rule out stories just because someone else has done them, not if we feel we can add dimension and context that would make readers experience the story in a fresh way. Then, once Phil, senior producer Josh Howard, and I have approved a blue sheet, the story goes up the line at CBS to make sure it doesn't clash or overlap with something being done on the *Evening News*, *Sunday Morning*, or another CBS News program.

Producers spend more time on individual stories than correspondents do, which is why we prominently feature each producer's name on screen when a story is introduced. To us, it's what a double byline is to a newspaper. In network news, the correspondent carries about 90 percent of the burden, the producer 10 percent. In an hour-long documentary, the percentages are reversed. On *60 Minutes*, it's roughly a 50-50 split, so a shared byline seems perfectly appropriate.

We have a big blackboard in our "newsroom" with seven names across the top—Wallace, Safer, Bradley, Kroft, Stahl, and our two contributing correspondents, Christiane Amanpour and Bob Simon. A story goes up under each name when the correspondent completes it and it's ready or almost ready for broadcast. When the blackboard is full, with four or five stories under each name, my job becomes a lot easier: I can look up on a Monday morning and say, "That Wallace story, that Bradley story, and that Stahl story will make a strong show."

Like any newspaper, the story mix is important. We do three pieces each Sunday, and we want to strike the right balance in tone, length, and subject matter among them. Getting there usually requires some last-minute adjustments. It goes something like this: "That Wallace, that Bradley, and that Stahl piece is the right mix for this week, but Lesley, you need to get a minute and a half out of your piece if we're going to make it all fit in."

We also have a very unique senior producer by the name of Esther Kartiganer whose principal job is to look at a finished piece and compare it to the unedited transcript to make sure what we are about to say on the air does not do violence to what a person had to say when he or she made himself, or herself, available to talk to us. If one of our producers puts two and two together and gets five, she catches it. If a story needs context, she catches it. What she does, essentially, is keep us from getting too big for our britches.

In that regard, I have found over the years that the oft-asked question put to reporters: "Who died and left you in charge?" is not always an invalid one.

What I most admire about the producers on 60 Minutes, brilliant as they are, is that they don't mind criticism, in fact, they seem to welcome it. The same goes for the on-air talent to whom I frequently say: "that pause is too long" or "that inflection is wrong" or "you're putting the emphasis on the wrong word." Is that dramatic coaching? No, that's editing—broadcast style. Inflections and pauses are to us what commas and semicolons are to writers.

When people ask me, "How long in advance do you produce the broadcast?" I tell them, "we don't produce a broadcast. We produce stories that once a week are assembled into a broadcast. That job falls to Merri Liberthal, who along with Kartiganer and Josh Howard, is a 60 Minutes senior producer. What I admire most about Liberthal is her uncanny eye and ear for mistakes and, that with the help of Arthur Bloom, the most accomplished director in television news, knows how to get the best out of all the disparate elements that have to be put together to become the finished product that gets transmitted to millions of homes every Sunday night. More often than not, she has each week's broadcast in the can by Friday night, but it can be opened up for late developments even as it goes on the air.

Josh Howard is another gem. His job is to keep everything running smoothly *before* it gets to the studio. It is rare to pass his office and not find a producer there asking his advice on how to solve a problem.

The broadcast has remained essentially unchanged since the very beginning. This is no accident. I have this crazy theory that we are the only thing in American life that still looks, feels, and smells the same as it always did. The supermarkets look different, the gas stations look different, the banks look different. But if you remember *60 Minutes* as a kid, you'll feel an intimacy with it today. People say, at some point, you have to change the ticking watch. And I say, no way. The watch is like the screen door at grandpa's house, the one that always squeaks and you never want oiled because it brings back such wonderful memories. In a changing world, we strive for constancy. I like the screen door to squeak a little.

What makes a television story different from a newspaper or magazine story is that a print publication can sic a reporter on someone who is essentially dull, and with some brilliant writing can make that person come to life.

In television, dull is dull, and what you see is what you get. So the trick is to find people who can tell their own story better than you can and marry them to a first-rate reporter like Mike Wallace, Morley Safer, Ed Bradley, Steve Kroft, or Lesley Stahl, with whom they'll feel comfortable. That reporter can then bring out the best in that person, and sometimes the worst in them. Here are just a few of the memorable moments from *60 Minutes* interviews, when we sat back and let the subject of a story give of himself or herself:

> Arthur Ashe volunteering to Morley Safer that "one day, I think not too far in the distant future, there will be many, many more black tennis players playing…and they won't talk like me and they won't look like me and they won't act like me and they won't dress like me, and they're going to upset a whole lot of people." And while there are many more black tennis players today (some of whom do talk, look, dress, and act like Arthur Ashe), the two most famous ones don't—

Serena and Venus Williams. But the Williams sisters seem to upset not "a whole lot of people," but just John McEnroe.

Art Buchwald telling Mike Wallace, "The thing about this country is if you attack the establishment and do it well, they make you a member of the establishment."

And how about Jesse Jackson ridiculing a lot of the theories that say "the reason the Negro can't learn [is] his daddy's gone and his momma is pitiful and he doesn't understand anything about education and [there's] not much food in his refrigerator and there's rats all in the house and that's the reason he can't learn. And we read all that mess, and then we come to school…and the teacher stands there feeling guilty. Says, 'These poor Negroes, they got all these heartaches and trials and tribulations and they're so pitiful and now I got to stand up here and try to teach them how to read and write and count.' Well, if we can run faster and jump higher and shoot a basketball straight off of an inadequate diet, we can read and write and count off of those same diets."

There was also Teddy Kollek, the mayor of Jerusalem, owning up to Morley Safer that the only difference between expropriating land from a Jew and expropriating land from an Arab is that "The Jews will call me a bastard and the Arabs will call me a Zionist bastard."

Katharine Hepburn, in 1979, after sounding off about how "disgusted" she was with what she called the filth and violence in the movies, being asked by Morley Safer, "Surely, you're not advocating censorship?" Her knock-your-socks-off reply was: "Don't be too sure!"

Barry Goldwater leveling with Harry Reasoner that he didn't think Richard Nixon "should ever be forgiven," because "he came as close to destroying this country as any one man in that office ever has come."

I particularly savor the interview when Nancy Reagan volunteered to Mike Wallace that "whenever somebody would say something about Ronnie that I felt was unkind and cruel and unjust and untrue, I'd go and take a long bath. And I would carry on imaginary conversations in the bathtub in which I was marvelous. I'd say all those right things that you hope you'd have the chance to say and all the right words would come to you and nobody could talk back to you.... By the time I finished the bath I was okay."

Nancy Reagan's son, Ron, telling Lesley Stahl many years later that if it hadn't been for his mother, he didn't think his father would have been president: "She has more ambition than he does.... If left to his own devices he might have, you know, ended up hosting *Unsolved Mysteries* on TV."

And was there ever a line out of the blue more memorable than Hillary Clinton putting Steve Kroft on notice, and also the millions watching her and her husband in 1992, that "I'm no Tammy Wynette standing by my man"?

See what I mean when I say that the best stories on television are those in which people come to life when the camera goes on and are sparked to share some of what makes them tick with a reporter? And nobody was ever blessed with more reporters who can do that, and top-notch producers who share a byline with them, than I have.

We aren't in the crusade business at *60 Minutes*, but we do right some wrongs in the course of developing good stories. In addition to drawing on our own knowledge and reading, we also pay close attention to tips and suggestions from viewers, which often result in terrific stories. We listened carefully when one viewer told us about a situation in the Dallas area in 1983 that had received a lot of newspaper coverage. It involved a young black engineer named Lenell Geter, who had been recruited out of South Carolina State College to work for E-Systems, a defense contractor in Greenville, Texas.

Geter had arrived there in 1982, his future seemingly secure—a clean-cut, twenty-four-year-old earning $24,000 a year and planning to get married. Six months later, he was arrested for the armed robbery of $615 from a Kentucky Fried Chicken restaurant in Balch Springs, Texas, then tried, convicted, and sentenced to life in prison.

As Morley Safer and producer Suzanne St. Pierre found out, there was both more and less here than met the eye. Safer and St. Pierre demonstrated that Geter could not have been at the restaurant at the time of the robbery and that some of the "evidence" against him was pure fiction. Morley interviewed Geter in jail, who, of course, denied that he had done anything wrong.

The next time any of us saw him, Lenell Geter was our guest at the George Foster Peabody awards luncheon, free at last. No new trial: They just opened the jailhouse door and turned him loose, case dismissed. Did our good, hard digging make *the* difference? The jurors for the Peabody, the prestigious awards program for television and radio administered by the University of Georgia and named after the famous banker-philanthropist, obviously thought so when they gave us the award. In truth, it's hard to say, but one thing I do know is that it is almost impossible to put something like that in a *60 Minutes* spotlight without something happening. When it does, and justice is done, we couldn't be happier.

For the last several years, we have augmented our all-star team with two ringers who are themselves stars, Christiane Amanpour of CNN and Bob Simon of CBS. For now, their role is limited to about five stories each per year. My gut tells me that before too many years go by, they'll be regulars. Even though they only appear every once in a while, they are one of us or—more accurately, two of us.

I don't remember fighting with management more than all of us on *60 Minutes* did to try to dissuade them from inaugurating a show that they wanted to call *60 Minutes II*, and as everybody knows, we lost. However, *60 Minutes II* has kept up the standards that we like to think we are dedicated to and has proved to be not only a credit to CBS News but a credit to us.

We were concerned at the time that a broadcast called *60 Minutes II* would diminish the name *60 Minutes* and we weren't sure that they wouldn't be expected to play the ratings game that we had always managed to avoid. Until I saw the product, which I thought was first-rate, management had trouble convincing me that what they wanted to do was a good idea. The fact is that Dan Rather, Scott Pelley, Bob Simon, Charlie Rose, and Vicki Mabrey rose to the occasion and their executive producer, Jeff Fager (who had been a *60 Minutes* producer for many years) has kept up the standards of first-rate broadcast journalism that we feared might not be the case. Not for the first time, I was wrong.

However, I refused to believe I was wrong in 1999 in giving Mike Wallace the green light to broadcast a videotape of an assisted suicide made by Dr. Jack Kevorkian, the celebrated champion of euthanasia. It all started when Dr. Kevorkian called up Mike Wallace to tell him that he had such a videotape and to ask whether we wanted to use it on *60 Minutes*. My first reaction was, Jesus, I don't want to put that on television. But the more I thought about it, the more I thought, why not? Mike and I thought airing the tape might reopen the debate over physician-assisted suicide, which had become dormant, and we were right.

We live in a country where people will pay money to watch all sorts of violent acts dramatized for big and small screens alike. Was this more horrifying than Janet Leigh getting stabbed in the shower scene in the original *Psycho*? Or any number of "realistic" portrayals of murder in more contemporary movies?

The scene on the tape was quiet and almost mundane, putting a man to death. There was no terrible moment of pain or suffering; he just slipped away. We hear at memorial services and funerals about shuffling off this mortal coil and the glorious moment to follow, leaving our earthly possessions behind and entering the Kingdom of Heaven. That's what I saw this man do. And if that isn't a beautiful moment, I don't know what in heaven's name all these clergymen are talking about.

We got praised and pilloried for that Kevorkian story. Bill Bennett, the self-appointed "virtues" czar and his sidekick, Joseph Lieberman (yes, *that* Joe Lieberman) gave us the Order of the Silver Sewer, which I suppose meant they didn't much like our broadcast. Bennett's brother, Bob, was defending President Clinton at the time, so I figured they gave us the Silver Sewer because Bill Bennett was saving the gold one for his brother, Bob.

Still, the critics had a point when they said we didn't show the other side of the debate, so we followed up with a piece about people in hospices who choose to live with their pain and suffering. I wish I could say it was my idea, but it wasn't. It was suggested to us by some of our viewers.

However, it was my idea to try to put Boris Yeltsin and Lesley Stahl together. There is no way I'll ever forget the off-the-wall Saturday morning that *60 Minutes* producer Rome Hartman, Lesley, and I spent at Yeltsin's tennis court at his dacha outside Moscow. I can't imagine a more bizarre setting for an interview with a head of state than between games of a doubles match between the president of Russia and his grandson on one side and a friend of his and the captain of the Russian Davis Cup team on the other. Each time Yeltsin sat down after a game—between his daughter wiping his brow and he himself blowing his nose into his tennis towel—Lesley peppered him with questions. One of the things she hadn't gotten around to and wasn't sure she wanted to was his drinking, when lo and behold he brought the subject up himself.

Out of the blue, he pointed at me and said, "You're the one who doctored the film to make me look inebriated."

I told him I didn't know what film he was talking about and if somebody did something like that, it wasn't me.

What happened next stunned me. "You cross yourself you didn't do it?" he said. Cross yourself? Did this old Bolshevik really say, "Cross yourself"? Now, to a kid brought up in a Jewish household, "cross yourself" meant you were old enough to cross the street by yourself, but I knew what he wanted and I did it, right there in front of God and everybody on Boris Yeltsin's tennis court. I crossed myself. And no sooner had I done it than he reached for my hand (the one I had just crossed myself with), shook it, and said, in English, the only two words I know that never have to be translated: "No problem."

I thought that calmed him down, but a few minutes later when Lesley asked him about the poor state of hospital care in Russia and told him that she had seen two babies die because there were no antibiotics to give them, he went ape.

"Why don't *you* give us antibiotics?" he said, angrily. "You're a rich country. I have my own mother who had a heart attack. She's lying in a hospital ward with ten other patients. There's no medicine to treat her"—as if that were Lesley's fault—"and I myself had to bring her medicine from Moscow and *this*," he said, "is the mother of a president!"

You want to try a Saturday morning of tennis that beats that one?

CHAPTER THIRTEEN

News Business, Show Business,

and Nobody's Business

The sad fact of life about television today is that the economics of commercial broadcasting have in large measure driven the networks out of the expensive and high-risk entertainment business, which they used to be very serious about and did very well, and into the less expensive and less risky news business, which they're not very serious about and don't do very well.

Now don't get me wrong. I'm not talking about Dan Rather, Peter Jennings, or Tom Brokaw. I'm not talking about Ted Koppel and *Nightline*, or Bob Schieffer's *Face the Nation*, Tim Russert's *Meet the Press*, or *This Week with Sam Donaldson and Cokie Roberts*. What I am talking about are the so-called newsmagazines that came along in our wake, which the networks use as filler when the ratings gods don't smile on a sitcom or an hour-long drama. If it's true, and it is, that behind every great man there's a woman, then behind almost every TV newsmagazine there's a failed sitcom. Had that sitcom not failed, that newsmagazine wouldn't be there.

The networks used to measure success by the kudos they got from the public and the recognition from colleagues and competitors for doing as well as they did. Traveling the high road was what made you proud to be a broadcast journalist, back in the days when broadcast journalism could hold its own with the best of print. Today, a lot of what passes for news on television couldn't hold its own with a supermarket checkout counter.

Today, the only measure that counts is what kind of promotable nonsense you can come up with to draw people away from the sitcom that's opposite you on another channel. News competing with entertainment has to mean cutting corners. You can't compete with a sitcom unless you have no compunction about being something you aren't, or, at the very least, being something you shouldn't be.

There is a line that separates news biz from show biz. The trick is to walk up to that line, touch it with your toe, but don't cross it. If you don't go near it, you're going to lose your viewership or your readership. If you step over it, you'll lose your conscience. For more than thirty years, 60 Minutes has walked up to that line but never crossed it.

So what is it that's happened to TV news? Andy Rooney says, "Most of the decisions made in television news are not about news, they're about money," and "Corporate America was late discovering there was a profit to be made with news, and it's trying to make up for a slow start." I don't think Andy would mind my pointing out that what he says about broadcast journalism could apply to broadcast journalists, among them one named Hewitt and one named Rooney. So, in essence, everyone has made out like a bandit, the people Andy and I work for and the people Andy and I work with. It makes no sense for people like us to get all high and mighty about the corrupting influence of money in the news business when we ourselves are the beneficiaries of this newfound prosperity. All the hand-wringing about the money in television reminds me of the marvelous answer the legendary Broadway producer George Abbott once gave to a student who had asked him disdainfully: "Mr. Abbott, when did the theater become so commercial?"

"I think it was in the early 1600s," Mr. Abbott said, "when the actor Richard Burbage said to Shakespeare, 'I think we need a bigger theater.'"

As I said earlier, when I came to CBS in 1948, what was called news and public affairs was a service, not a business—a service that broadcasters were obligated by the Federal Communications Commission to provide on a more or less regular basis. And they did it more often than not on what was called a sustaining basis, devoid of commercials.

When a news or public-affairs broadcast did go commercial, it was often with institutional messages that eschewed the hard sell and dwelt on corporate responsibility. It was a time when the FCC ruled broadcasting with an iron fist, deciding what broadcasters could do and couldn't do and decreeing which time periods—early Sunday evening, for example—had to be devoted to public affairs or children. Network news operations were the price we paid for use of the public airwaves; they were hardly money makers—loss leaders were more like it. So much so that even Murrow had to enter the entertainment arena with *Person to Person* to make a fraction of what Rather, Brokaw, Jennings, and even I make today.

What turned the tide was the enormous profit *60 Minutes* made before television got split into so many channels. *60 Minutes* proved that television news, done with flair, can be worthwhile and profitable at the same time, in fact, very profitable. In that regard, no one honestly believes that the heads of the networks woke up one morning and said to themselves, "You know, I don't think we are doing enough to inform the American people." What they woke up and said to themselves was, "Can you believe the money that *60 Minutes* makes?"

My biggest surprise in fifty-plus years at CBS was the day somebody came to me and told me that we were in the top ten. This whole bit about moving up into the top ten was a new country and a foreign language. All of a sudden, one day we were number one— four times, once in the '70s, once in the '80s, and twice in the '90s we were the number-one broadcast in America. And this was against *M*A*S*H* and *Cheers* and *Roseanne*. We are the only news show that has ever been in the top ten, and more than that, the only *day-*

time show that was ever in the top ten. After all, in the summer, we're on in daylight.

In 1990, when we were in a nip-and-tuck battle with *Cheers*, I was fortunate enough to be inducted into the Television Academy's Hall of Fame, along with three of the broadcasters I always considered to be legends in this business: Roone Arledge, who was for many years president of ABC News; Joan Ganz Cooney, the creator and guiding light of the Children's Television Workshop; and Barbara Walters. On the flight back to New York from that ceremony in Hollywood, Mike Wallace and I had just settled down, and the plane was ready to take off when Mike got up to get something from the compartment over his seat, and collapsed. Actually, he didn't collapse; he went down like a tree in a forest and lay there in the aisle of the plane, motionless. I am reluctant to tell you what I thought as I saw him lying there, but Mike loves the story and doesn't mind my repeating it. All I could think was, "Oh, shit, he's dead. Now we're never going to catch *Cheers*!" Am I competitive? Perish the thought. Happily, Mike turned out to be fine, but his doctors recommended a pacemaker. As everyone in the world knows, it didn't slow him down. And who won that year, us or *Cheers*? Neither. *The Cosby Show* and *Roseanne* tied for number one

Our twenty-two consecutive years in the top ten is a record we're proud of, and a record the network is more than proud of. For a while we were the single most profitable hour in the history of television, so it's our bottom line everybody's trying to clone, not necessarily the broadcast. A few years ago, Ed Bradley launched a new CBS News program called *Street Stories*, which focused on gritty, urban pieces. The morning after Ed's first show, he got a call from Larry Tisch. My *60 Minutes* colleague was expecting congratulations or criticism, some assessment of how he had handled himself, but that's not what he got from the other end of the line. "Ed," Tisch said, "I think we have a gold mine." That's it, not a word about whether the program was good, bad, or indifferent. Just, "Ed, I think we have a gold mine."

In TV-speak, a "gold mine" is a broadcast in which commercial spots sell for a fortune. The determination of how much to charge for a spot is made during what television calls "sweeps weeks," which is complete and utter lunacy. The networks load up their schedules with what they hope will be ratings blockbusters, then try to convince themselves and their advertisers—not to mention TV columnists—that the phony baloney is a legitimate gauge of how many people are watching when it's *not* sweeps week. The truth is, it's not a legitimate gauge of anything. The network executives know it. The sponsors, whose ad rates are set by this idiotic practice, know it. And yet no one comes up with a way to get rid of it.

One thing is certain: "Sweeps week" generally doesn't make for elevated television. Consider ABC's big-ratings exclusive during a sweeps week in 1998. Cambodia's strongman Pol Pot coming out of the jungle? No. Ellen DeGeneres coming out of the closet. And I'd venture a guess that ABC couldn't have cared less if she'd come out of the closet or stayed in the closet as long as she did it during a sweeps week. By the way, that's no rap on ABC: The same thing would have happened had Ellen DeGeneres been on CBS or NBC.

Ratings, for better and for worse, are the way television keeps score. I have never understood why, to newspaper reporters and columnists, *ratings* is a dirty word and *circulation* is a clean one or why *commercials* is a dirty word and *advertising* is a clean one. Newspapers run commercials on every page, but they call it advertising, and it took Katharine Graham, the longtime chairman of The Washington Post Company, to bring it all into sharp focus. At Ben Bradlee's seventi-

eth-birthday party, Kay told the assembled guests, "Everybody thinks
The Washington Post is all about Woodward and Bernstein. Well, let
me tell you, there's a lot of Woodward & Lothrop in there, too."
(Woodward & Lothrop was a prominent department-store chain in
the Washington area.)

Further, while reporters don't like to be reminded of it, the fact is
that, with a few exceptions, the size of tomorrow morning's newspaper is determined by the amount of advertising space sold, not by the
amount of news that has happened.

Newspaper reporters frequently look askance at television's tendency to "tease" upcoming stories, to get people into the tent. Newspapers do the same thing, only they call their teases "headlines."
Our friends in print also get annoyed at the salaries on-air journalists
get. When Barbara Walters became the first broadcast journalist to
crack the $1-million-a-year ceiling, the news was greeted with front-
page headlines and a great hue and cry throughout print journalism.

"What's wrong with it?" I asked the huers and criers.

"What's wrong with it? What's wrong with it?" they sputtered.
"This is journalism, not show biz." I could not help noticing how we
are "journalists" when they are appalled at what we earn and "per-
formers" when they write about what we do.

Frequently, newspaper people hold our feet to the fire for trans-
gressions they themselves are guilty of. Back in the '60s, when Alan
Shepard was about to make the first of the Mercury spaceflights, I
videotaped in advance some scenes of the engineers at Mercury
control doing exactly what they would be doing during the flight,
when our cameras would be barred from mission control. I ran the
scenes during the flight as pictures Walter Cronkite could talk over
as he described what was going on at mission control. Jack Gould,
The New York Times's TV critic, thought us remiss in not labeling
the pictures a simulation.

He was right, and I told him so. But I also referred him to a page one picture in his own newspaper of the Soviet Union's U.N. ambassador, Andrei Vishinsky, and his American counterpart, Warren Austin. "Jack," I said to him, "the caption says it's a picture of Vishinsky and Austin discussing the Berlin situation. You and I know that's a picture of Vishinsky and Austin *posing* for a New York Times photographer *before* the discussions began. Why wasn't that labeled a simulation?" He conceded that I had a point, but as Ed Murrow used to say, conceding "you have a point" is the best way to end an argument and it really concedes nothing.

Can you imagine how *The New York Times* would hyperventilate, for example, if 60 Minutes became so beholden to its sponsors that it allowed them to use quotes from the newsmen and newswomen who appear on our broadcasts to endorse products being advertised on the broadcast?

Yet *The New York Times* that sits in judgment of and looks down on—when they're not looking askance at—television allows its "sponsors" to do just that: use quotes from New York Times reporters to endorse products advertised in the *Times.* Or, to put it another way, they allow their own reporters' news stories to be excerpted—in ways no New York Times editor would countenance—to sell products in ads that run in *The New York Times.*

Take just one day's output. On a recent Wednesday, I examined the ads in *The New York Times's* arts pages, and this is what I found:

> "Wonderfully witty! Erotically charged!"
> —*The New York Times*

> "Marvelous!"
> —*The New York Times*

"Far and away the best musical."
—*The New York Times*

"Jumps and jives with pulsating energy."
—*The New York Times*

"Filled with songs of great beauty and evocative power."
—*The New York Times*

"Superior entertainment."
—*The New York Times*

"A rich, evocative rousing show."
—*The New York Times*

"Brilliant, exuberant and infectious."
—*The New York Times*

Is it a capital crime against journalism to sell advertisers space to run quotes that originally ran as news copy in your own newspaper? Good God, no. It's more a misdemeanor, just as are a lot of the things that *The New York Times* criticizes television stations for, including the things that appear on the eight television stations that the New York Times Company owns and operates (in Memphis, Tennessee; Wilkes-Barre/Scranton, Pennsylvania; Moline, Illinois; Fort Smith, Arkansas; Oklahoma City, Oklahoma; Des Moines, Iowa; Norfolk, Virgina, and Huntsville, Alabama). *They* can say what they want about *us*, but in those cities, *they* are *us*.

Good God, *The New York Times* can be annoying when it gets into its holier-than-thou mode. However, the mornings the *Times* lets Maureen Dowd out of the barn to canter across my breakfast table I can forgive them anything—anything but putting Russell Baker out to pasture.

And I have to admire *The New York Times* for letting me say, in an article they ran on their op-ed page:

> One of the things that *The New York Times*, among other newspapers, hardly ever tells its readers is…that it has dealt itself into the TV game to make money just as surely as Laurence Tisch, Capital Cities [the owner of ABC at the time], and General Electric have.
>
> In fact, no one tells you, unless you go digging for it, that one-quarter of the television stations in this country are now in the hands of newspapers or newspaper chains. What an opportunity for newspapers—the conscience of TV—to exert a real influence on what goes out over the airwaves, instead of just moaning about it….
>
> I've heard [these publisher-broadcasters], when they're wearing their publisher's hat or editor's hat, raise concerns about all kinds of issues threatening newspapers. Have they ever, when wearing their broadcaster's hat, even attended a National Association of Broadcasters meeting, let alone raised the issues of the need for more network news on TV or the lack of decent children's shows or the explosion of game shows? After all, TV is their business just as much as it is CBS's and NBC's and ABC's.
>
> What local station owners want and don't want often sets the tone for television. Without the local stations behind them, the networks don't stand much of a chance of changing the face of TV. Publishers apparently are not very proud of being station owners because they hardly mention it in their newspapers. But let's face it: That's what they are—the customers for the game shows and soap operas and cartoons.

How long are they going to sup at television's table without ever opening their mouths except to feed themselves?

One of the terms that newspapers love to level at broadcasters is "checkbook journalism." This is also a maddening double standard. CBS News got roundly criticized by *The New York Times* and others in 1984 when we purchased thirty-eight hours of taped interviews with former President Richard Nixon. To our critics, there were two issues—first, that we were practicing "checkbook journalism" by paying for the tapes and second, that a Nixon associate named Frank Gannon appeared on the tape with him as an interlocutor, prodding the former president for more information.

The first issue is nonsense. Print journalism pays for book excerpts and other writings by political figures all the time. In a letter to *The New York Times* on March 14 that year, I mentioned its own purchase of the rights to something Winston Churchill wrote—and even the *Times's* acquisition of serial rights to an earlier Nixon memoir. More recently, *Newsweek* published an excerpt of a book by George Stephanopoulos, the former top aide to President Clinton. The truth is that reputable newspapers and reputable news broadcasts pay for interviews all the time, not in cash but in something more valuable—newspaper space and airtime for an author to plug a book or a movie star to plug a movie or a politician to plug a pet cause. Who in his right mind sits down to be interviewed without getting something in return? And let's face it, "getting something in return" is the equivalent of "getting paid." And we all willingly go along with it, because if we don't, 20/20 will, and if *The New York Times* won't, *The Washington Post* will. Is there something wrong with it? No! Just stop all this "holier than thou" jazz that we don't pay for interviews because everybody does, all the time.

The second issue: Gannon was not a newsman and didn't pretend to be, so the tape we bought was not a journalistic interview. It was an effort to get from Nixon some things he'd never said before publicly, or quite so frankly. We made sure our viewers knew exactly what the tape was and what it was not, and that Gannon was not a reporter, but someone close to Nixon who got him to say more than anyone else had up to that point. We also weren't restricted to any portion of the thirty-eight hours. It was our choice to select from that tape anything we wanted to.

On another tack, both of us—print and broadcasting—sometimes have a tendency to be too big for our britches. Whether in print or over the airwaves, journalists have enormous power—the power to uplift, the power to degrade, the power to shield, and the power to attack. Too often, we take the low road, degrading and attacking with little thought about the consequences of our actions. We're also cowards about it some of the time. Instead of attacking in our own voice, which might expose us to ridicule or even retribution, we often hide behind a wall called the unattributed quote.

You've read it and heard it a million times:

"Informed sources said Politician X was spotted in a midtown bar with a woman who was not his wife";

"An official close to the commissioner said NFL Player Y was under investigation for possible violation of the league's drug regulations";

"A top studio executive said Actress Z has a 'temperament' problem, which is costing her roles and money."

To be sure, promising anonymity to sources is sometimes the price a reporter must pay to get critical information that belongs in the public domain. When Neil Sheehan broke the Pentagon Papers story for *The New York Times*, he did not reveal that he had obtained them from Daniel Ellsberg. Bob Woodward and Carl Bernstein would never have exposed the Watergate scandal if they had had to rely entirely on people willing to speak on the record.

We've used anonymous sources at *60 Minutes* as well, but I wish we hadn't and we're getting better about it. For example, in 1999, we did a story on police brutality and we had a sentence in the script that said: "According to credible evidence, one in three cops have been guilty of brutalizing their families." Credible evidence? What do you mean, credible evidence? I'm a guy at home and I hear that and I say, who says it's credible evidence? No way we broadcast that line. Finally, we were able to nail it down when a former police chief in Portland, Oregon, told us, "Those are the figures we came up with." Now we had a source and could go with the story.

Unattributed quotes should be used sparingly—and hardly ever when they are used to attack an individual. If you're going to publish or broadcast anything insulting or demeaning that one person says about another, that's put up or shut up time. If you want to use us to say something uncomplimentary about someone, you damn well better put a name and a face to the quote. *What* informed source? *Which* official of the league? *Who* said that about the actress? If they can't answer, count us out.

Anyone under attack ought to know who is doing the attacking. It's not only *fair* journalism, it's *good* journalism.

But there's more to this quote business than attribution. Just because a quote is accurately recorded and presented in a newspaper or on a news broadcast doesn't mean it is the truth. Attributed quotes can be as wrongheaded and damaging as unattributed quotes, and so, more and more, I think, journalism needs to be about truth as well as accuracy.

News and truth are not always the same thing. That's because the truth isn't always knowable. A good example is what Bill Moyers, back in 1970, discovered at Kent State right after the tragic incident in which National Guard troops fired on a crowd of students and killed four of them. Moyers talked to just about everybody in town. Finally, he talked to the editor of the local paper and told him, "Everybody I talked to gave me a different story. Who is telling the truth?" And the editor, to his everlasting credit, said: "They all are."

Truth can be the story behind the story, the forces that animate and motivate individuals and institutions, the raw stuff that gets at the ways people behave and conduct their lives. As Moyers learned at Kent State, truth and accuracy mean different things to different people. The only thing I ask of a reporter is: "Have you ever knowingly done violence to what you believe to be the truth? And do you believe the story you're reporting is an honest and accurate representation of what the viewer or listener or reader thinks it is?" If a reporter can answer those two questions to my satisfaction, that, in essence, is all I need to know.

As fragmented as my Jewish education was, I find myself from time to time recalling the sage pronouncement of Hillel, who said, in essence, that the golden rule was "the law" and that everything else was "commentary." Extended to journalism it could read — indeed, should read — "To never knowingly do violence to the truth is the law and everything else is commentary." Additionally, even though the phrase "the right to know" does not appear in the Constitution, I think it is a concept to which reporters should pay attention but should not claim that it justifies trampling on other people's right to be left alone if they so choose. If the public does have an appetite "to know" (if not a right "to know"), that does not translate into an obligation to publish or broadcast anything and everything that catches a reporter's eye.

And the best way to ensure that we go on having a right to

publish and broadcast is to guard against self-indulgence. Self-indulgence by the press is no more attractive than any other kind of self-indulgence, and is probably a lot worse. The question frequently asked of us—"Who died and left you in charge?"—is not always an invalid one.

That doesn't mean that citizens should be allowed to hide their malfeasance. Good journalism is confrontational by definition: You want information that other people would prefer not be made public. In that regard, my wife, Marilyn, who has worked in both print and television, has said on many occasions, "Breaking eggs isn't pretty, but it's an inevitable part of strong reporting. The problem in television, and it's unavoidable, is that when television breaks eggs, the whole world is watching; when a print reporter breaks eggs, no one sees him do it." To which I have to add, one of the things that neither print nor television should do is make omelets out of law-abiding citizens.

Exercising our freedom to publish or broadcast should further the cause of something worthwhile. The best way to ensure our continuing the freedom to publish and broadcast is to guard against self-indulgence, a trait as unattractive and undesirable in the press as anywhere else in our society.

Of course, we should hold politicians to account, because the record of dissembling—or fudging the truth—is rich and detailed. FDR said he'd balance the budget. Ronald Reagan said he'd cut the deficit. Lyndon Johnson said he wouldn't bomb Hanoi. If you're of a certain age, you probably remember the old joke. "They told me if I voted for Barry Goldwater, we'd end up bombing North Vietnam, and they were right. I voted for Goldwater and we ended up bombing North Vietnam."

But poking into the sex lives of public officials—or anybody else, for that matter? That's where a line should be drawn. In this century, journalists knew a lot about the private affairs of public officials that never saw the light of day. How much of Franklin Roosevelt's other life with Lucy Mercer did Walter Lippmann keep to himself? What did Ben Bradlee know about his pal, Jack Kennedy? It may have been off-limits once, but not anymore. If you think that's going to change, you're kidding yourself.

When Bill Clinton raised his hand and swore to preserve, protect, and defend the Constitution of the United States, he didn't swear to preserve, protect, and defend his marriage. Nowhere in the Constitution does it say a thing about extramarital relationships.

What I draw the line at is showing people's grief. I don't care about nudity and I don't care about blood and gore if it's pertinent to the story, but nobody has the right to televise moments of private sorrow. It's obscene to tape a mother watching the police drag a lake for her kid.

The week John F. Kennedy Jr. was killed in a plane crash was a hideous display of excess. I was particularly revolted that the *New York Post* ran a picture of Carolyn Bessette Kennedy's father coming out of their apartment carrying her belongings, including a little teddy bear. Nobody has a right to look at that; it's nothing but voyeurism. That man had a right to go into that apartment to find mementos of his daughter without a photographer tracking his every move.

The death of John Kennedy Jr. was a classic example of what happens when news doubles as entertainment. First, the cable news networks go to the story full-time. Then the news bosses at the Big Three networks see all the coverage and figure that they want a piece of the action, too. In a flash, everyone's on the air nonstop, way out of proportion to the story's worth.

Never have I seen a story played out of proportion to its worth than the media circus that grew up around Elian Gonzalez in the winter and spring of 1999–2000. I can understand why the O. J.

Simpson case commanded nonstop coverage, and I can understand why everyone was transfixed by the sudden death of Princess Diana, but that this Cuban child became a political football in an election year was excess piled on excess. Think about it: Giving Elian Gonzalez back to Cuba caused a bigger ruckus in the United States than giving the Panama Canal back to Panama.

Cover the news? Absolutely. But please don't stay on the air and fill time and tell us that, in effect, you can't get off the air.

However, I have to admit that the cable news networks did themselves proud during the time the presidential election results of 2000 were in doubt in Florida. Their coverage was authoritative, knowledgeable, and as professional as I ever remember any news team in television handling a complex and continuing story that was not fundamentally visual in nature. So much for those who say television is too involved with pictures and not involved enough in substance. CNN, MSNBC, and Fox were up to their ears in substance, and I couldn't help but sit there and marvel at how well they handled it.

What happened after November 7 was the exception to the rule. The rule is that the twenty-four-hour news stations usually go all-out when they can play to much the same audience that the supermarket checkout-counter magazines appeal to with stories like JonBenet Ramsey, Princess Di, and O. J. Simpson. Those kinds of stories are manna from heaven for a cable news network whose audience shrinks on normal news days.

Steve Brill, of the magazine *Brill's Content*, and I once crossed swords over that issue on the *Today* show back in 1995. Brill, the media entrepreneur who founded Court TV, had cameras in the courtroom during the O. J. trial. He maintained that his cameras had a First Amendment right to be there. And I said, okay, Steve, stop right there. Let's assume the judge, Lance Ito, comes to you and says, Mr. Brill, of course you have a First Amendment right to put your camera in my courtroom; far be it for me to say otherwise. But you don't have a right to televise commercials from my courtroom. If he said that to you, Steve, I asked him, would you stay or would you go?

Brill said that what I was suggesting was unconstitutional and that the judge cannot impose such rules.

Yes he can, I replied. It's his courtroom. So tell me, do you still want to broadcast from Ito's courtroom if you can't make money doing it? No one's screwing around with the First Amendment if you don't sell commercials. Here's how I put it later, in a letter to Floyd Abrams, one of America's best-known First Amendment attorneys and at the time, Court TV's lawyer: "No one, least of all me, is saying 'close the courtroom.' What I'm saying is that, as much as television likes to claim it is no different from the written press, it is. Is it unreasonable to think, had the authors of the First Amendment had the prescience to see television coming—television with its capability to shape and mold society beyond anything the written press is or was capable of—that they might have dealt with it separately from 'the press'?"

Did we at 60 Minutes think that covering the O. J. Simpson story was beneath us? No. The fact was that after everyone else had picked it over all week long, there was nothing that we could report that everybody didn't already know. But when a woman who would have voted guilty was removed from the jury, that we thought was a 60 Minutes story, and we told it.

Not following the herd has been a staple of 60 Minutes reporting. In fact, that's—one of the things that has made us so successful. People watch us because we're going to tell them stories that they haven't heard everywhere else. The only way to rise above the pack is not to be part of it.

CHAPTER FOURTEEN

The Televised Future

In many respects, this is a golden age of news and information. There are fewer daily newspapers than there were a generation ago as well as a generation before that, but the ones that remain probably are better and people have access to more of them through the magic of the Internet—the most extraordinary tool for dispensing information in all of human history.

Television news? It's everywhere. There was a time, before Roone Arledge made ABC a full player, and frequently a better player, in the network news game when viewers had to watch Walter Cronkite on CBS, or Chet Huntley and David Brinkley on NBC, to know what was happening in the world. Now, with the cable news networks, there is news all over the dial at any time of the day or night. The news divisions of ABC, NBC, and CBS have followed suit by feeding their local stations news they once kept exclusively for their own evening newscasts but are now forced to feed their affiliates to keep them competitive with the all-news stations.

My network was asleep at the switch in not noticing that over-the-air news broadcasting was becoming obsolete before its eyes (and ears) and that *cablevision* was a better business for news to be in than *television*. One CBS executive told me not to worry about CNN, ESPN, and the other cable channels. "They're boutiques; we're a department store," he said.

Well, the department stores are gone and boutiques are revolutionizing retailing in America.

It's true that CNN and the other cable networks show little restraint when they go nonstop on stories that didn't deserve the attention they give them. But it's also true that they are on the spot and can get information to the audience as the news happens or almost as it happens. And over the last few years, the Internet has compounded the competitive pressure in ways no one could have anticipated. Every news organization of any size now has its own Web site, and many of them have gone round the clock in their reporting and delivery of the news.

A survey conducted by the highly respected Pew Research Center in the summer of 2000 suggests the dimensions of the problem for the traditional TV networks. Fewer and fewer people feel the need to keep up with the news. And among those who do, network news is a diminishing force in their lives. Pew said that newspaper circulation and cable audiences were relatively flat, but the number of people who say they regularly watch one of the Big Three nightly news shows had slipped from 38 percent to 30 percent in just two years.

Having been present at the creation of the half-hour evening news as a staple of early-evening television, I fear that in its present form it has become an anachronism in need of a serious overhaul.

What to do? The three networks could tinker with their format and become more like 60 *Minutes*, 20/20, and *Frontline*. They could try to get beyond the headline service and provide more context, depth, and interpretation to their newscasts so viewers experience in fresh ways what they may already know. They could do this in many ways, from news features to interviews. One of the best ideas I ever heard for reconfiguring the evening news came from Andrew Heyward, the current president of CBS News. Heyward tried to lure Diane Sawyer back to CBS, and one of the things he wanted to have her do was to preside over a segment in the middle of the evening news modeled after Ted Koppel's *Nightline*. Diane certainly has the talent and presence to have carried it off, but she decided to stay put and help rescue *Good Morning America* for ABC.

In any event, the overhaul I envision would go well beyond small changes. Try this for a radical proposal: If NBC, ABC, and CBS can "pool" a White House news conference or pool a presidential debate, why can't they also pool an early evening newscast or even the coverage of breaking news stories? What I am proposing is a single newscast that would run simultaneously each evening on ABC, NBC, and CBS as a joint production of the news divisions of those three networks.

Because the individual ratings and share of audience of the Jennings News, the Brokaw News, and the Rather News frequently add up to more than a 20 rating and more than a 40-percent share of the audience—not far off, incidentally, the numbers that accrue to shows like *Survivor* and *Who Wants to Be a Millionaire*—combining them would be a ratings blockbuster and would attract the kind of advertising revenue that would go a long way toward giving the big three news divisions a bigger bang for their bucks.

The simple truth right now is that if you locked me in a room for a year and told me I could watch nothing but Dan Rather, and you locked somebody else in a room and told him he could watch nothing but Tom Brokaw, and you locked a third viewer in a room and told her she could watch nothing but Peter Jennings, at the end of the year, I dare say, all three of us would be more or less equally informed. None of us, I would bet, would know anything the other two didn't know.

Because television news is as expensive as it is repetitious, too much time is spent by news executives at the hopeless task of figuring out how to stay within budget and not enough time at the rewarding task of figuring out how to cover the news. Combine the three evening newscasts and you would save money that could be put into broadcasts like *60 Minutes*, *60 Minutes II*, *Nightline*, *Meet the Press*, *Face the Nation*, and a lot of single-subject one-hour broadcasts.

The editorial board that would run the combined broadcast would be the presidents of the news divisions of CBS, NBC, and ABC. And their three anchormen would play major roles in this radically new newscast. For example, Brokaw, Jennings, and Rather would each take turns—one week presiding over the newscast, two weeks out in the field reporting for the newscast. The result for them personally would be that they would become newsmen again, not merely "presenters" of the news.

Crazy? Maybe, but no crazier than laying out millions and millions of dollars each year to say more or less the same thing three times every night.

If that's too radical, we at least could at least steal a page from our brothers and sisters in print. The Associated Press, Reuters, Agence France Presse and other so-called wire services exist because their member newspapers cannot afford to post their own reporters in all the places that make news, which is everywhere. The wires and news services started more recently by the nation's biggest papers—*The New York Times, The Washington Post*, the *Los Angeles Times*, the Knight-Ridder chain and the *Chicago Tribune*—satisfy the appetites of smaller papers by feeding them a steady diet of national and international news.

We could do the same thing: Instead of AP, let's call it AT—Associated Television. Each network doesn't need its own man or woman on every river that overflows its banks or on every border where there's a skirmish or in every town battening down for the big hurricane. If the same competent AT reporter showed up on Rather, Brokaw, and Jennings, or better yet, on the combined broadcast I propose, who would know which network he was with—more to the point, who would care?

The AT could even file an A wire and a B wire. Via satellite, the A wire could feed the newsrooms of the three networks—and CNN and Fox News if they wanted to sign up—a finished, edited story complete with the service's reporter. On the B wire, any of the AT subscribers could request unedited footage fed via satellite to edit any way they saw fit.

Other options should be considered as well. For instance, a network could share the cost of one news team—reporter, producer, cameraman—at its key affiliates, although we'd select the team. The network would get first call on the team when a big story breaks, and the local station would have an extra unit for regular assignment.

If one of the key issues is money, and it always is, the idea is to stop spending it mindlessly.

Doesn't the idea of pooling a newscast raise some questions? First, wouldn't it be an anti-trust violation for three networks to gang up on the rest of the industry? If so, I think this could be solved by allowing anyone who wants to pay his way to become part of the consortium. The other question is, wouldn't such an arrangement stifle competition? I don't think so. I think what drives reporters and their editors to get stories is not the competition but their own desire to show their bosses and the world how good they are—at least, that's what has driven me and *60 Minutes* to the top of the heap of news broadcasting, with little or nothing else competing with us.

You could say the same about *The New York Times*. They're good because they're good, not because they have competition in New York, because they don't, perhaps with the exception of the *Wall Street Journal* when it comes to business news. Think about it: In general, the *Times* became even better after its only real local competition, the *New York Herald Tribune*, folded.

Never was there an event that illustrated better what I am proposing than the 2000 election night broadcast. Each anchor—Rather, Brokaw, and Jennings—sitting in front of ostensibly the same graphic displays of the states with the same numbers popping on at precisely the same time, were clones of each other. Having the three of them doing the very same thing, including being fed the same information from the same source (some of it wrong and correcting it at the same time) made it more apparent than ever that the public would have been just as well served if the three networks had gotten together and pooled one broadcast. They could have saved a bundle that could have been better spent than playing "follow the leader" and singing "Anything you can do I can do better." The plain fact is that anything one did wasn't better—not worse, but certainly not better.

The money they wasted "showing off" on election night would have paid for better and more complete coverage of things we give short shrift to now. The trick will be to convince the powers that be not to cut the news budget if and when they can agree on a way to pool the three networks' evening newscasts and breaking news specials, but to use the savings to provide the public with more and better-produced newsmagazines and hour-long specials that are—when done with flair and verve and good writing—a joy to behold. When they're cobbled together as substitutes for failed sitcoms, they look it.

Anyone who thinks one network's news division is head and shoulders over anyone else's is kidding himself. So is anyone who takes seriously boasts like the one recently made by WCBS-TV in New York that it has "better sources." It doesn't. No one has. And anyone who thinks that what I am proposing would be an easy sell is also kidding himself. Do I think it will fly? That they'll buy it? My guess is that they'll tell me what two CBS News presidents told me over thirty-three years ago when I proposed doing a weekly prime-time newsmagazine called *60 Minutes*: "It's a lousy idea"—so "lousy" that for a time in recent years it looked like a network's whole schedule would consist of nothing but newsmagazines. That, right there, is proof of my contention that, with the exception of *60 Minutes* (the broadcast that started what became a craze), behind every television newsmagazine there's a failed sitcom. It was during that blizzard of newsmagazines that the networks lost sight of something they used to know: that quantity is no substitute for quality. That's why so many shows fail the first test, which is to get the chemistry, which produces the quality, right? Whether in news or entertainment, successful broadcasts are made not by theme songs, not by stage sets, not by graphics, but by people who work well together.

It's no secret that what appeals to the public are pairings like George and Gracie, Desi and Lucy, Katie and Matt, Diane and Charlie. After ABC made a mistake putting together Barbara Walters and Harry Reasoner, which didn't work, and CBS made a mistake putting together Dan Rather and Connie Chung, which didn't work either, I would have thought that, in devising *The Early Show*, CBS would have given more thought to the *who* than to the *where*. Bryant Gumbel and Jane Clayson may yet make it, but laying out $30 million to build them a studio is like laying out $30 million for a picture frame before you've even found the picture to put in it.

But let's face it: CBS has *never* been able to put together a winning morning news program. They tried it with Walter Cronkite, Mike Wallace, Diane Sawyer, and Charles Kuralt, among others, and it never made it. Nothing sticks out for me more than what Cronkite's producer, a man named Paul Levitan, told the staff when we all came to look at a pilot he had made of a morning news show with Walter in the 1950s. He said, "The trouble with this broadcast is that it doesn't have any semblance." Because Levitan was best known around CBS for murdering the English language, something he did long before anyone had heard of George W. Bush, everyone guffawed — except me. I said to myself, "You know, he's right, the problem with this broadcast is that it doesn't have any semblance."

But that was not Levitan's finest moment. His finest moment in murdering the English language was in 1953, when I questioned him

at Eisenhower's first inaugural about why he was bringing so many
technicians from New York to Washington. I asked him, "Paul, what
are we going to do with all these guys?" He told me, believe it or not,
"We want everyone we can get. We don't want to lose the dike for
want of an extra finger." Try to top that!

But even as news and information becomes more and more available, I worry about the role we journalists have assumed, especially
in politics. We are the masters of ceremonies of their conventions,
we participate in their debates, we take it upon ourselves to call their
elections, and we make money selling them commercial time. It all
goes back to the first Kennedy-Nixon debate—one of the historic
broadcasts I got to produce and direct. If the number-one qualification to hold office in the greatest democracy the world has ever
known has become the ability to raise money, it winged off that
night in 1960 when politicians saw for the first time how valuable television exposure was to campaigning for office, and television and
politicians realized for the first time how much they had to offer
each other.

It's only in hindsight that I now realize that the night of the first
televised presidential debate was the night television and politics
became engaged and the marriage that followed was a disaster for
"free elections." What we now have in their place are "expensive
elections." Simply put, they married us for love and we married
them for money.

When the Founding Fathers decreed that an officeholder in this
wonderful new democracy should be freely elected, who knew that
two hundred years hence a gadget called television that could pick
pictures out of the air would make it impossible for anyone to be
"freely" elected and that the principal qualification for holding office

would be an ability to raise cash *and* who can do that without having a hand in some lobbyist's pocket and his hand in yours?

Money can bury a political opponent—and it can bury democracy in the process. It cost the Democratic National Committee $2.2 million to elect Franklin Delano Roosevelt president in 1932. That's close to $26 million in today's dollars, about what it costs in media buys on television for a couple of candidates to fight it out for a seat in the U.S. Senate. And it's getting worse with every cycle. Spending on the New York Senate race in 2000 between Hillary Rodham Clinton and Rick Lazio approached $100 million, and the presidential contest between Al Gore and George W. Bush, on television alone, was off the charts, at one billion dollars, more or less.

One thought that's occurred to me to clean up the mess is to make it illegal for any corporation that does business with the government to make contributions to political candidates. Yes, I know, that would bump up against the First Amendment, but I can't believe that the Founding Fathers had anything like this in mind when they devised the First Amendment. And I also can't believe that everybody doesn't know that a lot of that money comes from people who *want* "something in return"—and worse than that, are going to *get* "something in return."

So what to do? Giving officeholders free time on television is a lousy idea and would never fly; similarly, newspapers would never give politicians free advertising space. No, what I'd do is give airtime on a newscast when they do something newsworthy and not sell them time to toot their own horns. That's right, if I were king, I'd rule out paid political advertising on television. Political advertising has a greater impact on how people vote than what newspapers write and what we broadcast. Think about it: What you have is a guy making a one-sided speech in your living room, coached by his so-called media adviser. I see these things and I wonder whether I'm voting for a candidate or a copywriter.

First Amendment again? Yeah, probably, but maybe we could insist on a warning, like the one on cigarette packs: "Caution: Watching a paid political commercial could be injurious to your mental health and an affront to simple truth."

There must be some way to skin that cat. People have enough trouble sorting out news from propaganda, so think about how tough it is when the news runs alongside someone with an agenda peddling you an alternate "truth." The First Amendment has never kept anyone from refusing to broadcast or print obscenities, and I contend that political commercials are often just that—obscenities—and should be banned for that reason alone.

Wouldn't the playing field be just as level if neither candidate spent a buck instead of both candidates shelling out money, someone else's money, like it's the U.S. Treasury? And if broadcasters can't make ends meet without peddling wall-to-wall hard political commercials, I propose they take up the slack peddling wall-to-wall hard liquor ads. It's legal, even though it's seldom done now. I say run them 'til the cows come home, even if they come home drunk. Let's face it, Jack Daniels and Jim Beam, in my eyes, did a hell of a lot less harm to America than Dick Morris.

Presidential debates are supposed to give us a chance to see the two combatants—sometimes three combatants—in the same ring, but there is, as a general rule, more waltzing around than slugging it out.

It's hard to remember anything from those encounters, certainly anything of substance, even on the rare occasions when substance is aired. Some pundit will always recall that what Kennedy and Nixon said about Quemoy and Matsu was terribly important and maybe even memorable. To which, I always say: "Okay, which one said what and where in hell are Quemoy and Matsu?" Silence usually follows.

The only thing most of us remember about Kennedy-Nixon was Nixon's makeup. Gerald Ford and Jimmy Carter? Ford's gaffe about Poland. Reagan-Carter? Reagan taunting Carter, "There you go again." George Bush and Michael Dukakis? The latter's dispassionate response to a question by CNN's Bernard Shaw on how he would feel about the death penalty for someone convicted of raping and murdering his own wife. Lloyd Bentsen telling Dan Quayle, "I knew Jack Kennedy. And senator, you're no Jack Kennedy." Bush-Gore? There's nothing about those debates that anybody's going to be quoting years from now.

So what to do about it, to make a presidential debate more of what it should be—a heavyweight championship fight and not a *pas de deux* orchestrated by a journalist or group of journalists who have no business waltzing with the candidates? After all, there isn't one of those journalists who hasn't prepared himself or herself for his or her role in a debate without asking himself or herself what I can ask that will make me look smart but not partisan. Right, there's the rub: No one who isn't partisan should even be in a debate.

To give the spectacle more meaning, my pal, the late Theodore White (author of the *Making of the President* books) and I once proposed to the League of Women Voters—which was sponsoring debates then—that they manage it like a real debate. Each candidate would bring with him two top debaters from his party—a state governor or a member of the House or Senate. The two teams would then debate for one hour before a joint session of Congress, then spend another hour being queried by and otherwise taken over the coals by members of the opposing party, just as it's done during what is known as "Question Time" in Britain's parliament. This would have the added virtue of getting the ladies and gentlemen of the press out of the ring and into the gallery—covering the event, not participating in it.

And just as we need to get journalists out of the debates, we also need to get them out of the conventions. When did these things become the be-all and end-all of television reporting? Back in 1948, when I first got into television, what TV could do was pretty much confined to a studio except for the occasional side trip to a sporting event or a circus. We just weren't mobile enough to get around the way radio could. Radio could go anywhere and did. TV had big, heavy cameras and unwieldy cables, and TV was confined to events that happened within a walled enclosure or to predictable events like football games. We knew how long the game would take, when it would be played, what the field looked like, and where the goal line was.

Then came the epiphany. Hey, we can cover a political convention. We know where the rostrum is, we know where the podium will be, we know when they'll meet and how much time they plan to spend. Simple, just like covering a football game.

Thus was born the televised political convention, a bonanza for a fledgling industry trying to make an impact on the nation. But it may have been a bigger bonanza for politicians who can now seat the entire country at their conventions. And they don't even have to supply funny hats and noisemakers.

For more years than I care to remember, my job come convention time was to oversee the CBS floor reporters. In truth, my job wasn't much different from a circus ringmaster's. My responsibility was to make sure that what was happening in my ring was more exciting than what was happening in ABC's or NBC's. If one of our guys had to get into a contretemps with the mayor of Chicago or the governor of New York to keep my show moving, so be it.

Will it ever change? Here's a thought: Let's tell them to hold their conventions during the day and we'll cover them as we do other news events. If anything newsworthy happens, we'll put it on our evening newscasts. If it's something that needs more than five or ten minutes, we can schedule a special that night. You want to watch gavel to gavel, try one of the all-news stations or C-Span.

Or consider this: Suppose the two parties held their nominating conventions in the winter, in the middle of the television season. How much airtime do you think they would get? Today, the networks can manage preempting summer reruns. But preempting a new episode of a profitable show like *Frasier* or *ER* for a nominating convention in which the candidate has already been chosen by a primary? Not a chance. Schedule these extravaganzas in winter and see how fast television rethinks the entire enterprise.

In the real world, of course, the television types don't have the guts to tell the politicians they are not going to carry their conventions. What to do? I propose that we *give* them the airtime and tell them to produce their own television show. No longer would Rather, Jennings, Brokaw, Shaw, and Woodruff be the ringmasters of their circus. The Democrats could get Warren Beatty or Barbra Streisand or Steven Spielberg or Susan Sarandon to anchor. The Republicans could get Charlton Heston or Tom Selleck. We'd retire to the sidelines where we belong.

Has television gotten too big for its britches? I think so. Getting too big for your britches is how you trip over yourself, as we did on election night 2000. Isn't it time we all took a step back and examined who we are and what we are and if we couldn't have a bigger impact on what happens *in* our country and *to* our country if we came on a little more low-key than we do now. I don't think we are as bad as some people say we are, but at the same time, I don't think we're as good as we think we are. The trick for journalists, broadcast or print, is to take what they do seriously but not take themselves too seriously. Try it, you'll like it. It's worked wonders for me.

Epilogue

My judgment over the years has been pretty good, but it wasn't flaw-less. I'm the one Barbara Walters came to in the 1950s when she was a producer on the *Today* show and said she'd like to be a broadcaster. "Barbara," I said, "with your voice, no one is going to let you broad-cast."

I'm also the guy who told a kid named Marty Ehrlichman back in the early '60s, when he was working in the CBS film library for maybe $60 a week, to stop coming up with get-rich-quick schemes and pay more attention to his job. One day, he came to me and said, "I'm going to quit."

"Okay, Marty, now what?"

"I'm going to manage a singer."

"Oh, shit," I said. "What do you know about managing a singer? What singer?"

"Well, I saw her in a club. She's a Jewish girl with a big nose, but she can sing."

"Forget it, Marty," I said. "Get rid of her. Get rid of that girl."

That girl's name was Barbra Streisand and that kid who worked in the CBS film library for $60 a week got rich and famous ignoring my advice.

But, for the most part, I seemed to have guessed right more than I've guessed wrong. Maybe that's why I'm still around at age seventy-eight and Mike Wallace at eighty-three and why Senator Tom Daschle of South Dakota, when he toasted Al Neuharth, chairman of the Gannett Co. and founder of USA Today, at his retirement, told the assembled guests that Al had an impossible problem. He was "too old to work for a newspaper and too young to work for 60 Minutes."

It's true, of course. We have been around a long time, and as Bill Paley said on the occasion of our twentieth anniversary, "When 60 Minutes went on the air in 1968, I'm sure Don Hewitt didn't expect to be producing it twenty years later." In fact, not too long ago, someone at ABC or NBC—I can't recall which—said of Mike and me, "Hewitt and Wallace can't live forever." And we said, "You wanna bet?"

When you've been around as long as I have, you get a lot of awards. I'm not sure I deserve all of them, but I'm always happy to get any award, especially one that isn't posthumous. Also, when you've been around as long as I have, you get somewhat set in your ways. For example, I am computer illiterate and have no desire to be otherwise. There is nothing I need that I am not willing to go to a store to buy, although I am prepared for the possibility that before too long there may not be any stores (as we know them) or schools (as we know them) or hospitals (as we know them)—that anything we need, from a pair of socks to a college education to medical treatment, will come from a Web site.

Today it's said that the Internet is the new national and even global community. Maybe, maybe not. I sure don't feel comfortable saying it is. But perhaps I shouldn't judge, since I may be the only male I know who has never received or sent an e-mail.

I got to thinking the other day about what we all took for granted before the computer age and worked up a scenario in which a man comes home and tells his wife that he had heard about a great new gadget that worked without any connection to the Internet—no screen, no laptop, no mouse, no gigabytes. A guy named Alexander Graham Bell came up with it. He calls it a telephone, and all you'd have to do is punch in a bunch of numbers that would be listed in something called "a telephone book" and you could talk to anyone in the world—even in Chechnya, if you knew someone there and could find his or her number in the book. Dollars to donuts, his wife would tell him: Oh, God, you're so gullible, you believe anything anyone tells you.

Okay, you say. You don't go for Bell's telephone. Try this. I heard about a guy who has invented something called a "post office." There would be one in every town. If you wanted to write a letter to your mother, for thirty-four cents, a man would personally deliver the letter to her house.

How can anyone be as on top of the world as I am and not want to come to terms with the twenty-first century? Maybe, liking it "the way it was" gives me a perspective on the way it is, perhaps even the way it will be—and for reasons I can't explain the ability to transmit a little light through the tube every Sunday night.

I'd like to believe that providing a little light is what my life has been all about. What is it that adorns the masthead of Scripps Howard newspapers? "Give Light and the People Will Find Their Way." If that's not a credo for an honorable working life, I don't know what is.

A postscript: One morning, Darryl Kemp, who mans the front desk at 60 Minutes, greeted me with "Mr. Hewitt, when I grow up, I want to be just like you."

And I said, "That's funny. So do I!"

The 60 Minutes *Honor Roll*

There isn't enough space here to list each individual award *60 Minutes* and its correspondents, producer-reporters, and others affiliated with the broadcast have received. But here are the cumulative totals of three of the most prestigious awards at the time this book went to the printer.

Emmy Awards from the Academy of Television Arts and Sciences for news and documentary programs and individual achievements: 73

The Alfred I. DuPont-Columbia University Awards: 11

The University of Georgia Peabody Awards: 9

Index

Abbott, George, 225
ABC, 4, 50, 57, 74, 114–115, 158, 168, 228
ABC Close Up, 108
ABC News, 55, 120, 180, 210, 227, 242, 243, 244
and Philip Morris story, 193, 194, 195, 197, 210
Abell, Bess, 87–88
Abortion, 5, 6
Abrams, Floyd, 240
Academy of Television Arts and Sciences, 259
Accident mills, 146
Acme Newspictures, 45–46, 47
Adidas, 208
ADL. *See* Anti-Defamation League
Advertising, 143, 228, 229, 230–231, 244
political advertising, 250–251
See also Commercials
Affirmative action, 7

Agence France Presse, 245
Agnew, Spiro, 4
Agronsky, Martin, 87, 88–89
Al-Aqsa mosque, 169
Alexander, Shana, 137–138
Alfred I. DuPont-Columbia University Awards, 259
Amanpour, Christiane, 213, 219
American flag, 8
Amos 'n Andy, 54, 108
Anchormen, 3, 55, 76, 120, 254
and joint production by networks, 245
teams of, 70
Andrea Doria (luxury liner), 62–63
Andy Capp (comic strip), 138
Anglo-American relations, 31–32, 37
Anonymity, 234, 235
Anti-Defamation League (ADL), 170, 172, 174
Anti-Semitism, 17, 93

Anti-trust violations, 246
AP. *See* Associated Press
Apollo space program, 76
"Appalachian Spring," 114
Arabs, 216. *See also* Palestinians
Arad, Ron, 177
Arafat, Yasir, 156
Arledge, Roone, 180, 227, 242
Armstrong-Jones, Anthony, 59
Arnaz, Desi, 99
Arvold, Frances, 72, 73
Ashe, Arthur, 215
Associated Press (AP), 44, 45, 183, 245
Associated Television, 245–246
Assumptions, 146–147
Astor (Lady), 36
Attorneys general, state, 203
Aubrey, Jim, 95, 98
Audience share, 244
Austin, Warren, 230
Awards, 4, 54, 218, 256, 259

Baird, Petey, 132
Baker, Russell, 231
Ball, Lucile, 51, 99, 108, 115
B&W. *See* Brown & Williamson
    Tobacco Company
Barr, Bob, 188
Basketball, 15, 208
Battle of Britain, 31
Beatty, Warren, 254
Bendick, Bob, 46–47
Bennett, Bill, 220
Bennett, Bob, 186–187, 220
Bentsen, Lloyd, 252
Berger, Marilyn, 15–16, 132, 147–149,
    157, 184, 237
Bergman, Ingrid, 120
Bergman, Lowell, 192, 193–194, 195

accused of lying, 207–209
    and *The Insider* film, 204–206
Berle, Milton, 47
Bernstein, Carl, 235
Better Government Association of
    Chicago, 139
Bias, 5
Bigart, Homer, 24, 26
Black Americans, 8, 17–18, 216
Bloom, Arthur, 182, 214
Blue sheets, 212
Bosnia, 183
Botha, P. W., 153
Boyer, Charles, 111
Bradlee, Ben, 168, 228, 238
Bradley, Ed, 2, 29–30, 150–151,
    153–156, 157, 180, 183, 185, 213,
    227
Bradshaw, Brad, 171
Braille, 53
Brenner, Marie, 204, 207
Brill, Steve, 239–240
Brinkley, David, 70, 89. *See also*
    Huntley-Brinkley Report
British-American Tobacco, 201
British Parliament, 252
Brokaw, Tom, 33, 244, 245
Brooke, Ed, 112
Brown & Williamson (B&W)
    Tobacco Company, 192–204,
    206, 207
additives used by, 199, 201
Brunvand, Jan Harold, 153
Brynner, Yul, 48
Buchanan, Pat, 5
Buchwald, Art, 216
Burbage, Richard, 225
Burdett, Winston, 52, 61
Burke, David, 171, 180
Burlesque, 49
Bush, George, 4, 5, 252

Bush-Quayle campaign (1992), 184–185
Bush, George W., 5, 203, 250, 252
Businesses, 142–145. *See also* Corporations
Butterworth, Bob, 203
Bylines, 213

Cal-Neva Lodge (Lake Tahoe), 99, 102, 103
Cameras in the courtroom, 239–240
Camery, James, 141
Cam Ne village (South Vietnam), 124
Cancer, 141, 142
Carmichael, Stokely, 112
Carpenter, Liz, 126
Carter, Hodding, 142
Carter, Jimmy, 5, 252
Carville, James, 182, 183
Casablanca (film), 120
CBS, 4, 5, 47–49, 57, 60, 70, 74, 98, 168
  Black Employees' Association, 150
  CBS News, 3, 47–48, 55, 58, 61, 63, 75–76, 78–79, 92, 95, 110, 111, 112, 124, 130, 136, 150, 162–167, 171, 180, 195, 205, 210, 219, 227, 233, 243, 244
  CBS Radio, 41, 46, 49, 50, 51, 158
  CBS Reports, 97, 100, 108, 114, 137
  CBS Sports, 208
  cost cutting at, 168
  legal department, 195, 196, 207
  mistakes/problems of, 162, 166–167
  sale of divisions of, 163
  and Westinghouse, 195, 196
Censorship, 216
Chandler, Bob, 112
Cheers, 226, 227

Chernowsky, Celia, 132
Chicago Tribune, 245
Childers, Frankie, 75, 76, 147
Children, 226, 232
Children's Television Workshop, 227
Christian, George, 87, 89
Chung, Connie, 248
Churchill, Winston, 31, 38, 128–129, 233
Chyrons, 56
"Civil War at CBS—The Struggle for the Soul of a Legendary Network" (*Newsweek*), 166–167
Clayson, Jane, 248
"The Clinic on Morse Avenue," 139
Clinton, Bill, 5, 8, 181–183, 185–189, 220, 238
  impeachment hearings for, 188
Clinton, Hillary, 182–183, 185, 188, 217, 250
CNN, 239, 245
Cohan, George M., 14
Cold war, 60
Collingwood, Charles, 51, 52
Columbia Journalism Review, 207, 209
Columbia University Graduate School of Journalism, 209
Commercial Appeal (Memphis newspaper), 44–45
Commercials, 16, 226, 228, 240. *See also* Advertising
Communism, 8, 18, 60, 51
Competition, 57, 61, 66, 130, 224–225, 243, 246
Computers, 48, 256. *See also* Internet
Confidentiality agreements, 193, 197, 199–200, 206
Connal, Scotty, 94–95
Conservatives, 4–5, 5–8
"Conversation with the President," 89

Cook, Greg, 141
Cooke, Alistair, 54
Cooney, Joan Ganz, 227
Copland, Aaron, 114
Coronations, 58–59, 131
Corporations, 108, 109, 250. *See also*
    Businesses
The Cosby Show, 227
Court TV, 239
Crack cocaine, 199
Cronkite, Walter, 1, 32, 51, 54–55,
    57–58, 70, 75, 76, 77, 78, 79, 80,
    91, 92, 96, 100, 102, 167, 168, 210,
    229, 248
    and Charles Lindbergh, 92–93
    retirement of, 150
    See also under Murrow, Edward R.
Cutler, Lloyd, 184

Daly, John, 55
Darnton, John, 205
Daschle, Tom, 256
Day, John, 65, 67
Dayan, Moshe, 176
Death penalty, 5
Defense Department, 210. *See also*
    Pentagon
de Gaulle, Charles, 121
DeGeneres, Ellen, 228
DeMoisey, Fox, 198
Desilu, 99
Devine, Frank, 182
DGA Magazine, 206
Diana (Princess), 239
Dimbleby, Richard, 58
Diplomacy, 31
Directors' Guild of America, 206
Disney Company, 168, 206
Documentaries, 97, 99, 108, 112, 114, 115

Dome of the Rock (Jerusalem), 169
Domino Theory, 123
Donaldson, Sam, 159
Douglas Edwards with the News, 51,
    53, 75, 112
Dowd, Maureen, 231
Downs, Bill, 52, 57
Dukakis, Michael, 4, 252

The Early Show, 248
Eastern Airlines, 89–90
Editing, 58, 214, 246
Edwards, Douglas, 47–48, 49, 52, 55,
    62–63. *See also Douglas*
    Edwards with the News
Edwards, Margie, 30
Ehrlichman, Marty, 255–256
Eisenhower, Dwight, 5, 27, 39, 57, 61,
    74, 100, 171
Eisner, Michael, 168, 210
Elections, 5
    of 1932, 250
    of 1960, 71, 103
    of 1988, 4
    of 1992, 184–185
    of 2000, 5, 239, 246–247, 250, 254
    spending for, 249–250
    See also Nixon-Kennedy debate;
        Political conventions
Elizabeth II (Queen), 58–59
Ellsberg, Daniel, 235
Emmy Awards, 259
Euthanasia, 219

Face the Nation, 181
Fager, Jeff, 219
Farrow, Mia, 101

INDEX

FCC. *See* Federal Communications Commission

Federal Communications Commission (FCC), 4, 98, 225–226

Films. *See* Movies

Firestone tires, 143

First Amendment, 5, 92, 210, 239–240, 250, 251

Flowers, Gennifer, 181

Ford, Gerald, 5, 252

Ford Motor Company, 143, 144, 208

Foreign Correspondent (film), 20

Foreign correspondents, 44. *See also* War correspondents

Forty-five Minutes from Broadway (musical/song), 14

42nd Street (film), 19, 46

Four Star Playhouse, 111

Foxman, Abraham H., 172–175

Fox News, 239, 246

Frankenheimer, John, 48

Freon, 199

Friendly, Fred, 53–54, 89–90, 95–96, 99, 108, 110, 116, 130, 133–134

Frontline, 243

The Front Page (film), 19, 24, 46

Frost, David, 185

Fulbright hearings, 110

Galloway, Carl, 146–147

Gannon, Frank, 233–234

Gardella, Kay, 151

Gavshon, Michael, 208

Gays, 9

Gemini space program, 76

General Electric, 168

Geter, Lenell, 218

Getty, Gordon and Ann, 158

Ghost surgery, 145–146

Giancana, Sam, 103

Glantz, Stanton, 198–199

Glenn, John, 77, 78

Goldenson, Leonard, 4

Goldin, Marion, 140, 141, 142

Goldstein, Tom, 209

Goldwater, Barry, 9, 73, 217, 237

Goldwyn, Sam, 10

Gonzalez, Elian, 238–239

A Good Life (Bradlee), 168

Good Morning America, 243

Gore, Al, 5, 203, 250, 252

Gould, Jack, 229–230

Graham, Katharine, 228–229

Grand Central Terminal. *See under* New York City

Great Depression, 16, 128

Great Society, 127

Grief, 238

Grunwald, Mandy and Henry, 182

Guerin, Eric, 54

Guess Who's Coming to Dinner? (film), 8

Gumbel, Bryant, 248

Guns, 7–8

Hall, Philip Baker, 207

Hammerstein, Oscar, 129

Hartman, Rome, 208

Hawkins, Eric, 44

Headsets, 57–58

Hear It Now, 53, 131

Hepburn, Katharine, 216

Herrick, John, 122–123

Heston, Charlton, 254

Hewitt, Frieda and Ely (parents), 16, 19

letters to, 32, 33–39, 40–41

Hewitt, Jeff, Steve, and Lisa (children), 75
Heyward, Andrew, 210, 243
Hidden cameras, 139, 140
Higgins, Marguerite, 24
Hillel, 236
Hipple, Bill, 28–29
Hitler, Adolf, 19, 153
Holocaust, 153, 176
Hospices, 220
Hottelet, Richard C., 52
House Un-American Activities Committee, 61
Howard, Josh, 212, 214
Howard, Roy, 130
Howe, Irving, 10
Howe, Quincy, 55
Humphrey, Hubert, 5, 103, 115, 116
Humphrey, Hubert, III, 203
Humphrey, Muriel, 115
Huntley, Chet, 70. See also Huntley-Brinkley Report
Huntley-Brinkley Report, 75, 112, 242
Hussein, Saddam, 169, 170
Hutton, Bud, 26
Hyde, Henry, 188

I Can Hear It Now (record album), 131
Illinois Power, 144–145
Improvisation, 56
In Retrospect: The Tragedy and Lessons of Vietnam (McNamara), 123
The Insider (film), 204–206
Internet, 194, 242, 243, 256, 257
Interviews, 57, 215–217, 233
Intifada, 169
Investigative Reporters and Editors (organization), 205–206

Iraq, 169
Ireland, 8
Islam, 169
Israel, 169, 171, 176. See also Temple Mount incident
Ito, Lance, 239–240
Ivins, Molly, 133
Iwo Jima, 28–29

Jackson, Jesse, 216
Jankowski, Gene, 164–165
Jennings, Peter, 133, 244, 245
Jerusalem, 169, 216
Jews, 16, 17, 93, 169, 216, 236
Johnson, "Lady Bird," 89, 124, 126
Johnson, Lyndon, 61, 80, 86–90, 100, 122, 123, 124–127, 237
Johnson & Johnson, 143
John XXIII (Pope), 131
Journalism, 3–4, 19–20, 22, 42, 46, 51, 60, 114, 129, 210, 229
checkbook journalism, 233
as confrontational, 237
personal journalism, 108, 110
truth and accuracy in, 235–236
Journal of the American Medical Association, 199
Joyce, Ed, 163, 164, 165, 166

Kaden, Ellen, 195, 196
Kahn, Irving, 53
Kama, Ezra, 171, 173, 175
Karmazin, Mel, 168, 210
Kartiganer, Esther, 213–214
Katz, Oscar, 136
Kelly, Grace, 61
Kemp, Darryl, 257

INDEX

Kennedy, John F., 5, 61, 74, 76, 89,
  100, 103, 127, 238, 252
  assassination of, 73, 79–83
  and South Vietnam, 79
  See also Nixon-Kennedy debate
Kennedy, Joseph P., 103
Kennedy, Robert, 82, 103, 112
Kennett, Tom, 23
Kent State incident, 174, 236
Kervorkian, Jack, 219–220
Khomeini (Ayatollah), 142, 151–152
Khrushchev, Nikita, 65
Kickbacks, 139
Kilpatrick, Jack, 137–138
Kinescopes, 58
The King and I, 129
Kissinger, Henry, 98, 148
Knight-Ridder chain, 245
Kollek, Teddy, 216
Koppel, Ted, 243
Kroft, Steve, 2, 103, 180, 181, 182–183,
  213
Kuralt, Charles, 65, 66, 248
Kuwait, 169

La Belle Simone (yacht), 148
Lack, Andy, 180
Lando, Barry, 139, 156, 170
Langley, Norman, 154
Lardner, John, 109
Lasky, Jesse, 10
Lawrence, Bill, 89
Lazio, Rick, 250
League of Women Voters, 252
Lehrer, Tom, 132
Leonard, Bill, 3, 94, 96, 110, 112, 121
LeSeuer, Larry, 52
Levitan, Paul, 54, 248–249
Levitt, Simone and Bill, 148

Lewinsky, Monica, 185, 197
Lewis, Boyd, 47
Liberals, 4–5, 5–8, 18
Lieberman, Joseph, 220
Lieberthal, Merri, 182, 214
Life magazine, 10, 81, 109
Lincoln, Abe, 128
Lindbergh, Anne Morrow, 93
Lindbergh, Charles A., 19–20, 91–93
Lindsey, Bruce, 186
Lippmann, Walter, 134, 238
Livingston, Robert, 188
Llewellyn, Ensley, 26
Loewenwarter, Paul, 132–133
Loews Corporation, 168, 195–196
London, 25–26, 27–28, 29, 30–32, 33,
  35, 36, 38, 41, 44, 58, 154
  Kensington Palace in, 59–60
Lorillard Tobacco, 196
Los Angeles Times, 173, 245
Louis, Joe, 18, 47
Love affairs, 32, 33, 34, 38
Loyalty oaths, 61
Lumet, Sidney, 48
Lupino, Ida, 111
Lyndon Baines Johnson Memorial
  Library, 124, 126

Mabrey, Vicki, 219
McCarthy, Joseph R., 60–61, 210
McCloy, Ellen and John J., 111
McCurry, Mike, 183, 186, 187
McEnroe, John, 216
McGovern, George, 5
Macmillan, Harold, 97
McNamara, Robert, 122, 123
Maddox (destroyer), 121–123
Mafia, 102, 103
Magnuson, Warren, 98

Mahoney, Hillie and David, 15
Mahoney, Jim, 99
Making of the President (White), 252
Manatt, Chuck, 158
Mann, Michael, 204, 206–207
"The Man Who Knew Too Much"
    (Brenner), 204
Mapplebeck, Tamara, 34–35
The March of Time, 114
Marcus Welby, M.D., 115, 136
Margaret (Princess), 59, 60
Marianas (islands), 42
Maryland legislature, 4
Mayer, Louis B., 10
MCA, 165
Medals, 31
Memphis, Tennessee, 44–45
Mercer, Lucy, 238
Merchant Marine (Maritime Ser-
    vice), 26–27, 28, 34, 37, 39, 41
    Merchant Marine Academy, 25
Mercury astronauts, 76, 229
Meredith, Burgess, 35
Mickelson, Sig, 52, 55, 58, 80
Middle class, 8–9, 16
Middleton, Drew, 59
Miss Rheingold (title), 15
Mistakes. *See* CBS, mistakes/prob-
    lems of; *60 Minutes*, mistakes
    made by
Mitchell, George, 8
Mondale, Walter, 158
Montgomery, Bernard Law "Monty,"
    28
Moonves, Les, 210
Moora, Bob, 26
Moore, Mike, 203
Morgan, Beverly, 150–151
Morris, Dick, 251
Movieolas, 58
Movies, 18–19, 24, 25, 33, 35, 46, 54

Moyers, Bill, 89–90, 164, 165, 236
MSNBC, 239
Mudd, Roger, 150
Murrow, Edward R., 1, 2, 49, 51, 52,
    53, 57–58, 60, 108–109, 116,
    128–129, 137, 226, 230
    "high Murrow" and "low Mur-
    row," 109, 110
    and Joseph McCarthy, 60, 210
    and Walter Cronkite, 70–71
Music, 114
Myers, Dee Dee, 189
My Lai incident, 174

NASA. *See* National Aeronautics and
    Space Administration
National Aeronautics and Space
    Administration (NASA), 76. *See
    also* Space program
National Rifle Association (NRA), 7,
    8
Native Dancer (race horse), 54
NBC, 4, 49, 50, 54, 57, 64, 65, 66, 67,
    70, 74, 101, 148, 168
    NBC Convention Plans, 94–95
    NBC News, 242, 244
    NBC White Paper, 108
Network (film), 10
Neuharth, Al, 256
New Haven Tug (company), 64
New Rochelle, New York, 11, 14, 16,
    17, 18, 20, 34
News broadcasts, 2, 9–10, 47–49, 54,
    88, 91, 213
    of Big Three networks, 238, 243,
    244–245. *See also* ABC, ABC
    News; CBS, CBS News; NBC,
    NBC News
    breaking news, 57, 244, 247

cable, 238, 239, 242–243
and CBS commercial interests, 207–208
vs. entertainment, 50–51, 108, 109, 168, 224–225, 238
expanded to thirty minutes, 78–79
joint production by networks, 244–247
money made by, 225, 226, 244, 246, 247
morning news programs, 248
News conferences, 57, 244
Newsmagazines, 224, 247, 248
Newspaper Guild, 24
Newspapers, 228, 231, 232, 242, 245, 250. *See also* Television, and newspaper practices
Newsweek, 166–167, 233
New York City, 29, 45
Grand Central Terminal, 46, 48, 78
plane crash in East River, 63–65
WCBS–TV in, 247
New York Herald Tribune, 22–23, 24, 25, 26, 44, 246
New York Post, 238
The New York Times, 24, 51, 59, 151–153, 205, 209–210, 229–233, 245, 246
corrections column in, 152–153
Hewitt article on op-ed page, 232–233
reporters' quotes endorsing products in, 230–231
television stations owned by New York Times Company, 231
New York University (NYU), 22
Nicotine, 199, 201, 210. *See also* Tobacco industry
Night Beat, 112–113
Nightline, 243

Nike, 208
Niven, David, 111
Nixon, Pat, 115
Nixon, Richard, 5, 9, 57–58, 73, 115, 116, 138, 217
and Dan Rather, 136–137
and Kennedy assassination, 82–83
See also Nixon-Kennedy debate
Nixon-Kennedy debate, 9, 71–72, 81, 249, 251–252
NRA. *See* National Rifle Association
Nuclear power, 144–145
NYU. *See* New York University

Oban, Scotland, 39–40
Ober, Eric, 195
Olivier, Laurence, 153–156
Omnibus, 54, 97
O'Reilly, Tex, 24
Oswald, Lee Harvey, 82

Pacino, Al, 204, 205
Paige, Satchel, 129
Palestinians, 156, 169
Paley, Kate, 149
Paley, William S., 4, 50–51, 75, 148–149, 162, 163, 165, 167, 171, 210, 256
Panama Canal, 239
Parnis, Molly, 167
Parr, Jeanne, 101
Patterson, Gene, 140
Paul White Award, 150
Peabody Awards. *See* University of Georgia Peabody Awards
Pegler, Westbrook, 18
Pelham Sun, 23, 45

Pelley, Scott, 219
Pentagon, 122, 123, 208, 210
Pentagon Papers, 209, 234–235
Perot, Ross, 184–185
Perrin, Arthur, 22
Persian Gulf War, 169, 170
Person to Person, 109, 226
Pew Research Center, 243
Philip Morris Company, 193, 194, 195,
    197, 203, 210
Physician-assisted suicide, 220
Piscopo, Joe, 139
"Point-Counterpoint" (*60 Minutes*
    segment), 137–138
Police brutality, 235
Political correctness, 7, 18
Political conventions, 49–50, 54,
    55–56, 57–58, 70, 93–95, 98, 115,
    253–254. *See also* Elections
Pooling, 242. *See also* News broad-
    casts, joint production by net-
    works
Powell, Dick, 111
Powers, John E. "Shorty," 77
Presidential debates, 244, 251–253. *See
    also* Nixon-Kennedy debate
Presidential trips, 61
Privacy rights, 140, 145, 236, 238
Producers, 3, 48, 52, 61, 74, 89, 132,
    153, 156, 170, 182, 185, 192, 205,
    207, 212, 213, 214, 217, 218, 219,
    255
Public-service responsibilities, 51, 98,
    108, 225–226

Quayle, Dan, 184–185, 252
Quemoy and Matsu islands, 251–252
Quotes, unattributed, 234, 235

Rabin, Yitzhak, 176–177
Race, 17–18
Radio and Television News Directors
    Association, 150
Radio broadcasting, 49, 50, 51, 53, 55,
    57, 253
Radutzky, Michael, 29, 185
RAF. *See* Royal Air Force
Rainier (Prince of Monaco), 61
Ramparts magazine, 193
Ramsey, JonBenet, 239
Rather, Dan, 51, 80–81, 136–137, 146,
    150, 163, 164, 165, 166, 219, 244,
    245, 248
Ratings, 3, 4, 109, 110, 115, 219, 228, 244
Rat Pack, 103
Reagan, Nancy, 9, 217
Reagan, Ron, 217
Reagan, Ronald, 5, 98, 158, 217, 237,
    252
Reasoner, Harry, 65, 66, 100, 111–112,
    114, 120, 180, 248
Redstone, Sumner, 168
Reid, Ogden, 24
Religion, 17
Reuters, 245
R. J. Reynolds, 197
Rockefeller, Happy and Nelson A.,
    148
Rodgers, Richard, 129
Rogers, Ted, 72
Rogow, Bob, 46
Rooney, Andy, 2, 26, 100, 138–139, 225
Roosevelt, Eleanor, 18
Roosevelt, Franklin, 81, 93, 128, 237,
    238
Roseanne, 226, 227
Rose, Billy, 32, 33
Rose, Charlie, 219
Rosenfield, Jim, 164, 165

Rosenthal, Joe, 28–29
Roth, Eric, 206
Royal Air Force (RAF), 25, 29, 31
Rudd, Hughes, 58
Rudd, R. J., 141, 142
Rudin, Mickey, 99, 102, 103, 104
Ruff, Charles, 186
Rustin, Bayard, 7

Safer, Morley, 2, 93, 121–123, 145, 152,
   164, 165, 180, 183, 213, 216, 218
St. Pierre, Suzanne, 218
Salant, Richard S., 110–111, 112
Salaries, 3–4, 22, 44, 45, 168, 193, 229
Salinger, Pierre, 79
Same-sex marriages, 9
Sandefur, Thomas, 193, 201
San Francisco Chronicle, 95
Sarandon, Susan, 254
Sarnoff, David, 4
Saroyan, William, 35
Satellites, 58, 142, 163, 245
Saturday Night Live, 138, 139
Sauter, Van Gordon, 163, 164, 165, 167
Sawyer, Diane, 157–159, 164, 165, 180,
   197, 243, 248
Scanlon, John, 202, 207
Scheffler, Phil, 116, 195, 196
Schmeling, Max, 18
Schoenbrun, David, 51, 52, 61, 75–76,
   133
Scripps Howard newspapers, 257
Scruggs, Dick, 196
Scud missiles, 170
Second Amendment, 5
Secret Service, 86, 90
See It Now, 2, 53–54, 60, 97, 108, 109
Self-indulgence, 237

Selleck, Tom, 254
"The Selling of the Pentagon," 97,
   210
September 11 terrorist attacks, 29–30
   volunteers at Ground Zero, 30
Severeid, Eric, 51, 52, 89
Sex, 15, 237–238
SHAEF. See Supreme Headquarters,
   Allied Expeditionary Force
Shaffner, Frank, 48
Shakespeare, William, 225
Shamir, Yitzhak, 169–170
Sharp, Ulysses S. Grant, 122–123
Shaw, Bernard, 252
Sheehan, Neil, 234
Shepard, Alan, 229
Simon, Bob, 208, 213, 219
Simpson, O. J., 238–239, 240
Simulations, 229, 230
Sinatra, Frank, 99–104, 105
Sinatra, Tina, 102–103
Sitcoms, 224, 225, 247, 248
60 Minutes, 11, 93, 103, 243
   audience for, 10, 111, 218
   audio in, 129–132, 198
   awards received by, 4, 218, 256, 259
   first broadcast of, 114
   and friends of executive producer,
      207
   genesis of, 109–111, 247
   memorable moments from inter-
      views, 215–217
   mistakes made by, 144–145
   money made by, 226
   move from Tuesdays to Sundays,
      136
   people of, 1, 2, 48, 180, 219
   pilot for, 111, 112
   "Point-Counterpoint" segment,
      137–138

60 Minutes (cont.)
    process of generating/broadcasting
        stories, 212–215
    success of, 52, 116, 130, 139,
        226–227, 240, 246
    ticking stopwatch used, 2, 114, 215
    title of, 110
    tobacco story, 192–204
    as unchanged, 214–215
60 Minutes II, 209, 219
Smith, Gordon, 203
Smith, Howard K., 51, 52, 120
Smith, Red, 24
Snyder, Harry, 45
Solomon, Jeanne, 153–156
Sondheim, Stephen, 129
Sorenson, Ted, 73, 82
South Vietnam, 79, 123, 124. *See also*
    Vietnam War
Space program, 76–78, 229
Spielberg, Steven, 254
Sputnik, 56–57
Stahl, Lesley, 2, 158, 180–181, 183, 184,
    208, 213, 221
Stanton, Frank, 50, 54, 72, 75, 80, 124,
    149, 162, 210
Starr, Ken, 187
Stars & Stripes, 26–27, 28, 36
Stephanopoulos, George, 182, 233
Stevenson, Adlai, 5, 171
Stockholm (liner), 62
Stollmack, Fred, 74
Stone, Peter, 133
Street Stories, 227–228
Streisand, Barbra, 254, 255
Stringer, Howard, 132, 167
Super Bowl (1992), 181, 182
Supreme Headquarters, Allied Expe-
    ditionary Force (SHAEF), 27
Survivor, 244
Sutton, Willie, 127–128

Swayze, John Cameron, 49
Sweeps week, 228

Taliban, 31
Taylor, Elizabeth, 132
Teases, 2, 229
Teleprompters, 53
Television, 32, 54, 70, 80, 83, 127
    cable, 238, 239, 242–243
    early days of, 46–47, 47–48, 49–50,
        51, 111, 253
    local stations, 232, 242
    and NASA, 76–77
    and newspaper practices, 140, 168,
        210, 212, 213, 215, 228–231, 237
    and politics, 249–251. *See also*
        Elections; Political conven-
        tions; Presidential debates
    preemptions in, 254
    stations owned by newspapers, 231,
        232
    superimpositions in, 56
    See also News broadcasts
Television Academy's Hall of Fame, 227
Temple Mount incident, 169–170,
    171–175
"This Year at Murietta," 140–142
Thomas, Lowell, 2
Tiananmen Square, 174
Tiffany Network, 163
Tisch, Andrew, 199
Tisch, Laurence, 167–169, 170–171,
    177, 195–196, 210, 227–228
Tisch, Preston Robert, 167, 195
Tobacco industry, 192–204, 206, 207
Today show, 64, 239, 255
Tortious interference, 194, 195, 200
Town Meeting of the World, 97, 98
Truth, 235–236, 251

Turner Joy (destroyer), 121
20/20, 243
Tylenol, 143

United Press, 45, 75
University of Georgia Peabody
    Awards, 218, 259
U.S. Marines, 124

Vance, Cyrus, 142
Vanity Fair, 204
Viacom, 168
Vieira, Meredith, 180
Vietnam War, 5, 110, 126–127, 181, 237
    Gulf of Tonkin incident, 121–123, 124
Villa Venice Club (Chicago), 103
Vishinsky, Andrei, 230
Von Elling, Emil, 22
von Hoffman, Nicholas, 138
Voting, 5, 250–251. *See also* Elections

Waddington, Pauline, 32–33
Wallace, Mike, 1, 2, 90, 91, 112–114,
    116, 124, 125, 137, 139, 141, 142,
    145–146, 148, 151, 156, 164, 165,
    166, 167, 168, 169, 170, 180, 183,
    208, 213, 219–220, 248, 256
    collapse in plane, 227
    and depression, 113
    and Lowell Bergman, 209
    and Lyndon Johnson, 126–127
    and tobacco industry story, 192,
        195, 196, 197, 198, 199–204, 205
Wall Street Journal, 184, 199, 200, 203,
    246

Walters, Barbara, 120, 133, 180, 227,
    229, 248, 255
War correspondents, 26, 27. *See also*
    Foreign correspondents
Warren Commission, 82
War Shipping Administration (WSA),
    27
The Washington Post, 140, 148, 173,
    209–210, 228–229, 245
Wasserman, Lew, 165
Watergate scandal, 235
WCBS–TV (New York), 247
Weaver, Mary, 45, 75
Welch, Jack, 168
Wells, Kendrick, 201
Wershba, Joe, 121, 122, 123
Western Wall (Jerusalem), 169, 172
West 57th, 180
Westinghouse, 177, 195, 196
West Side Story, 129
White, Joan, 32–33
White, Paul, 51
White, Theodore, 252
Whitelaw, Bobby, 42
Who Wants to be a Millionaire, 244
Wigand, Jeffrey, 192–193, 196, 197,
    200–203, 206, 207
    dossier on, 202–203
    indemnified by CBS, 204
Willey, Kathleen, 185–188
Williams, Merrell, 198
Williams, Palmer, 116–117
Williams, Serena and Venus, 216
Winter Olympics (1998), 208
Wire services, 245. *See also* Associated
    Press; United Press
Wolf, Perry, 97
Woman of the Year (film), 24
The Wonderful World of Disney, 136
Woodward, Bob, 235
World of Our Fathers (Howe), 10

World Trade Center. *See* September
11 terrorist attacks
World War II, 19, 20, 24–25, 28, 31, 33,
36, 42, 51, 58, 128, 131
end of, 44, 59
European invasion, 39, 40, 41
Writing, 127–133
WSA. *See* War Shipping Administration
Wussler, Robert, 65–66, 94
Wyman, Tom, 162–163, 165, 166, 167,
169

Wynette, Tammy, 217

Yeltsin, Boris, 221–222

Zapruder film, 81
Zastafayev, Viktor, 152
Zionism, 176, 216
Zukor, Adolph, 10

PublicAffairs is a nonfiction publishing house founded in 1997. It is a tribute to the standards, values, and flair of three persons who have served as mentors to countless reporters, writers, editors, and book people of all kinds, including me.

I. F. STONE, proprietor of *I. F. Stone's Weekly*, combined a commitment to the First Amendment with entrepreneurial zeal and reporting skill and became one of the great independent journalists in American history. At the age of eighty, Izzy published *The Trial of Socrates*, which was a national bestseller. He wrote the book after he taught himself ancient Greek.

BENJAMIN C. BRADLEE was for nearly thirty years the charismatic editorial leader of *The Washington Post*. It was Ben who gave the *Post* the range and courage to pursue such historic issues as Watergate. He supported his reporters with a tenacity that made them fearless and it is no accident that so many became authors of influential, best-selling books.

ROBERT L. BERNSTEIN, the chief executive of Random House for more than a quarter century, guided one of the nation's premier publishing houses. Bob was personally responsible for many books of political dissent and argument that challenged tyranny around the globe. He is also the founder and longtime chair of Human Rights Watch, one of the most respected human rights organizations in the world.

———

For fifty years, the banner of Public Affairs Press was carried by its owner, Morris B. Schnapper, who published Gandhi, Nasser, Toynbee, Truman, and about 1,500 other authors. In 1983, Schnapper was described by *The Washington Post* as "a redoubtable gadfly." His legacy will endure in the books to come.

Peter Osnos, *Publisher*

Breinigsville, PA USA
28 August 2009
223146BV00001B/15/A